WITHDRAWN

Transitions:
Concepts + Drawings + Buildings

Design Research in Architecture

Series Editors

Professor Murray Fraser
Bartlett School of Architecture, UCL, UK

Professor Jonathan Hill
Bartlett School of Architecture, UCL, UK

Professor Jane Rendell
Bartlett School of Architecture, UCL, UK

and

Professor Teddy Cruz
Department of Architecture, University of California at San Diego, USA

Bridging a range of positions between practice and academia, this Ashgate series seeks to present the best proponents of architectural design research from around the world. Each author combines innovative historical and theoretical research with creative propositions as a symbiotic interplay. In offering a variety of key exemplars, the book series situates itself at the forefront of design research investigation in architecture.

Other titles in this series

Furniture, Structure, Infrastructure
Making and Using the Urban Environment
Nigel Bertram
ISBN 978 1 4094 4927 0

Design Research in Architecture
An Overview
Edited by Murray Fraser
ISBN 978 1 4094 6217 0

Marcel Duchamp and the Architecture of Desire
Penelope Haralambidou
ISBN 978 1 4094 4345 2

Architectures of Chance
Yeoryia Manolopoulou
ISBN 978 1 4094 3536 5

Digital Poetics
An Open Theory of Design-Research in Architecture
Marjan Colletti
ISBN 978 1 4094 4523 4

Transitions: Concepts + Drawings + Buildings

Christine Hawley
Bartlett School of Architecture, UCL, UK

Published by
Ashgate Publishing Limited
Wey Court East
Union Road
Farnham
Surrey, GU9 7PT
England

Ashgate Publishing Company
110 Cherry Street
Suite 3-1
Burlington, VT 05401-3818
USA

www.ashgate.com

British Library Cataloguing in Publication Data
A catalogue record for this book is available from the British Library.

The Library of Congress has cataloged the printed edition as follows:
Hawley, Christine, 1949-
 [Works. Selections]
 Transitions : concepts + drawings + buildings / by Christine Hawley.
    pages cm. -- (Design research in architecture)
 Includes bibliographical references and index.
 ISBN 978-1-4724-0909-6 (pbk) 1. Hawley, Christine, 1949---Themes, motives. I. Title.

 NA997.H38A35 2014
 720.92--dc23
                                                                        2013023967

ISBN: 978-1-4724-0909-6 (pbk)

MIX
Paper from
responsible sources
FSC
www.fsc.org   FSC® C013985

Printed in the United Kingdom by Henry Ling Limited,
at the Dorset Press, Dorchester, DT1 1HD

Contents

List of Illustrations

URBAN COLLAGE

PECKHAM HOUSE

TKTS

PALOS VERDES ART CENTER, CALIFORNIA

Preface

At the outset my intention was to explore the way discussion and observation influence the way we design. My approach is not naturally process led; I do not use an inviolate set of systems that lead the decision-making regardless of the formal consequences. I have realised that the approach to these projects is far more intuitive, and surprising relationships emerge where the route is more unfathomable. This manner of working is associative, but the way in which these relationships are forged still remains in a realm that I still cannot always analyse. I set out to try to understand how random observations and a multitude of conversations could be categorised and understood in a logical manner. I wanted to challenge the mythology that surrounds the act of designing, where collective understanding and consensus exists in silence between members of informed groups. This tribal behaviour still remains compelling and indecipherable. On occasions I have found the development of a design drawing to be visceral yet there is still a requirement to develop a rationale and in many cases this takes place in retrospect. It is important to understand how we arrive at conclusions. Yet it is the parts that defy rationality that are intriguing.

In the last 30 years I have been in conversations that have drifted from the dreamlike to the acutely economic and what has been produced as ideas and drawings has evolved and acquired nuance through the turn-mill of conversation.

The projects are influenced by memory but the complexity of memory compromises the ability to transcribe. There are obvious contrasts in creating a concept and the struggle to produce an accurate drawing. These drawings go through another act of translation to produce information that has the necessary precision to construct a building. The process of design that wanders through dreamlike exploration always runs the risk of losing the essence of the original idea. The three chapters describe the ideas, buildings, texts, films and artwork that have been a major influence in the process of translation. The references have been used repeatedly but in every instance the interpretation has been different and always adapted to suit a particular context.

There are two projects in the book that were experiments created through a methodological process – The Shadow House and Peckham House – and both are projects that have been revisited after a period of 25 years. There was no anticipated outcome, yet both designs use the subject of the essays as repeated references. These projects are both ongoing and I anticipate that they will evolve in ways that I cannot possibly imagine. The exploration will take unforeseen turnings and make unexpected observations and sit alongside the more formally predictable processes for construction.

The architectural community is usually divided into the majority who build and the minority who explore the margins of the architectural world without the constraints of practice. I see both activities as interdependent; hypothetical exploration does not immediately translate into construction but there are unforeseen influences that ebb and flow between the two realms. I have explored concepts in more self-conscious detail to understand a little better how and why certain ideas have worked and others not, yet I am still a long way from fully understanding the process of translation.

I would like to take the opportunity to thank all those who have worked with me and to acknowledge their invaluable contribution, without which the projects and this book would not have been possible: Peter Cook, a unique professional partner whose enthusiasm is unparalleled; CJ Lim, with whom I taught and whose extraordinary talent has cast an enormous influence; Abigail Ashton and Andrew Porter, who effortlessly supported the design and construction of Gifu and with whom I have entered innumerable competitions.

I have had drawing support from Nichola Czyz, Yoonjin Kim, Kamen Leung, Nick Wang, photographs of models by Danny Lane and Mike Pugh and the photographs of Gifu by Tomio Ohashi. Throughout one year I have had an invaluable design and organisational input from my research assistant Charlotte Reynolds and advice on graphic layouts from Sam Watson. Clyde Watson has had the patience to look through my references and Kate Ahl my text. It is quite clear that the making of this book has been the result of enormous collaborative support, for which I am so grateful.

Urban Collage

There are two complex processes in the way the human brain perceives image and text. The first involves visual scanning and the latter constrains the reader to a pre-constructed route that is normally horizontal and must be read from one side to another or in some instances top to bottom. The first act of scanning involved in image perception has no decipherable rules and no system for sustained focus; the second act has pre-determined rules and demands unbroken attention. When both visual symbols are brought together the demands on the brain intensify, and the methods of simultaneous cognition are still not fully understood. The co-existence of word and image can be hierarchical where one of the symbols has a supportive or explanatory role, it can be deliberately in conflict, or it can have a collaborative relationship, as we usually see in advertising. All patterns of presentation impact differently on the process of perception and the re-contextualising of image and word into three-dimensional space is even more fascinating. The intrusion of the word and image onto the urban surface creates a complex synthesis of cognition where icon symbol and space have a visual interdependence. The interruption of urban space by information displayed through advertising, street art, urban signage, unauthorised graphics and fly-posting fundamentally alters the way we perceive the city, yet this phenomenon of altered space is rarely considered within the construct of formal analyses. Planning legislation may acknowledge the need for constraint, but the Advertisement Control Act (2007) executes authority in a limited and bureaucratic manner, abdicating control over many parts of the city but, more importantly, ignoring any form of qualitative discussion.

It was during the nineteenth century that the combined result of technical advances in reprographics together with a burgeoning consumer culture resulted in an unrestrained *blizzard* of typography and images. There was little planning legislation in place that even acknowledged the presence, let alone the impact, of this new and highly assertive form of communication that was using the urban surface as a message board.

'All that is solid melts into air' declared Karl Marx and Friedrich Engels in the stirring evocation of the modern era in *The Communist Manifesto* (1848) and, as if in response to these new forces, written words began to overflow into the wider environment, sometimes in the most chaotic ways. Where once they had been confined to ordered ranks on the pure white of the book page, they now seem to roam uncontrollably within the vertical visual field – on walls, shop fronts, billboards, advertising pillars, street signs, passing vehicles, even people. (Morley 2003)

While certainly familiar to us today, this visual cacophony of word and image was clearly a heady new experience in the mid nineteenth century. (Morley 2003)

The introduction of words into the visual realm and words and image into the spatial domain has the potential to create a dramatic impact, in that it offers both a reinforced and deconstructed understanding of space. Using words and images as a focal part of the spatial lexicon has been part of a thematic pursuit within particular design proposals that considers the architectural impact of this intrusive culture.

Streets at night or in Shinjuku, Tokyo, a forest of neon signs flash, defying translation, street signs direct speeding vehicles, advertisement screens relay their messages, loud music from a passing car drowns out the engines; hum. Recorded in a photograph, a film memories of a scene frozen in paint. (Leaman 2010)

There is now a greater spread of signage and graphic disruption in the contemporary city but the origins of using the city surface to communicate to the public are found in early history and there is even earlier evidence of combining image and letter.

This spatial coexistence has an ancient history dating back to the Palaeolithic period and the earliest written (commercial) signage can be found in both early Roman and Greek inscriptions. Logographic symbols predated the use of cuneiform vocabulary (found in Mesopotamia around 3200 BC) and early Chinese written characters have always historically combined both written and pictorial signifiers. There have been periodic surges of interest in Chinese calligraphy, a typographic medium that was not immediately readable to the European observer, and which therefore became allied to the optical function of the semiograph, a visual caricature that conveyed meaning through an image without words. The Chinese calligraphic symbol is interesting in that it retains a symbolic relationship with the referent, suggesting that there could be a unity between the referent and the referred. The use of simple pictorial images or logos as associative symbols is now a deeply embedded part of current culture but these early symbols were important, as they were to facilitate a fundamental desire to communicate. Epigraphic writing originated on hard surfaces and the earliest cunaeic form was found on clay,

creating a form of concrete poetry; these marks were ultimately to bring ancient graffiti into the public realm. Unlike the subsequent use of soft writing material, inscription onto built surface conveyed information into the public domain. These inscriptions, often communicating contemporary news, were typically positioned on the walls of public buildings in order to capture the attention of the largest audience. Historically graffiti was considered a form of urban disfigurement, unlike commercial typography. There may be complex cultural reasons for this, but an explicit distinction is the relationship to surface: one was inscribed and was usually an authorised sign and the other was cut or applied and often unauthorised. The permanency of graffiti and the lack of authorisation established this as a fundamental act of desecration.

While commercial signage seen both in the Greek and Roman period were discreet plaques, medieval signage became larger and more florid, with some assuming the status of 'art', in particular the Guild signs of the City of London. The historic development of both formal and 'guerrilla' typography must be considered as a formative influence on the cultural acceptance of the contemporary phenomenon. Public writing and imagery cannot be disconnected from the evolutionary development of word/image in associated fields and it is important to consider its inevitable influence on the development of writing in the public realm. If one were to trace the development of communication on the urban surface, it would have an intractable thread through other forms of literature, art and word/ image conflation.

Maps, concrete poetry, illuminated manuscripts, emblems, art deco book design, advertising, film and video and all manner of digital formats like websites – these modes rely on words so involved within the graphic medium and its message that, in the first place, words may seem to be transfigured as graphic imagery and, second, the graphic imagery itself aspires to the condition of linguistic denotation. (Hunt et al. 2010)

This association of word and image has often produced conflicting interpretations. William Mitchell argues that text and visual image have a dialectic relationship characterised by the need for dominance where either linguistic or pictorial signs must exert overriding primacy, whereas Michel Foucault considers word and image to have a more blurred relationship (Hunt et al. 2010). Direct and indirect influences are found throughout history, where word and image have impacted on other creative genres such as fine art, print, film-making and latterly, of course, contemporary graphics. It is important to remember the complex inter-relationships between these media that ultimately impacted onto the surface of the city.

The still life painting and portraiture of the sixteenth and seventeenth century, the content of which had moved beyond figurative recordings, began to include items and signs that were emblematic. In these pictures there was an implied narrative that underpinned the understanding of the image. In these examples and, in this case, Foucault's more nuanced view of the relationship between word and image seems more apt. During the eighteenth century a more explicit relationship between word and image emerged where landscape architects and painters such as Joseph Turner and Humphrey Repton would embellish their paintings with notes and verse. At this time the making of print and the making of image on paper were two separate technical skills executed by two different craftspeople. The physical act of production was considered a craft where figurative and literal description never existed side by side, and it was William Blake who pioneered the technology that created illuminated printing, where text and image were executed together. To understand the impact this had, one had to understand the calligraphic nature of the text that was to reinforce and contribute to the meaning of the whole. The creation of illuminated text illustrated the precise force of both methods of communication working together – and the status of creating words into text that sat alongside illustration, now enhancing this process from a craft to an art.

The nineteenth-century painter John Martin was one of the first to use alliteration, a painterly form of accentuation when depicting hell through 'Satan Presiding at the Infernal Council' (1827), where the foreboding atmosphere was created by Claude-Nicholas Ledoux's architecture used as a background reference. The use of emblematic alliteration is still used in contemporary advertising where images have precisely associated connotations. Martin's work was amongst the first to use a reverse relationship with the city, where the urban monument was not used as the surface for communication but rather as the vehicle of implied atmosphere.

David Lomas (2010) noted that the introduction of words into the physical environment transformed the twentieth century and was to have far-reaching consequences.

Guillaume Appollnaire, playwright, art critic and poet, was one of the first to create with his work 'Mandolin Carnation and Bamboo' the '*calligramme*', a form of concrete poetry that adopted the form of the subject matter to create a surreal suggestion of object. The reductive outline, constructed from letter and word, relied on the symbolic codes reassembling meaning through the imagination of the observer. These associative forms in painting and text were seen many generations later in contemporary advertising. At the same time the art critic Raoul Hausmann noted that both the Russian Constructivists and the Italian Futurists had discovered that the force of image and text when superimposed created successive adversarial scenes played out amidst a flourish of image and statement. Their graphic art reinvented the notion of form and the word image compound, within which they celebrated notions of technology and dynamic simultaneity. While this work was stylistically detached from the intellectualised compositions of both the figurative painters and the abstraction of Cubism, the graphic work of the Futurists and the Cubists did share the technique of utilising printed form to accentuate or counterpoint the background subject. Much has been written about Cubist collage that has undoubtedly influenced contemporary advertising, yet the critic Clement Greenburg's reading of Cubist typographic composition was that it was a formalist interpretation 'for whom words … served merely to emphasize the flatness and autonomy of the picture plane' (Lomas 2010).

The emergence of collage at the beginning of the twentieth century challenged the notion of art as autonomous and developed the influence of symbolism that then began to emerge, in urban scale advertising. In the same period Fernand Légers' 'The City' used collage technique to emulate both the discordance and simultaneity of the city and produce work that echoed the style of contemporary advertisement. Léger used the style of contemporary advertising, yet many others who were either in, or aligned to, the Cubist movement understood the potency of graphic communication (Morley 2003). This period was the beginning of a cultural flux that saw the emergence of a more assertive graphic style of communication where the immediacy of word/image conflation had an intensity that influenced a coterie of artists. These artists in turn reflected a new and emerging image of the city that was one of 'message' and 'image' rather than architectural iconography. It is difficult to ascertain exactly how fluid the influences were across the fine art and commercial world, but it is absolutely clear that the concept of the modern city was now being represented with text and in some cases the detritus of urban living. It may have been those associated with the ethos of the Futurists, that were the most assertive proselytisers of the concept of 'modernism', but it was Cubist technique that had the more enduring influence. The issues of both temporality and simultaneity were central to their thinking, but their ability to represent these ideas, particularly in the context of the city, only emerged after encountering the work of the Cubists, where lettering began to occupy the space of the image. Georges Braque was one of the first artists to use text as a structural part of the composition and in doing so drew attention to scale, space, texture and position, contributing to the development of a language that was much closer to graphic abstraction. The deconstructed nature of print in this context meant that the letter or the word could be detached from its role as signifier and from its position and sequence in a sentence. This form of deconstruction enabled the painting of the city to depict a different form of spatiality that bore little relationship to traditional urban iconography. The texts were often gathered from all parts of the environment – whether surfaces of buildings, newspapers, labels or billboards. The city was an instrument that could now be read in many different ways and reinterpreted through painting and collage (Morley 2003).

Word and images can have a synergistic relationship where cumulatively they reinforce both a concept and a message. Conversely the relationship can be contrapuntal, where the intent is to disrupt and undermine, and within this context the Dada or Anti Art movement emerged, with a critical commentary on the city that was to have a latent influence on urban graphics. One of the early figures, Francis Picabia, *a disabused commentator on the Parisian art world* (Lomas 2010), critiqued the art world through a socio-economic lens that launched a sustained attack on what he thought to be the socially and economically excusive world of the painters and the galleryists. In his view art could be found in the everyday and therefore the world of typography and urban graphics was a natural focus for his work. His goals coincided with the underlying spirit of the Dada movement, where the disruption and disengagement of meaning created illogical and de-contextualised typography. For many, the traditional subject matter of visual representation was of no interest and there emerged a fascination with reflection of the everyday – particularly the working parts of the city and all its residual traces – which seemed to be an expression of a new authenticity.

Consider the intertwined emergence of graphics, used within an urban setting, and the polemic that developed within the European art community at the beginning of the twentieth century. Commercial typography contributed to the awareness of the changing 'opticality' of painters in that they became increasingly aware that the flat graphical language of typography had an assertiveness that figurative painting lacked. Their ideology and in some instances their politicisation was to challenge the exclusivity of the product as imagery appeared in public places and access became democratised.

Although word and image had existed in the public domain for centuries, the most dramatic emergence and one that profoundly impacted on the fabric of the city was at the beginning of the nineteenth century. The emergence of a commodity-driven economy drove the demand for public advertisement. The advance in printing methods meant that there was an almost unparalleled choice of typographic style and, more importantly, the scale, colour and dimensionality could be exaggerated to create competitively assertive information designed to capture attention. By the late nineteenth century changes in commercial trading, law and reproduction technology resulted in the city both in Europe and the USA being festooned with posters on almost every available wall. Commercial advertising was not confined to the discreet presence in a shop window, but configured as building-scale paintings often extolling the efficacy of the product (Trifonas 2001).

The evocation of the city as a dense forest of signs to be read and interpreted indicates that the symbolist belief that sense data are symbols that we interpret was in the process of acquiring an experiential reality. Artists and poets registered the rapidly changing urban environment colonized by words and images in the form of billboards and posters that are celebrated by Apollinaire in Whitmanesque fashion. (Lomas 2010)

Rue St Jacques Paris at the start of the nineteenth century was dominated by billboards and posters, the discordance and raw vitality of this graphic imagery was changing the face of the city and to some extent echoed the Futurists' ethos in the visceral quality of modern urbanism. The emergence of the combined text/image was to have a synergistic relationship across the fields of fine art, architecture and the emerging discipline of graphic design. Signs and advertising were to become the 'standard props' of a vision of modernity that was evident both in illustration and in the city.

> Have you ever thought about the sadness that streets, squares, stations, subways, first class hotels, dance halls, movies, dining cars, highways, nature, would all exhibit without the innumerable billboard, without show windows (those beautiful brand new toys for thoughtful families), without luminous signboards, without the false blandishments of loudspeakers, and imagine the sadness and monotony of meals and wine without the polychrome menu and fancy labels. (Eliel et al. 2001)

Our current interpretation of context has developed from 'Beaux Arts' thinking and the need to substantiate our values is by reference to an abstract neoclassical system. Planning references are made through the abstracted codes that refer to building fabric; there is a requirement when relating a new development to context that the architect must observe local scale, materiality and the language of articulation. What this ignores is the plethora of signage which often renders the context invisible. What we *actually* see is quite different – the urban streetscapes are a collage of partly seen building elevations overlaid with an un-absorbable plethora of graphic information. Roland Barthes was perhaps the earliest cultural commentator to reflect on the importance of contemporary signage and urban typography when he considered the nature of representation in *Empire of Signs* and describes the city through the surface of image and writing. This was less an exercise in linguistic semiology than a broader enquiry into the influence of mass media and popular culture. Barthes' observations brought attention to the underlying influence signage had in contemporary communication and how both the message and the image were able to subvert and shape people's understanding of the contemporary experience.

By the 1960s *Time* magazine was claiming that,

> the typical American was likely to be exposed to an average of 1,600 advertisements per day, and thanks to new technologies of illumination the spectacle was now a twenty four hour one, with neon filaments pulsing through the night. Furthermore, the billboards were now so large and colourful that they often hid the buildings to which they were attached. (Morley 2003)

It is impossible to measure just how much influence the world of fine art had on commercial signage. Urban writing as a typographic expression of territoriality and urban graphics as freestyle imagery were unauthorised forms of communication on the walls of the city. It is difficult to unravel exactly how much influence flowed from the formal arena of fine art to the illicit expressions of the street and vice versa, but there is evidence that they were mutually aware, as elements of language and expression overlap.

Complex socio-economic circumstances, together with a political context that would challenge the elitism of the gallery, provided the momentum needed to bring visual imagery into the streets as a gesture of democratisation. It is therefore important to mention the work of certain twentieth-century artists whose work undoubtedly influenced both the structure and content of commercial typography and the *freestyle* of street writing.

At the outset of the twentieth century Marcel Duchamp was amongst those who pioneered a form of expression that magnified the art of the *ready-made*, raising the status of everyday objects and creating, in part, a commentary on urbanity and commoditisation, which certainly over time was to have an indirect influence on what was found on street walls. It was Duchamp who publicly derided the 'retinal' disposition of the Cubists and began to introduce prominently stencilled graphics onto his canvases. There were of course far-reaching philosophical and cultural questions about the status of art and authorship, but another intriguing aspect of this period was breaking the barrier of pure pictorialisation and incorporating text into pictorial culture. If the political protagonists within the Dada movement began their moves against the cultural position of the art establishment, the work of Duchamp, Max Ernst, Paul Klee and Man Ray propelled the art/text genre further. Duchamp's *Anaemic Cinema* and Man Ray's *Etoile de Mer* intercalated lines of text with film image,

so the multifocal phenomenon created forms of expression from collage to photomontage, film/text expression to mechanically transforming installations that challenged the canvas and the gallery as the classic form of exposure and subversively began to democratise both the venue and the medium (Ades in Mundy 2008). The artwork now began to confer a different status onto the walls of the city, illustrating views, philosophical, commercial or otherwise. In parallel to the work being produced in the world of fine art, one also needs to consider the technical developments in photography and photographic technique. These technological advances were undoubtedly instrumental in altering the classic palette of visual communication. The ability to disrupt overlay and suggest allowed images to convey more sophisticated and nuanced messages and these early technical advances still have resonance in the commercial photography and typography used in contemporary advertising. Subsequent development in the techniques of photomontage was another interesting progression into the phenomenon of disrupted reality, where the photograph, an emblem of reality, was de-contextualised and stripped of its purpose to represent a realistic arrangement. Within the photomontage the spaces and the interjected typography contributed to the intention of creating an image that had no immediate coherence but was intended as a provocative catalyst. The optical arrangements were interesting in that compositionally they were carefully considered, therefore if there was no desire to analyse the geometric arrangement, they created a degree of aesthetic attraction (Richter 1965).

Conversely the early work of Lazlo Moholy Nagy began to construct form with the use of sans serif letters stripped of ornament (Typo Collage 1922) and used the structural geometry of the letters and hyphenation as a form of aesthetic composition that was devoid of both pastoral or philosophical narrative and was constructed as purely an abstract compositional arrangement (Morley 2003). Perhaps the most compelling – and, I would argue, one of the most powerful – forms of textual image to emerge within the urban content at architectural scale is the work of Kurt Schwitters and the construction of the Merzbau in Hanover (Elderfield 1985). From the outset his work straddled literature and art, where the juxtaposition of words was contrived to create a rhythmic sequence. However, this work is not easily categorised, as his use of everyday detritus and disposable objects had a stronger affinity to Cubist collage than the politically strident art position of the day. The 'assemblages' were made from discarded objects: bus tickets, bottle tops, handbills, wrappers, cigarette butts were all to leave a fragmentary trace of people and their engagement with the city; it is impossible to view these compositions without attempting to construct an imaginary picture of time, place and person. This imagined world is, of course, a fiction, but no more so than the textual recollections of history. The work imbues enigma and has a fluidity of interpretation, yet also provides an exact record of how the artist and the subject physically interacted with the urban space. Schwitters' observations were to chronicle the actions of the everyday, the most mundane and repetitive events that form part of city life. In one sense his recordings of these miniscule acts represented a more accurate reflection of the way we lived in the city than any formalised strategic study. He was also one of the first artists working in this particular genre to simultaneously use his skills as both a fine and commercial artist, by undertaking advertising contracts set up through his own company, the Merz-Werbenzentrale (White, in Hunt et al. 2010). Fascinated by the interaction of words, letters, image and material, he created a holistic link to the world that illustrated the everyday. This work is the most architecturally evocative, as the disconnected images speak of the city not through the grandiosity of iconic building but through the small actions of the individual. There is a fascination with these serendipitous arrangements in that they have the possibility of creating new meanings and new connections, and they were also compelling in that they were blind tests, the outcome of which were always unknown. The constructions, originally built in his house, were the first significant installation that took art out of the galleries and into the wider world, also demonstrating how textualised image could be used as a three-dimensional construct to create an architectural alliteration. Unlike many of his contemporaries, Schwitters was also interested in the process of commercial marketing and for many years he worked as an advertising designer. He was initially categorised as an academic artist; he worked repeatedly with compositional language, continually inviting the challenge of message interpretation. Although there are few analysed links with the work of Schwitters and that of contemporary *urban writers*, the requirement to decode is shared by both. The geometric structure of the Merz assemblages together with their combination of symmetry and asymmetry and the rotational repetition echoes some of the formal compositional gambits of modern typography. The words used in his compositions were always structurally integrated, a legacy of his advertising skills. He was one of the first to consider the neurological impact of collage, where the eye scans the surface and tries to make sense of forms, whereas in figurative painting the eye is drawn into the perspective beyond the painting (Richter 1965). During the 1920s Schwitters became increasingly aware of the work of Constructivist artists, and because of the politicised nature of its graphic content, this work was more suited to public display than his own. This graphically constructed propaganda skilfully combined photographic image with text to create ideological message with formal imagery. It was in a different way that Russian artists were also demonising the bourgeois phenomena of fine art and using the public fora of the city as the vehicle for their message. However, one cannot consider the role and influence of typography and image in the urban realm without observing the darker and more political role it played in the totalitarian regimes in both Russia and Germany, where the control of communication and its power of persuasion was totally understood by the political authorities. Their stylistic adaptations were possibly rooted in the elemental form of the Soviet Constructivist art, where the abstraction of verbal language hinted at forms of utility and standardisation, and this became an implicit driving force of the message. Public advertising in urban space profoundly altered the conventions of reading. Assertive and arresting commercial messages were presented to the public confrontationally – and the method of delivery was unavoidable, unlike in other media such as books or newspapers that demanded individual intellectual choice. This phenomenon

used the city as the page and democratised the action of reading as the process of display brought written language to a wider socio-economic group. During the late 1920s and early 1930s the influence of commercial typography was to have a reciprocal relationship with architecture. Buildings appeared in paintings; urban surface and their typographic layers were used as a contemporary commentary on the urban condition, particularly in the works of Edward Hopper (Wagstaff 2004) and the photographer Walker Evans (Nau 2007).

A more poetic interpretation of words and the city was to be found in the work of the poet André Breton, who, working in collaboration with the photographer Jaques André Boiffard, produced a contemplation on the city entitled *Nadja*, where the entanglement of urban text and image were inseparable. This was to become a surface of the city where the two worked harmoniously as one. Although abstraction within painting developed through multiple influences emerging through the work of Klee and Miro, it was Magritte who developed a more profound relationship between word and image. In his work he confronts the viewer with visual puzzles presented largely through the arbitrary character of linguistic signs.

> The typographic elements along with collage and assemblage, were weapons in a campaign against painting as conventionally understood. (Lomas 2010)

Although text may have had the function of undermining *haut bourgeois* figurative painting, text was now being used in a dissociative manner to detach it from the purely instrumental function of delivering a message (Morley 2003).

The cumulative influence of pre- and post-First and Second World War art had, if not a direct, then an indirect influence on advertising. Magritte's semiotic exploration into the relationship between word and image may have influenced the view that advertising was often said to be the false resolution of word and image. If so, this prepared a generation of artists several decades later to challenge the concept of commodification and create a genre loosely labelled 'Pop Art', where the text image construct used in advertising was pressed into the service of fine art. The lens had revolved yet again. A parallel critique on commercialism and the consumer society in American Pop Art appeared at the same time in the more cynical work of the Independent Group in the UK, who were particularly aware of the cultural context to which they responded. A more 'spectacular' denunciation of commodity culture could be found in the work of Jacques Villegle and Raymond Hains, who produced work coined *décollage*, whose technical assemblies once again recalled the techniques of Schwitters (Corris 2010). The cacophony and discordance of these constructed images had remarkable parallels with the naturally evolving layers of text and urban writing that causes the urban surface to metamorphose. There emerged in the early 1950s an interesting characteristic that was to link the act of writing formally with *urban writing*, the spontaneous and uncontrolled act of creating marks in urban space. This was an emancipated form of writing, an act of physicality that created a spatial manifestation; once again there were close links to Eastern calligraphy, where embedded spatiality, the ability to represent message and space simultaneously, was a fundamental characteristic. Henri Michaux was one of the earliest to articulate the relationship between the act of bodily movement and the residual marks made in space. It was clear in this form of representation that there was a total abandonment of the formal linear arrangement and understanding; these were instinctive and primal marks that were to register little more than presence. But this, in the context of contemporary graffiti, was a critical move forward, away from the predictive formalism of linguistic communication (Lomas 2010).

Graffiti did not exist exclusively on the street wall; its visceral energy was a compelling force not ignored by those who wanted to make strident statements of intent and position. Both calligraphy and graffiti merged in the work of Antonio Tapies (1923–2012), where the use of reference alluded to the walls of his native city Barcelona and these were inscribed with marks that bore no trace of legibility. Although his spatial forms have close links with the harmonies of cosmic order, he also used these marks on the wall as an act of defiance in an era of fascist totalitarianism. This form of subversion was sufficiently abstract or perhaps primal that it avoided obvious legibility, but by its nature the act of writing on the wall is a natural act of protest (Borja-Villel 1993).

Unlike the graffiti-inspired work of the immediate post-war period, artists such as Rauschenberg, Dufrene, Hains and others were to take the surface of the city into the galleries. They attached torn posters and city detritus to canvases, redirecting the platitudes of the advertisers into much more elusive forms. Compositionally the works were vibrant and the work created an implicit 'eye' more common in the world of the graphic artist. In many ways this echoes and acts as a commentary on the work of the collagistes 50 years earlier.

At the same time as the art community was developing a dialogue with the city, there were lawless insurgents whose act of inscription 'and graffiti mark the very fabric of the city as an actor in the construction of urban life' (Corris 2010). It is debatable whether the inscription itself or the act has superior influence on the viewer. If it is the latter it denotes a culture of defiance and marks a form of possession that could only take place as part of urban life. Urban graffiti continued to offer a dynamic model, rooted in opportunism, exuding an energy that was lacking in the formally and commercially constructed images of the art world. The appropriation of such naïf forms has been criticised as little more than a stylistic cliché, but the taste of urban sophisticates showed little understanding of the primary forces that youth gangs needed in order to create both image and word with such visceral power. Much of the earliest graffiti had military origins – from the Viking warriors to Napoleonic troops and more recently the armed forces of the First and Second World Wars. All were concerned with stating the nature of conquest, and perhaps the subsequent armouring of letters into weapons has its cultural references in the professional activity of the warrior wall-writers of previous generations.

Graffiti became inextricably associated with local territoriality, a notion Gordon Matta-Clark explored in 1973 when he invited local residents to graffiti his delivery truck. The brash socio-political commentary of graffiti became an attraction for artists, who wanted this sub-cultural association. Basquiat was possibly the most notable artist to trade on this association; however, the unstructured lawless images that originally existed on the city surface lost their visceral power when translated into forms on canvas through a loss of physical and social context. Paradoxically, an unforeseen commercial success was the branding aimed at the youth market that emerged from this outlawed urban activity (Corris 2010). Contemporary urban graphics are regarded differently according to cultural genre and geographic location. Barthes' *Empire of Signs* (Trifonas 2001) establishes a commentary on Tokyo and the cultural acceptance of a city where the overwhelming overlay of typography and image is the commonly understood face of the city. The major cities of south-east Asia may be extreme examples, but during the 1950s and 1960s in Europe and the USA the same pattern was being followed. In London there was then, and is now, little if any legislative control over aesthetic language or typographic scale and yet this constitutes a very assertive and visual part of the urban surface. After the two World Wars an economic resurgence supported a consumerist economy that generated advertising covering significant areas of the city. Parts of the city were becoming devoid of visible buildings and were replaced by stylistically uncontrolled graphic images. The result was a visual cacophony that was simultaneously exhilarating and utterly confusing. The considerations of adjacency, material and scale, in fact any form of traditional contextualisation, was lacking from the protocol, the idea of 'blending in' must have been an anathema to the advertisers whose aim was to be as visually assertive as possible. This liberated (un)regulatory system existed in tandem with the growth of manufacturing. This emergent economy needed not only production but also consumption and, to that end, the mechanism of public communication became critical.

On successful advertising sites the buildings were and are still subordinated by messages designed to persuade the public to consume. This form of public communication has a scale that is unique and profoundly important, immediately arresting and largely determined by its architectural substructure; the image/message was to use a scale that was never seen in art galleries, painting, books or the media. The audience was often hijacked into paying attention, as the presentation of all forms of urban image and typography are an act of confrontation.

Contextually, there are major differences between the Asian cities of Tokyo and Hong Kong and European cities such as London. The south-east Asian cities share one characteristic in that neither has a venerated urban heritage that stretches back centuries; Tokyo was destroyed during the Second World War and rebuilt afterwards and Hong Kong is a city that is less than a century old. Both cities have a culture of consumption that fuels all aspects of commercial advertising. London, by contrast, has a markedly different history and culture that goes back to antiquity and, with it, a controlling regime of conservation. This attitude towards the preservation of the city fabric is nuanced by politics and the current *zeitgeist*, yet there is still a paradox in that control over the substance of the city is executed through fidelity to form, material and existing architectural language, yet often none of this is visible. The inescapable force of consumerism and how it began to alter our cultural thinking was captured by the work of Richard Hamilton, *Just What Is It That Makes Today's Homes So Different, So Appealing?* (1956) (Lippard 1966). Using a collage technique similar to Schwitters, he combined photography, painting and montage to produce a parody of consumerist desire. This differed from the images of the everyday that deified the object, in that Hamilton's work was a subtle yet cynical commentary on the facile nature of advertising and the implicit gullibility of those who want to believe the dream. This work was also a commentary on the media and how our lives are saturated with image and message, most insistently in the city, where it was quite simply inescapable.

Do the legitimate advertisers or the illegitimate graffiti artists choose to ignore the nature of urban surface, or do they actively deface it? Whether the displays are large and digital or hand-produced, they all share one characteristic in that they create a vertical surface that becomes a fragment or a complete urban wall, a 'new façade' and a new urban presence. This visual disturbance can be either an irritant or an accepted part of the urban visual language. From the seemingly neutral and un-politicised surface of the city, commercialised typography and unauthorised urban writing share a fundamental function in that the images, words and logos must communicate. Corporate investors make explicit statements to encourage consumerism and the scale of corporate power enables huge promotional images to cover the elevations of entire buildings. Throughout the last six decades there has emerged aggressive commercialisation and marketing; the growth of consumerist culture has led to the transformation of the city's surface. One has to ask about the nature of legislative controls, the influence of politics and the significance of lobbying and economic power as parts of the inner city disappear under a blanket of exhortations to buy. By contrast, those cities that have developed under different political and commercial regimes are remarkably naked. Prior to unification, the starkest contrast was to be found in a divided Berlin, where the West had all the overlay of commercial graphics and the East starkly presented itself through buildings alone. This contrast marked a historic moment that has now changed as the country's fiscal policies have developed a united culture. During the 1970s and 1980s the work of a younger generation of artists was inextricably linked to the developments in media technology and the cultures of documentary, journalistic photography and the cinema.

Perhaps the most influential work that utilised text as art is the later work of Jenny Holzer and Barbara Kruger, where messages usually political in nature are displayed in the public arena. Holzer was one of the first of her generation to exploit urban space to situate art and demonstrate that the combination of image and text could be more effective outside the effete world of the gallery or the economically inaccessible printed portfolio. However, there were installations that had a particular association with specific architectural space, as for example the Holzer installation in the Guggenheim in Bilbao. One might argue that this particular physical siting removes democracy from the audience and takes the work back into the arena of elite art; however, it does emphasise that art, particularly text, is now a mode of public address.

The geometric dynamism of the city aggressively accentuated in places such as Times Square in New York, Ginza in Tokyo and Piccadilly Circus in London, with their saturated neon emblems, captivated the American painter Stuart Davies, whose work appropriated the cultural associations of contemporary branding. But the cross-cultural influence between the commercial advertisement and the fine art statement was to be further adjusted with the advances in media technology. It cannot be underestimated how the process of communication has changed over the last 20 years. The influence of personal electronic media has not only changed the technical means by which we communicate; it has also adjusted the way we absorb information. The process of scanning has allowed us to understand message through headline and inference, thereby rendering the urban caption even more potent.

The visual din of the contemporary metropolis forces the observer to filter information; unlike the flâneurs of the nineteenth century, who were able to drink in every detail at their leisure, the contemporary walker is assaulted by typographic insistence and images of persuasion. The natural tendency in many must be to defy and resist. Alongside this emergence of visually riotous urban surface was the emergence of another set of skills through the development of electronic and digital media, which offered alternative ways to understand and process information. Electronic billboards displaying rolling information, mobile phones, digitised timetables and personal computers have all contributed to creating a synoptic language, either through text or image, that allows us to absorb information quickly. The nature of this information has created multiple and parallel strands of understanding that now demand simultaneous attention. The essence of this language is that it must communicate quickly and effectively through globally understood signage where words and images can be recognised simply, yet these simple statements often have multiple layers of inference.

There were those artists such as Mel Bochner and Ed Ruscha, who worked with text and image, whose messages were both superficially explicit yet were also enigmatic in that the artworks contained multiple interpretations which became even more potent when the observer was left to construct their own meaning. This could also be seen in the work of multimedia artists such as Bruce Nauman and Gary Hill – Nauman more explicitly manipulating language and Hill exploring the dynamic of word and images and its impact on space – perhaps more notably the phenomenological effect of installations such as *Tall Ships* and *Crux* (Cooke and Quasha, in Mignot and Eleonor 1993).

While the Conceptualists were analysing the construction and interpretation of word, an even more dynamic and visceral language emerged from its genesis in the 1950s in New York; in the 1960s, *urban writing* emerged as a counter-cultural phenomenon. Spray-can graffiti used cheap, easily available material; the 'wild style' artists were essentially expressing forms of individual or collective presence. The 'wild style crews' colonised different parts of the city, their dynamic signature and political invective as much a statement of cultural identity as a means of communication. The walls of the city offered a blackboard for each group, who would carefully select their sites, all of which had to be appropriate for purpose. In most instances the intention was to make a statement that claimed territory, therefore these sites had to be geographically specific. For others, a demonstration of bravado needed sites that were inherently dangerous, such as railway bridges and tunnels. For those who had extraordinary graphic skills, the sites were chosen to be as publicly visible as possible

(Mai and Remke 2003). The city surface is therefore stratified and prioritised; location and ownership are important to both the commercial and guerrilla groups, as are the economic and demographic status of the audience and the restrictions of authorised and unauthorised control. The position of wall writing is determined by its purpose, its cultural role and the nature of the message, particularly statements about the importance of risk. While the urban artist may be driven to make an individual statement, statements of social cohesion and political invective also have positions within the city and create identity for different areas and streets. The scale and complexity of street art vary, and the need for obviously designated public space may not be a priority for those who create spontaneous graphic statements; however, ethnographic boundaries provide understood territory for information that is often encrypted and displayed as part of the local sub-culture. Carlo McCormick comments that graffiti has now spread across the globe as a '*dominant language*' and considers that these forms of systematic display need to be read.

> Urban art is a measure of our relationship to the urban experience, and as such we need to understand the role of the city as muse in order to contextualise the kinds of expression it engenders … and we need to take up the questions that are actually being posed. (McCormick, in Deitch 2011)

The act of 'tagging' was a codified form of territoriality. It was primitive and explicit, using forms of presentation that were only alluded to by the informal art community. The 'tag' is a simple outline of letters usually spray painted onto a wall to signify identity.

This 'free style' expressed the sweep of bodily movement and some were embellished to the point of illegibility. However, these marks were illegal and seen as aggressive acts against the fabric of the city, suggesting a counter-cultural status of significant import. The acts of tagging, bombing and fly-posting were far removed from the slick commercial images of the advertising agencies, yet both relied on the city as the canvas to provide a public arena where the message was both insistent and unavoidable, yet rarely considered in formal terms or evaluated as a valid part of the urban panorama. At first glance tagging appears to be an activity that is not only implicitly but also explicitly antithetical to both the law and any form of authority. Despite its dissociation with the formalised world of art, there emerged tenuous links through artists such as Basqiat and Haring that created an intellectual and vital thread back into the established form of commercial and fine art. A critical study into the socio-economic catalysts that were at the core of this explosive form of expression has yet to be undertaken; social and economic factors were an obvious determinant, but the desire to create illegal, subversive statements in public venues had never been seen before so assertively and in such volume. This form of urban writing is inextricably linked to other forms of street culture, music, dancing and street sport in that it expresses the need for identity in a world where the formal routes of expression are restricted to commercially backed media. Much of the early graffiti that came from New York was sprayed onto trains and the style was such that they needed to be understood through movement; those who wrote on moving objects were conscious of the fact that, stylistically, they were quite different from static images (Corris, in Hunt et al. 2010, Mai and Remke 2003).

In London, the origins of wall-writing existed through political messages, many of them stylistically inspired by the exaggerated typography of the comic strip. The more complex pieces were not only about statement and identity but also developed artistic signatures that were both recognised and respected. Much of what was painted was illegal and often sited on parts of a wall surface that were so physically inaccessible that the status of the artist was enhanced through the element of danger that painting necessitated. The complexity of some of the work attracted the interest of the local councils, who then commissioned artists to spray in areas where the young would gather. The audience for these pieces was, for a long time, adolescent youth. This form of communication was also an expression of something much more onerous – youth unemployment.

The reception of this urban art was polarised. If painted onto walls in a fashionable, expensive part of the city, it would be considered vandalism and a call would be made for its removal. If, on the other hand, an art piece were constructed on the walls of a derelict site, it would rarely be admonished. McCormick makes the point that what we see on the walls actually describes a much larger social and economic picture that needs to be understood.

> This then is the nature of writing on the wall today: it is not only about what is written but also fundamentally about reading what is already there. (McCormick, in Deitch 2011)

The tactics of urban writing are intimately connected with the infiltration or possession of public space. Urban surface is the critical canvas and without the surface of the city the impetus to make these marks disappears. There was therefore a fundamental difference between those who created visual images on paper for galleries and publication and those who used the democratised surface of the city. The substance of urban writing is also distinguished from its commercial counterpart by transience; graffiti is now removed from some surfaces almost more quickly than it can be created. The production of any mark involves an understanding of the creation of form. In the case of urban writing, this form must be both concise yet also assertive. It must take possession of space and must deliver a message with subliminal impact. Much of the action is to establish territory and execute an act that is primal and instinctive, an act that lacks complex premeditated strategies. However, the physical action involved is disciplined and choreographed, as stylistic refinement is honed to a higher level. There is a unique chemistry that bonds the writer, their action and the calligraphic trace, left on the surface of the city that in turn becomes a submissive collaborator in the act.

> Writing is culture ... Nowadays, tags are so ubiquitous that they have become practically invisible in an urban camouflage. (Klanten and Ehmann, in Mai and Remke 2003)

Does urban writing denigrate the city or does it enliven it? These acts are interesting in that they can be acts of improvisation, as we see from the term 'jazz style', a term coined in the 1950s as a metaphor of jazz improvisation. The quality of anticipation is inherent in an action where the outcome is unknown. The calligraphy is loosely based on the Latin alphabet and the stylisation has an inherent rule system, which does not necessarily extend to the linear construct of semantic coherence, and is therefore a system of codification. Within the system of code there can develop a framework of extended geometry and balance that can only be produced by those with an intuitive design 'eye'; the balance of the form must work and the gestural dynamic of the letter must deliver the right implication. The city becomes a surface of gestures and messages, a book of curiosities to which the formal language of architecture rarely refers. However, there are some, if not conscious, then subliminal, references to the work of contemporary de-constructivist architects such as Liebskind and Hadid, where the liquidity of form and the rejection of platonic geometry influences writing style.

Some have taken their skill as writers and sought references outside the artificial surface of the city. Akim is one of the contemporary artists who has produced work that reflects both organic and inorganic, resulting in three-dimensional models, that echo and challenge the spaces they occupy. Environment becomes a critical component in the evolution of these pieces, yet the balance of the constructed piece can be made without the constraints of architectural process (Akim, in Mai and Remke 2003).

For those writers who develop their work into three dimensions, similarities can be drawn with the work of the early Constructivists. The use of digital technology has supported the exploration of the object in three dimensions, which does not appear as a transformed visualisation on a flat surface but as a physical reality in space; therefore the evolution of this highly stylised calligraphy occupies not only the surface of the city but now space within the city.

The social aspect of this phenomenon is unique among these artists in that groups will come together and work in an improvised way with one another. The outcome is therefore the sum process of interaction and spontaneity, its value being the creation of the unexpected experience. For some, this may merely be regarded as a visual intrusion; for others, the creation of urban writing is a phenomenological experience.

The process of applying information onto the wall starts with the line and in a sense one might see this as the most reductive form of codification. All the information is contained within the outline and the rest is merely decorative. This shares some characteristics with the production of architecture, where all information is initially contained and held within the line, yet both languages use at their core a highly abstracted vocabulary.

More recently there is evidence that the urban writer and the commercial advertiser have created a combative relationship. Politically strident artists and writers (Zevs, in Mai and Remke 2003) use the city as a vehicle for anti-propaganda and engage in 'visual kidnapping', where critical parts of the commercial text are removed in order to radically undermine the message.

The web of influence is complex and in many ways impossible to untangle, but consider the city as a surface for message, a collage of image, word and line. The visual, polemical and philosophical principles of this group of artists have not only leaked into the formal arena of the galleries, but also into all forms of commercial identity and branding. There is an unspoken consensus that this characterises a type of dynamic and positional lifestyle; it is this association with un-named images that now carries subliminal importance and commercial value. The primary structure of urban writing, the Latin alphabet, has had typographical styles added to create an urban dynamic on the walls of the city's streets. Caricatures that emanated from the culture of the comic strip, which strongly influenced the urban writers, are now absorbing street style as part of their vocabulary.

Is this applied notation an architectural substitute? By this I do not imply that it is a second choice or inferior quality to the architecture it conceals, but a reality that now constitutes a large presence in the inner city. One might argue that it is now possible to subvert the formal lexicon of architectural language through calligraphic representations, but this will tell us nothing about the nature of the enclosure, only about the nature of the synthetic façade.

Perhaps one should finally meditate on the observation of Roland Barthes, who talks about the city as the 'City of Signs'. At what point do we experientially distinguish between the substance of architecture and the surface of information that wrestles to attract our attention? One might argue that the phenomenological experience of the city is an assault of information, not the formal spatial sequence one would find only in cities whose political regime denounced capitalism.

Urban writing is vibrant, aggressive and often confusing. It can become a historic trail, an archaeological layering of fragmentary information to be put together in memory, but it is unquestionably embedded into the urban fabric.

PECKHAM HOUSE

Peckham is an area in south-east London that was originally established as an eighteenth-century village; the community were tradespeople and craft workers who supplemented their existence through small-scale arable allotments. The area underwent rapid redevelopment during the nineteenth century and, while it still remained an artisan community, there were now pockets of comparative affluence on the southern boundaries. Within the area, early Victorian bourgeois housing emerged and later isolated examples of neo-modernist commercial buildings. The impact of the First and Second World Wars arrested the burgeoning prosperity and the area then fell into what many would consider irredeemable decline. The socio-economic history of an urban community is critical, not only recorded in text and photograph, but because it also leaves behind material traces that are the memory of waves of human activity and endeavour. The fabric of the city is rarely examined for the evidence of everyday activity. It was artists such as Picabia and Schwitters who were more intrigued by the mundanity of the everyday where, for example, Schwitters' Merz constructions tried to make sense of the world around him through the discarded objects that were the residue of human activity.

1.3a   Reference material: timber

1.3b   Reference material: metal mesh

1.3c   Reference material: window frame

1.3d   Reference material: urban writing

More recently Rauschenberg's *Combines* found that reference to contemporary objects illustrated a subsumed commentary of the everyday, but this was in an art, not an architectural, context. Architects have only relatively recently realised that the exposure of historic layering has some value. Scholarly conservation retains and restores the fabric of the past yet reconstructs a falsification in that it denies the impact of time. There are a small number of architects who have worked with the concept of exposure, allowing the act of decay or material transformation to be seen and understood (Fehn's Hamar Museum, d'el Co's Castelvechio). Among contemporary architects there is an appetite (often driven by economics) to retain and reveal where the patina of historic layers becomes an aesthetic construct. If individual buildings contain inherent information that can be revealed, the surface of the city should accept similar scrutiny.

This project was first initiated in 1986 and was a conscious attempt to define a methodology that incorporated a contemporary reflection of the city's surface rather than the orthodoxy of architectural reference. The site in Peckham, south-east London, was deliberately chosen as it displayed signs of a richly evolving history. Amidst the decay and neglect there was a multicultural community that, despite economic deprivation, maintained a vivid sub-culture. The sub-culture had one compelling aspect of expression: visual 'vandalism'. To categorise the wall coverings as graffiti is simplistic, as it carries a bureaucratically negative image; it could be interpreted as a vibrant expression of identity, which combines political commentary with visceral presence. This was a London neighbourhood that had little commercial investment and very little technically sophisticated advertising; the writing and marks

1.4 Writing fragment circa 1987

of this area were evidence of the energy and the anxieties of a disenfranchised yet culturally vocal community.

There are many ways one can look at the city and it is critical to understand that a formalist approach used by the planning system to control architectural reference is not the only option to maintain urban integrity. If one chooses to look at another form of reference – and I would argue one that is equally authentic – one can see antique scars, the remnant of fliers, overwriting and decay; it is an extraordinary testament to time that so much information is evident. The layering of information as one handbill is posted on top of another is often non-political and socially neutral. There are, of course, handwritten and hand-painted statements that exhort the observer to beware; some are threatening, some are ironic, tags are written as symbols of identity and marks of territoriality. This is the city's blackboard, where messages can be written, overwritten and erased, leaving evidence and memories of people, whether they be communities, activists or the dissolute. The area was ideal to observe where one could trace and construct the memory of generations of human activity. The formal process of architectural reference neutralises the trace of human dynamic; there is little consideration of human intervention; all references are object based, yet the physicality which is observed contains no narrative.

This project therefore offers an alternative form of reference that looks at the nature of urban surface with both intrinsic historic narrative and of the signs of how time has affected its material composition.

THE PROCESS

Navigating an area half a mile in circumference established an area where the photographic survey could be constructed. Initially these images were intuitively selected, but during the process I became aware that these images needed a thematic thread that showed the effect of time and intervention on surface. Some images simply showed the effect of weather, while others showed how the surface had been used for expression and communication. Economically neglected, it was in many ways a perfect destination to show the unrepaired ravages of time. Many of the walls bore marks, whether statements or damage; much was indecipherable but these graphic marks were evidences of a rolling tide of events. There was something evocative about these surface collages that had developed opportunistically through anarchic acts of writing, to register a form of communication that was invisible in conventional arenas. These images displayed a different lexicon; unfettered by the classic edicts of composition, the marks were gymnastic arcs. This form of street writing was direct, immediate, sinuous and aggressive. Other traces on handbills and posters were passive reminders of events, constructed through crude typography, torn and overlaid, fractured images that needed memory to reconstruct.

Hidden within the area was a small piece of land that encapsulated the local character, a site of an abandoned Victorian school, which had been abandoned and empty for over 50 years, a scene of ill-regarded remnants, crumbling walls and rotten fences; corrugated sheet used to protect the site had also become the victim of time. The surface was both rusted and burnt, displaying a potent

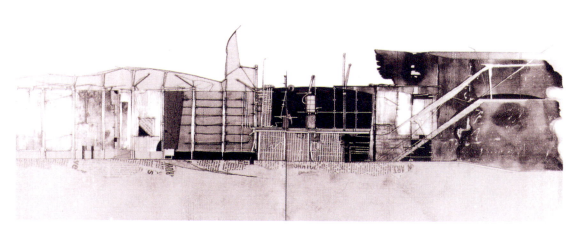

1.5a   Material references: weathered timber frame (original image turned into black and white photograph)

1.5b   Distorted metal (original image turned into black and white photograph)

1.5c   Weathered boards (original image turned into black and white photograph)

1.6   Sketch of internal long section using materials from the site (original image turned into black and white photograph)

creating a collage of indiscriminately broken words, demonstrating both opportunism and circumstance. The metamorphosis was not entirely negative; there was visual appeal in the patina as well as the objects of deformation. Here was evidence that time and people had created new colours, new textures and new geometries. There was also a philosophical appeal in that within the idea of cyclical change there is the possibility of reinterpretation or transformation.

The project not only occupied the same site as the fragments, but also borrowed from them in both an aesthetic and inspirational sense, incorporating pieces of material found on site. The ambition was to create a form of spatial enclosure that had at least a symbiotic if not a parasitic relationship with the derelict structure and, by incorporating non-standard references, challenge the familiar protocols of context and create a lexicon that could deviate from the familiar.

A methodological programme was established that took the photographic record and subjected it to a series of transformations. It was important that the process was an exploratory tool and not a method of representation; therefore there was a conscious decision not to strategise the outcome. Each stage revealed new information; the act of taking a pictorial image and transforming it involved making hierarchical decisions about content. The process was iterative and with each stage minor decisions about form, relationship to content and image changed.

After carefully scrutinising the site, all material and objects considered relevant to the concept were photographed, but at this point the decisions were instinctive; inevitably surplus

burst of colour yet also revealing a more ominous tale of accident and decomposition. Other building material had been gradually eroded; these crumbling forms were now overrun by the tangle of nature. A rectangle existed to indicate a door opening; nearby the frame lay discarded. There were sweeping gestures of wall writing – some dynamic, others uncomfortably geometric – time and weather had eroded some of the more vivid marks, others remained legible.

The site also displayed torn layers of printed paper, several layers pasted over one another,

1.7   Political rhetoric

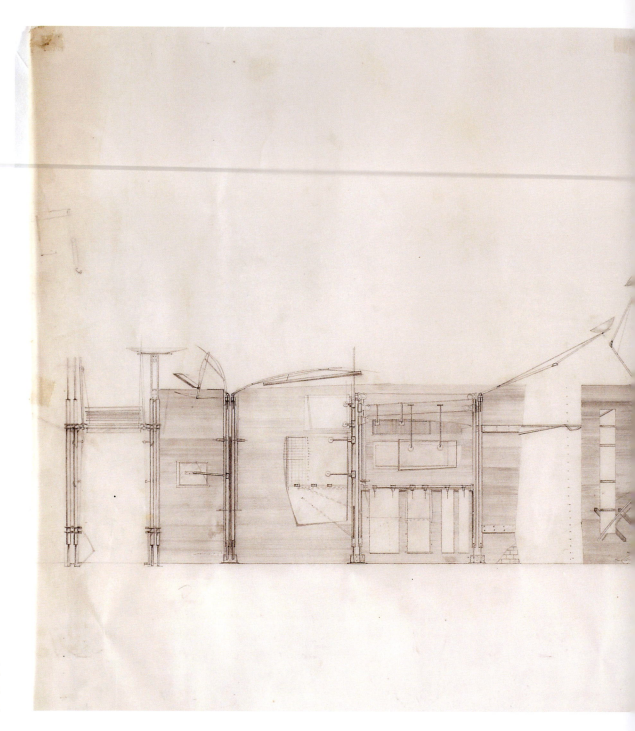

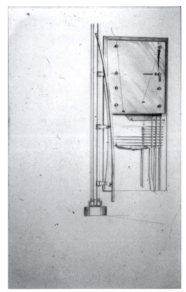

pictorial information was edited out. These early photographs were in colour and the information was distractingly figurative; the images were changed to black and white, and, by doing so, some of the realistic associations were removed. Elemental abstraction was necessary at each level of the process. These black and white photographs were then re-interpreted as hand-drawn sketches, introducing mimetic texture and shape that maintained some visible relationship to the original materials. The process of pencil-sketching was used as a developmental tool to try to extract as much formal and textual potential as possible. The synoptic language produced an abstracted geometry that combined with a number of textures to produce surfaces of infinite variability.

The challenge was how to interpret this information and use it in such a way that a spatial proposition could be constructed. Initially the information was drawn as a series of flat panels with frames, enabling them to be connected. The combination of panels was intuitive but it

also offered the opportunity to make a further referencing system by incorporating into the drawing many of the 'as found' objects from site.

An analysis of the site suggested that if any enclosure were feasible, it would have to have a close structural relationship with the original frame of the school. A process was developed to utilise the abstracted images and site material into a unitised panel system that formed the basis of an enclosure. Any direct association with function could compromise the concept, and at this point the drawings were still used only for the process of translation. In retrospect it is clear that when the drawings emerged there were too many implicit references to architectural orthodoxy and this in hindsight compromised the process as the final volume had identifiable floors and spaces with an implied functionality.

The panels were developed, first by systematically recording a motif onto each panel of the screen; the panels recorded script, commercial typography and materiality. The second part of the

1.11   Sketch ground plan
1.12   Sketch first floor plan
1.13   Sketch second floor plan
1.14   Sketch roof plan

1.15   Sketch interior perspective
1.16   Sketch panel detail

process was to ingrain the images with material found on site and it was important that the material evidence could be clearly read. There were, of course, issues of scale and these were adapted wherever possible. Sand, burnt wood, metal, newsprint, discarded objects were all incorporated. The technique of course is known through Dadaist assemblage, yet this seemed an appropriate technique to try and capture some memory of place and human activity.

1.17   Final ground plan using site materials

1.18   Final first floor plan using site materials

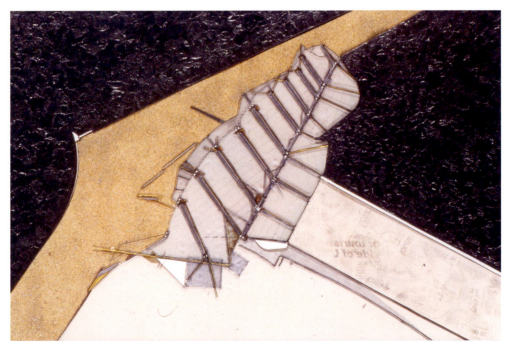

1.19   Final second floor plan using site materials

1.20   Final roof plan using site materials

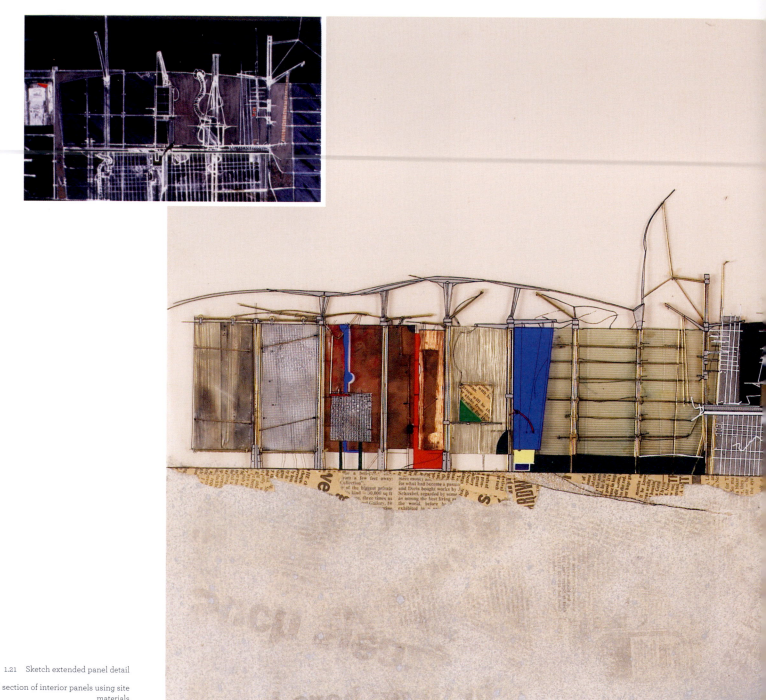

1.21　Sketch extended panel detail

1.22　Final section of interior panels using site materials

THE PROCESS, 25 YEARS LATER

I revisited the project to consider whether the fundamental concept was still valid and, if so, whether it could be further developed. The project was essentially a reflection on the process of time and the traces it left for us to read; the original site of the school no longer exists and the area has become more sanitised. Residual traces still exist in hidden corners, but the overwhelming character of the area covered with opportunistic graphics has disappeared. It has been replaced with a more orderly system of commercial advertisement, but groups that still needed guerrilla tactics to communicate chose their locations carefully: the messages are still there if you look for them.

In retrospect the process of empirical analysis and translation was a useful developmental tool and one that could in part be used again. On this second occasion there was the challenge to recall memory and, in doing so, explore how to represent the nature of the invisible.

1.23   View of interior panel, constructed 2012

If memory lacks material reality, there needs to be a visible tool that suggests the intangible. As a tactic, the plans of the previous scheme were remodelled and stripped of all colour; they were to represent ghosts from the past. While still pursuing the original idea, this iteration was liberated from architectural protocols. However, the references are now contemporary and the physical process of constructing the drawing allows certain ideas to emerge that would have been impossible through a premeditated process. There is an interior corridor, now built as a *bas relief*; the pieces are constructed with the more contemporary technology, so there is an interesting symmetry in the idea that the line as memory is incised through laser technology as a negative mark. Following the aesthetic language of the original, the screens are slightly more articulated and bear the graphic images that exist 25 years later. One of the primary intentions of this exercise was to explore memory; the construction of the assemblage deliberately uses light and shadow to suggest the ephemeral quality of the imagination. The project is still ongoing.

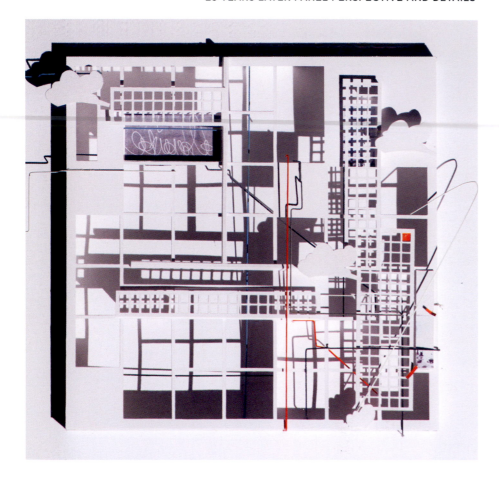

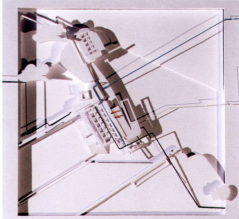

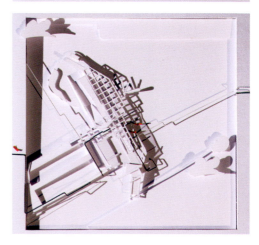

1.24   Final interpretive paper model, 2012

1.25   Paper and wire details of all levels, 2012:
             lower level

1.26   Mid level

1.27   Upper level

TKTS

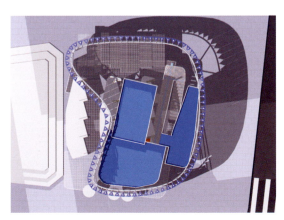

1.28   Ticket booth advertising panel

1.29   Ticket booth roof plan

1.30   Ticket booth advertising screen showing
blank surface

WITH ABIGAIL ASHTON AND ANDREW PORTER

Architecture is not physical; it is electronic, or it might be in certain parts of the city. The urban metropolis constructs a digital veil that conceals architectural presence yet constructs a new architecture that is produced electronically. The fascination with urban collage as an alternative form of city reference started with the application of paper and paint onto the architectural surface. However, advances in electronic technology have made synthetic urban-scale images possible. These are obviously the realm of corporate sponsors and lack the wit and spontaneity of guerrilla art. The images and the slogans may be predictable and sink into the background of human perception, but collectively they form an impression of the city not built with orthodox materials but constructed out of wires and light. The city is an illusory object – a fiction that exists at its most forceful at night and becomes slightly more muted during the day – and it is this facet of the city that was both overpowering and the most notable landmark of Times Square in New York.

The organisers of the competition required a replacement ticket booth to sell cinema and theatre tickets directly to the public. These booths, wherever they are in a major urban metropolis, are architecturally anonymous and only announce their presence through a barrage of typography informing the public what is currently available. The principle of message and communication needed to be maintained, not only to inform but also to prompt the spontaneous buyer. In the hierarchy of architectural planning, the structure assumed secondary importance and the role of typography became primary. The principles of the canopy were similar to the rotating corner of the Pravda building by Vesnin (St Petersberg 1924), the function of which was to keep the public periodically updated with headline announcements. Even at this early stage of the twentieth century, the city and its surface were seen as a suitable vehicle for typographic communication.

The centre of Times Square is a lacklustre space during the day, when the alternating lights of advertising space compete with each other and ambient daylight. During the night the tawdry equipment transforms into a blaze of colour and completely erases the spatiality of this urban landmark. The architectural presence of the ticket booth therefore became secondary and the references were only to the coloured images visible at night. The point of sale was organised at pavement level through three glass kiosks. The material of these enclosures was to be as unobtrusive as possible. An electronically activated screen, conceived as the most assertive architectural statement, surrounded the administrative office at the first level. The screen was made of a series of triangulated fins, each edge of which had a different surface. The integral motors periodically rotated the fins to enable either a pictorial or typographic statement to be seen by the public. Rotated for the second time the surface is mirrored, enabling the upper part of the building to reflect everything around. If the sensory experience of Times Square is visually incoherent, the purpose of this structure is not only to bring order but also to enhance and magnify the dynamic chaos. Rotated for the third time the fins are blue and provide a visual pause. There are a number of variables: on some occasions the fins rotate in a synchronised manner, producing a unified surface, whether typographic or reflective; and on other occasions they may not be synchronised to produce images that are on occasion reflection of urban chaos.

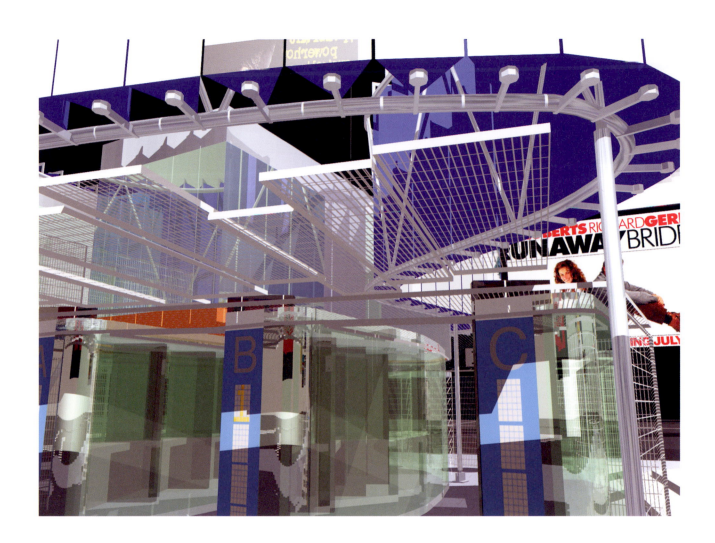

1.31   Ticket booth entrance perspective

PALOS VERDES ART CENTER, CALIFORNIA

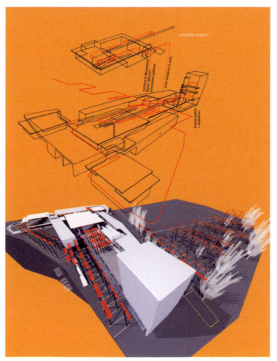

1.32   Entrance sign on textile wall

1.33   Palos Verdes Art Center, exploded view

1.34   Palos Verdes Art Center car park and
        photovoltaic sun shades

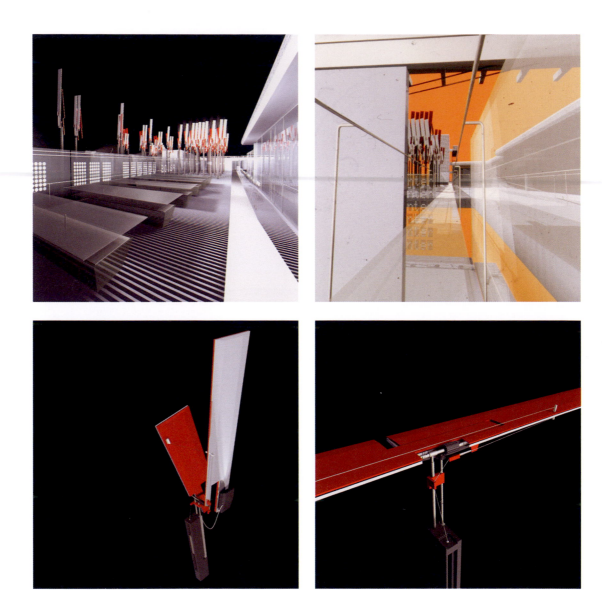

WITH CJ LIM

An existing community arts centre on the edge of an arterial road leading to Palo Alto, California, required an extension to its existing facilities: the accommodation needed to be doubled in size and the obvious response was to adapt the original house. However, the property, built in the 1920s, was designed as a large family house and little had been altered despite the function having changed. There was little interest in making major alterations and simply leaving the shell; somehow the historic integrity of the old house was more important. Therefore attention was turned to a large area adjacent to the property that was currently used as a car park.

Provision for cars is an unavoidable part of the Californian lifestyle, but the excess space dedicated for cars suggested that part of it might be utilised in other ways, satisfying the needs of expansion and addressing the conceptual and aesthetic problem of car use.

Before the development of a synthetic landscape could be addressed, some modification to the house was necessary to understand both the logistics of sequence and also how movement could be made smoothly from one function to the next. Most functions of the centre were craft based and it was therefore necessary to maintain some physical fluency in the design processes. The spatial and functional adjacencies were opened up where possible to create more visual connections between the existing house and the exterior. A reviled form of landscape, the car park was, in the Californian climate, not only an eyesore but at the height of the summer also a suntrap and heat island. Although one of the central problems was environmental and about car use, one had to accept that vehicular access was inevitable and, in doing so, develop it as a dynamic part of the project.

The challenge was therefore not only to extend the working space of the building but also to consider how to make the dominant feature of the site less hostile. The existing landscape was already synthetically constructed with no evidence of anything natural; therefore there was some logic to extend a synthetic concept into a spatial reality. Two components created the formal addition: the first was a synthetic hedge and the second was a series of synthetic flowers used as sunshades.

There was a need for simple spaces that could support craft activity that did not rely on complex technical infrastructure, therefore small rooms were located within an artificial hedge that formed the boundary of the extension. The dedicated activity in these spaces centred around textiles and therefore a wall was designed made from a series of small receptacles capable of holding textile samples and the wall was seen as a changing display of product from the craft studios. The receptacles were small to make it possible to create both images and text to act as either a graphic display or signage for the centre. The cellular nature of the construction created high thermal insulation, negating the need for supplementary environmental control.

Sun shading constructed as the metaphor of a flower offered not only a critical form of environmental control over the car park but also provided shade in the open-air social area at the rear of the house. These pseudo-organic elements were abstracted to have a residual formal similarity to plants, but their functional purpose was to provide shade, particularly during prolonged periods of hot weather.

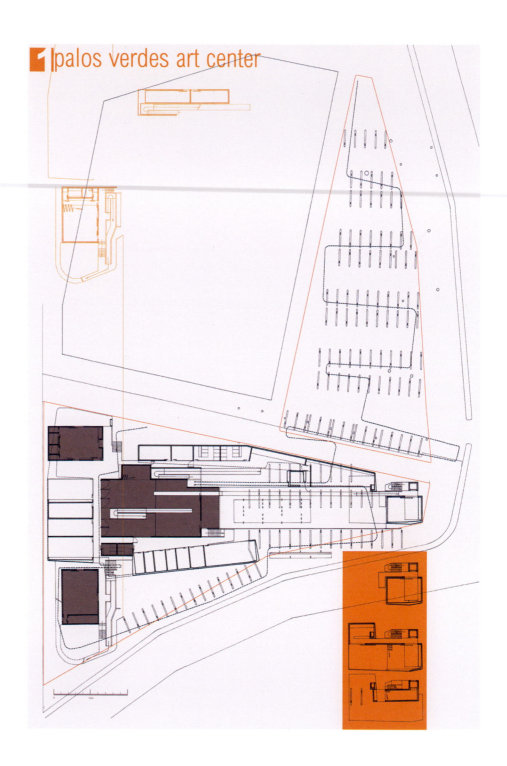

palos verdes art center

1.39   Ground level plan

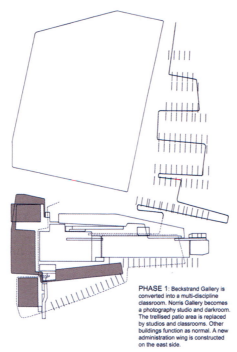

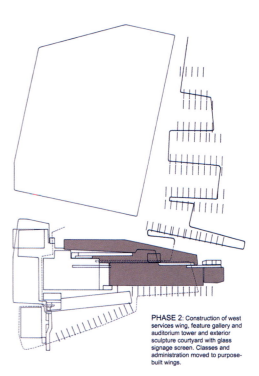

PHASE 1: Beckstrand Gallery is
converted into a multi-discipline
classroom. Norris Gallery becomes
a photography studio and darkroom.
The trellised patio area is replaced
by studios and classrooms. Other
buildings function as normal. A new
administration wing is constructed
on the east side.

PHASE 2: Construction of west
services wing, feature gallery and
auditorium tower and exterior
sculpture courtyard with glass
signage screen. Classes and
administration moved to purpose-
built wings.

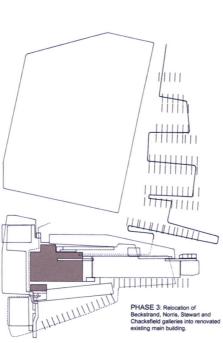

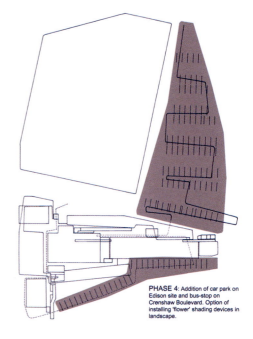

PHASE 3: Relocation of
Beckstrand, Norris, Stewart and
Chacksfield galleries into renovated
existing main building.

PHASE 4: Addition of car park on
Edison site and bus-stop on
Crenshaw Boulevard. Option of
installing 'flower' shading devices in
landscape.

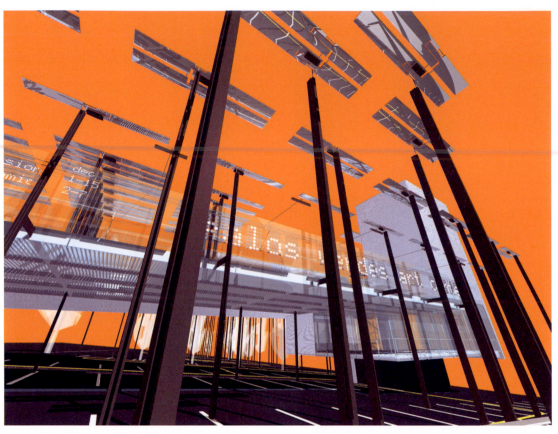

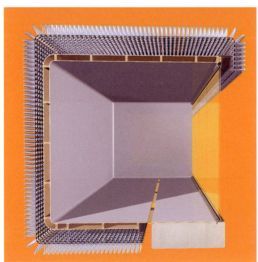

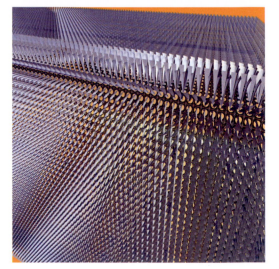

1.44   Bus stop shading

1.45   Cross section through workshop and
textile wall

1.46   Detail of textile wall

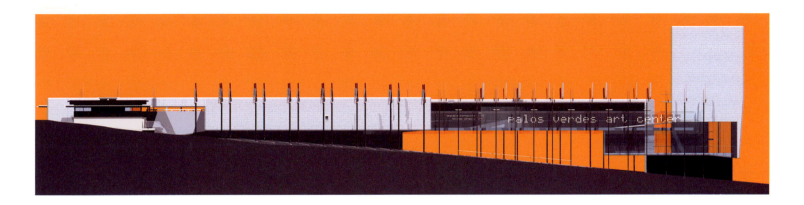

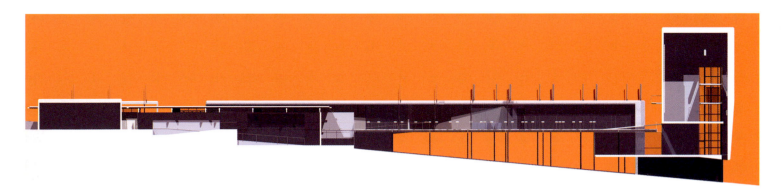

1.47 Section through shading and original
building

1.48 Elevation of bridge link

1.49 Section through bridge link

Individual structures were controlled by a light sensors, that activated the blades allowing them to ultimately open into a horizontal position. The upper surfaces were faced with photovoltaic cells, enabling each structure to be self-charging and therefore not need supplementary power. Once the sun had set the blades would return to the closed position; these were sited throughout the area to the rear of the house and formed a landscape that created greater environmental control through a synthetic interpretation of nature. There are certain parallels within this project to the augmented reality found in film and text, where a mechanistic horizon acts as a substitute for nature. Although not as apocalyptic, there is some association with the images created in E.M. Forster's *The Machine Stops*, where in a post-nuclear world the surface is barren and only through artificial support humanity can survive. This may be a paradox with the functions contained within a craft centre, where its very purpose is to create by hand, not by machine, however, the contrapuntal nature of the organic and the mechanistic serves to heighten the importance of each. Although this project focuses on the car park, it also uses the wall surface of the artificial hedge as a form of communication that changes with time, communicating both the function of the centre and displaying craftwork. Palos Verdes as a design uses both urban typography as a form of communication and also challenges the nature of the ground. It is a project not neatly categorised, referencing both the conversations of Urban Collage and Ground Surface.

Ground Surface

The relationship of architecture to the ground is fundamental not only in a physical sense but in that it demands an awareness of history and how elements have forged reciprocal relationships. The land is a rich source of cultural references that has allowed writers, painters and filmmakers to appropriate both the spectacle and its poetic concepts. It offers a medium of translation, which has great potential to deliver insight into the meandering route of the imagination. The ground as a tool of evocation provides reference that moves from mythology to social iconography, with the capacity to carry a complex implicit narrative. The land and its associations use personal narratives and the evocation of memory but it is also a place of death. The land is both a physical reality but, more interestingly, it is also a construct of our imagination. We look at it with our eyes but we use other senses to interpret and create a relationship with 'place' that is quite unique. This chapter tries to connect discussions of the ground, where an association with the etymology of the land (scape) has shaped the thinking around a spatial project.

There is an arc of reference often used that engages with topography, historic landscape and the garden, where the translation of critical characteristics with their numerous syntactical similarities is arguably easier to appropriate than other metaphorical or allegorical language. The projects to which this chapter refers reflect on the associative nature of land/garden; these oneiric and exploratory proposals are as much a product of unconscious affinities as they are of direct literary reference. The projects contain a fascination with the micro vocabulary of ground, illustrating how the textual and visually visceral play an important part in propelling ideas forward.

There is a long and deep history of land representation in classical art and literature and, more recently, the philosophical deliberations of the landscape urbanists have been at the forefront of a contemporary environmental debate. This text does not claim to be either a methodological or ideological declaration, only a statement of awareness, where certain facts or views are important because they linger at the forefront of one's consciousness and others are notable by their absence. This cannot be an exhaustive historic review, as these are ubiquitous and have been executed with commendable academic precision. The chapter will, however, suggest connections and use observation to raise questions about the nature of influence during the process of design. In some ways this must sound like an apologia, but in my experience there is often no clear linear route from idea to proposition; it is the circuitous bye-ways that are much more interesting. Sources of interest and influence have been wide ranging, including painting, film, installation art, photography and literature; some have been forensically deconstructed and moved into the architectural realm, but many others have just prompted a reflexive response. Methods of representation and physical reality have both been considered equally legitimate forms of influence; occasionally the material has metaphorical connotations which produce oblique translation; at other times the evidence is direct; more often it is no more than a background suggestion. During the development of some design proposals, primary observation has been used, but this has never excluded the interpretive work of others that over time has provided a cumulative influence, threading its way in and out of each project.

In my watery daydreams the shoreline itself mysteriously
dissolves, its ratty pubs and rusting cranes into a sombre
riverbank woodland where the tops of trees emerged from
an ancient funereal fog. (Schama 1995)

At the early part of the twentieth century, architects
and theorists (at the CIAM Conference) examined
ideas about the binary nature of space only to
resolve an ambiguous interpretation. An agreement
was resolved where territory (land) would be
difficult to categorise as it underwent continuous
transformation. This, of course, contrasted with the
popular impression where ground was an element
of stasis; in reality, both synthetic intervention and
geological rupture make it one of the most dynamic
forces in the natural world. The ground is commonly
understood as a physical reality, yet within its
history it has been used as the cultural force of
poetic inspiration, the deification of religious belief
and has the ability to express status, wealth and
to become a potent political tool. Its influence on
design is expressed in a variety of ways, as explicit
backdrop, or a catalysing force. Whatever simplicity
or complexity lie in the reference, in all of the
associated projects it has been applied through a
personal and prejudiced filter. Although the work
shows a sustained scatological interest in the syntax
of the land, these references were not applied through
self-consciously constructed dogma. References are
both pictorially direct and theoretically oblique,
often emerging opportunistically, segueing between
speculation and direct description and back again.
These associations can be embodied and easily
recognisable, but it is more likely that the references
will surface through a miasmic layer of memory.
Within much of the work there is the desire to

create a figurative object, or a sequence of spaces
that is evocative. There is no simple description
of a process because the convoluted journey that
captures the imagination is far from transparent.

To refer to concepts of land, there is some virtue
in placing aspects of physicality and speculation
into a loose cultural context. The influence of
historic precedent may be latent or wilfully exposed,
but often the traces of contextual reference become
the keystone to the project.

Historically, the cultural significance of land is
both complex and manifold; it has been illustrated
as a symbol of power at one end of the spectrum and
a poetically nuanced symbol of memory at the other.
It has been the professional domain of landowners,
land workers, planners, landscape architects
and gardeners, all with their designated right to
intervene for singular or the communal good. Land
is inextricably linked with wealth, politics, ethics
and environmental and social well-being. Poets,
artists, filmmakers and writers all claim the land as
their inexorable source of inspiration.

Throughout history, landscape design has embodied and
expressed the values of a culture: at times the power of the
state, at times the aesthetics of those at a distance from
power. (Treib 2002)

The lexicon of the land or natural surface has
repeatedly been interwoven with the language of
abstraction and 'land' has been a vital medium
through which artists have explored and produced
the earliest forms of representation, illustrating
issues of the day. For the urban dweller, painting still
arguably offers the most accessible relationship to
the countryside. Paintings of the land, distinct from

'landscape paintings', offer us a value-laden world seen through the cultural lens of the moment.

Although the term 'landscape' formally re-entered the English from the Dutch 'landschap' in the early eighteenth century, the earliest depictions of the land existed in Minoan, Greek and Roman friezes. Later, in the fifth century, 'land' was to become a central theme of the Chinese 'shan shui' paintings. These images showed pure landscape, where only the merest glimpse of human life was detectable. The pseudo-figurative, fictitious landscapes of the 'shan shui' ink paintings gave way several centuries later to the mythological, monochrome paintings of the 'wang wei' genre. Although the historic status of landscape painting was notably different between Europe and Asia, the iconography shown in Chinese landscape drawing uses complex cultural narrative that was to influence painters many centuries later.

European paintings of the land were initially no more than a historic record and had little cultural status. In contrast, landscape illustration in Asia was held in high regard and its value was based on a prerequisite of imaginative, intellectual narrative. The influence of these very early oriental paintings were not confined to Asia, as the opening of the historic trading routes transported their influence, to be seen many centuries later in Europe. It has been argued that even the romanticised land and cloudscapes of Turner and Constable owe their conceptual stance to the legacy of this early oriental work.

Linguistically the word 'landscape' was originally used to identify a patch of cultivated ground. It was not used to describe an idealised, picturesque vista until the late eighteenth century. The historically diminished status of landscape painting in Europe was further devalued in the eighteenth century as

it also lent itself too easily to the recreation of the 'gentleman painter'. It has been argued, however, that the emergence of the idealised 'rustic' landscape painting coincided with the accelerated enclosure of the English countryside, where the acquisition and sequestration of land by the wealthy created a hitherto unrecognised commodity of power. At this time landscape painting was considered a conceit of the wealthy; the paintings were to contain clear social messages, where land was no longer for production, but for the display of wealth and social status.

Images of the land also began to include totemic language used to illustrate epic social struggles, these paintings first emerged in northern Italy, then Flanders, and finally in the politicised manifestos of the Soviet Russia. With few exceptions, illustrations that were to emerge in the late eighteenth and early nineteenth centuries perpetuated an ideological, perhaps mythological, image that masked reality; rural poverty was virtually concealed. Painting the land, therefore, served several functions, the least important of which was figurative representation. Social stratification, wealth, ideology and folkloric fantasy were all found, using land as the interpretive icon. It was therefore the synthesised images containing motifs of symbolic or mythological value that were sought after, and their creators (including painters such as Nicholas Poussin and Claude Lorrain) were no longer regarded as journeymen painters, but now had acquired the status of poet.

The political and social context in which European painting developed was critical and it served as a reminder that much art emerged under the patronage of the Church or the land-owning aristocracy. The role of landscape painting as propaganda or at least as a reflection of society's mores indicated that 'ground' had a translated totemic value. The linguistic style of these paintings undoubtedly influenced future generations; whether the translational agenda was circumstantial or not, similarities can nonetheless be found in both the incipient technique and symbolism emerging in the paintings of the early twentieth century in the work of artists such as Hopper, Diebenkorn and later Hockney. Contemporary artists depicted land with a greater degree of abstraction, often resulting in more desolate compositions lacking any human element. Whether these paintings contained figurative or symbolic elements, representational language of the land also began to emerge as a powerful tool of symbol and enigma.

Painters do not have a monopoly on the representation of land and space, of course, film and video artists have tools at their disposal that enable them to create work with equal if not greater resonance, particularly within an architectural context. The power and understanding of an image often lies in the observer's subjective imagination, rather than the explicit message of the author; the challenge then lies in how to observe certain techniques of painters and filmmakers and exaplore how these could influence an architectural process, technically and conceptually.

Installation artists, sculptors and photographers such as Andy Goldsworthy, Olafur Elliason and Roger Hiorns use an entirely different range of media, creating immersive environments – *Storm King Wall* (Goldsworthy 1997), *Melting Ice on Gunnars Land* (Elliason 2008), *Seizure* (Hiorns 2008/9/10). These installations relate to surface, synthetic or otherwise, to create a 'land' or 'surface' scape within the imagination, dominant materials, colour or texture create the spaces, where each installation's ambiguous title acts as a mnemonic guide. The distinction between these constructions and architecture is a lack of pre-ordained functionality. At what point must a physical purpose be ascribed to space and, once assigned, should this limit the boundaries of interpretation? Gary Hill occupies the realm of immersive art through highly sophisticated video technology; installations such as *Crux* (1983–87) and *Tall Ships* (1992) (Cooke et al., in Mignot and Eleonor 1993) do not represent the usual orthodoxies of landscape, but both pieces suggest a journey through geographic space that is neither occupied nor unoccupied; it is a place of ambiguity. This is achieved through the capacity of video to offer complex 'non-linear narrative that encourage active engagement on the part of the viewer'. In Roland Barthes' terms, Hill's video narratives can be understood as 'writerly texts' (Barthes 2012).

The work of these artists has the freedom to use levels of abstraction and disassociation in a way that is certainly more difficult than the technically explicit realm of architecture. The audience is not in a position in these installations to be entirely conscious of either space, the physical reality of the gallery or the virtual reality of the journey and the levels of imaginative engagement will always be an unpredictable response. Paradoxically the observer might be left reflecting on nature and significance; whereas engagement within architectural space (with some exceptions) is normally through functional expediency. In accepting a lesser degree of control the architect needs to search for a means of expression that captures the audience and encourages greater reflection.

The Turkish filmmaker Abbas Kiarostami by contrast, produces films that explore the intimacy of human relationship to the land using techniques that distil the power of evocation. Kiarostami, heavily influenced by the Japanese filmmaker Yasujiro Uzo, developed a form of cinematic minimalism that undertook to describe themes reflecting the land through gradual revelation. His seminal work *Five* (2003) (Elena 2005) observes the ebb and flow of the water along the Caspian Sea. Filmed with a motionless camera, events drift in and out of focus, the land and the sea are a timeless backdrop and as the film deliberately lacks a constructed narrative, the audience is obliged to interpret these images through association and memory. The architectural challenge faced by capturing aspects of equivalent nuance is to explore ways of refining the conventionally static palette. A possible technique might be found in the eighteenth-century stratagem of the journey through constructed natural space (landscape) which if interpreted architecturally could create a synthetic alternative offering both dynamic and interpretive parallels. There are, of course, many other references in contemporary film where spatial enigma is played out against the backdrop of carefully contrived landscapes. Ozu's *Late Spring* (1949) and *An Autumn Afternoon* (1962) typify the director's minimal style, suggesting a complexity of narrative through the emptiness of the land. Ozu's obsession with composition and its power to evoke are seen in the opening shots of *Floating Weeds*, where the landscape is noticeably empty except for the beer bottle and lighthouse (Ritchie 1977). Ingmar Bergman's *Seventh Seal* (1957) (Bragg 1998) and *Faro Documents* (1967/1969) are films similarly empty of explicit narrative, encouraging a form of existential imaginative exploration. The impact of the film genre lies not only with its ability to convey wordless narrative through image but also through the control of the director and the highly attuned compositions of the cinematographer. The dialogue and systematic partnership between director and cinematographer is vital in sustaining a dynamic interpretation relationship of complementary skills.

The cinematic work of Christopher Doyle is perhaps the first to have major popular impact through his collaboration with Ang Lee, Wong Kar Wei and Yimou Zhang. The combination of dynamically choreographed camera work and immense focus on the power of physical context creates layers of interpretation that far exceed the simplicity of the story line. Doyle's work creates resonance through the relentless dynamic of the camera's eye (Doyle 2003). Derek Jarman's photography and film of Dungeness in contrast, suggests an immense power of stillness capturing a different quality of evocation, a sense of isolation, if not desolation. These works primarily engage with space and the power of the land to create an explicit resonance that conveys a depth of meaning that would otherwise be dissipated through words.

The filmic experience is understood through translational control, together with the timing and sequencing of visual imagery. The journey the audience takes through this responsive experience is highly orchestrated, yet film is unable to control the level of interpretive interaction. One of the compelling allures of film is the degree of absence that can be tolerated. The experiential construct of film is obviously different from that of 'being in space', but there could be an opportunity to examine some of these essential characteristics and consider how these could influence physical language.

Consider a parallel construct that has often been described as of frozen film, found in the physical minimalism of the 'Karasansui', or Royal Japanese Stone Gardens (Young and Young 2005), where reductive compositions of stone are positioned to create abstracted symbols of folkloric truth or legend. These compositions demand that the audience not only understand the iconography but also experience the vignettes through a prescribed series of compositional frames. The control of the spatial visual framework is, of course, less controlled than that of the filmmaker, as the journey is three dimensional and immersive rather than two dimensional and mono directional. Differences in the physical relationship to object are critical to the way in which the audience comprehends both space and the attendant narrative. While it is complicated to make comparisons between visual genres where the method of construction, constraint, delivery and physical relationship are so different, the fascination lies in the fact that they often share the same intellectual platform. The challenge for the architect is to try to capture nuance that linear drawings and constructed space lack and consider how to explore translational technique. Architectural tools, whether on paper or constructed, have an explicit format – the line, the edge, the boundary, the wall – but the phenomena of fading and conflating a non-linear time sequence are difficult. One must consider levels of dynamic, objects of significance, editorial control and narrative delivery. These must be seen as essential parts of the architectural composition – how do they compare with the techniques of painters and filmmakers?

It is impossible to appreciate the ground as a medium of translation without also considering aspects of the work undertaken by those who have had either a direct physical involvement with the land or those who have produced text that explores the concept and reality of the land. This synoptic commentary provides references and observations that have emerged as part of continual design discussions in the studio.

Dennis Cosgrove's and Stephen Daniel's edited volume *The Iconography of Landscape: Essays on the symbolic representation, of design and use of past environments* argues that land should be read as symbol of our economy and social status (Cosgrove and Daniels 1988). Barbara Novak's text, *Nature and Culture: American landscape and painting 1825–1875*, examines the scientific, philosophical and theological influences in landscape painting (Novak 1995). Leo Marx's *The Machine in the Garden: Technology and the pastoral ideal in America* (1964), by contrast, examines the pastoral concepts in nineteenth-century technology and the tensions created by the emergence of industry in the landscape. Contemporary theoreticians such as James Corner in *Recovering Landscape* (1999) and Charles Waldheim in *Landscape Urbanism Reader* (2006) demonstrate how the 'meta' principles of natural landscape and landscape structure can be translated into a theorised polemic that underpins urban planning strategy, which offers an alternative planning methodology to the traditional mechanisms of socio-economic and functional data.

There is no cogent argument or absolute logic that affords privilege to one polemical position, only an ability to recognise that some pieces of work have resonance with spatial design.

Sheila Harvey and Ken Fieldhouse's edited essays, *Notes from the Cultured Landscape* (2005), continue to illustrate a further range of opinion. Within the collection is Simon Swaffield's seminal essay 'Landscape and a Way of Knowing the World' (2005), which considers the divergent levels of representation and significance landscape has, both historically and in the twenty-first century. He maintains that 'landscape embodies knowledge' and suggests the range extends from geological science to poetic reading, from the formal significance of classic landscape ornament to the understanding of 'self' in the wilderness. The essay references the pioneering American landscape architect Garret Eckbo, who argued that landscape architecture could be used as a tool to enhance social justice, to Corner (1996), who sees landscape as an 'active agent of culture'; finally, the texts of Sylvia Crowe (Collens and Powell 1999), describe the personal expression of human values through the evolution of the garden. The critique these essays offer is less about the way we understand land in a biophysical sense (from the point of view of geo-morphologists or the land evaluators), but more about different ways of understanding the significance of the ground. These polemical positions are important in that they refocus the conventions of physical understanding and are persuasive as land is the primary context for much design. The complexity and interpretive symbolism create an alluring reference or tool and produce a palette of unimaginable richness.

Donald Meinig, in his essay 'The Beholding Eye: Ten versions of the same scene' (1979), outlines the critical context in which we can understand the land.

Thus we confront the central problem: any landscape is composed of not only what lies before us but what lies within our heads. (Meinig 1979)

Meinig's analysis uses ten different perspectives, arguing that visible land and what you see is not simply a set of surfaces and objects but critically an interpretation of that vision, and that each interpretation reflects the cultural history and professional knowledge of the viewer. It is a fascinating analysis, yet it rather too neatly compartmentalises theoretical views and I would argue that the boundaries between each are more ambiguous. His essay illustrates landscape as nature, habitat, artefact, problem, wealth, ideology, history, place and aesthetic – a broad reading that does not become congested with the linguistics of specialists. The interpretative models that I think are most useful in an architectural context are those of nature, history and aesthetic. The principles contained within Meinig's 'aesthetic' interpretation are that the relationship to the fundamentals of visual composition becomes increasingly important. He encourages assumptions to be made about the value of compositional elements, prior to any consideration as to how and whether they can be translated into an architectonic language. This form of referencing is not 'landscape architecture': it is spatial design that borrows from landscape – line, form, texture, geometry, colour, the placement of the object, their adjacencies and the metaphors attached to each – these will ultimately have some role to play in an architectural project.

The twentieth-century American philosopher John Dewy (1929) argued in contrast that the force of economic argument has increased the homogeneous nature of land and the isolation of art as a form of expression. The connection between art and the land, he maintained, had always been a way of expressing identity and perhaps some of the reason for the popularity of the land artists in the 1970s and 1980s was that their work forcibly reconnected with nature.

The work of the English academic David Cooper (2006) on literary geographies argues that there are two distinct cultures evident on either side of the Atlantic. The American view of open space has historically been drawn from the culture of the social common good, unencumbered by centuries of pictorial garden tradition where the pioneers of landscape were interested in public space. In contrast, the English tradition, in particular, idolises the 'romantic' and the 'picturesque', where landscape was destined to become a sequence of aesthetic arbours. The American model also acknowledged the progressive use of open space as a functioning forum for playing sport, swimming, picnicking and so on, which all rely on access to open space in the public realm. This was complemented by the growing need to also use private open space (domestic gardens) for a range of social activities. There were interesting precedents set outside the USA and Europe, in Japan, where for generations there was vital cultural importance embedded in the relationship between the miniscule gardens attached to the traditional family house where the garden was artfully composed and seen as an extension of the interior domestic space.

> In both these respects, readers of Murasaki's 'The Tale of the Genji' will be reminded of the Heian Japanese conception of the garden – a place at once the main theatre for the everyday, if unusually refined, activities of the Kyotan aristocrats, like poetry reading, and one so minimally separated from the house by sliding paper screens that 'the open sunny garden was no mere decoration but the very pivot of Heian domestic architecture.' (Morris, in Cooper 2006)

Cooper also argues in a dense philosophical manner about what he calls 'garden practices' and that the phenomenological experience of executing functions in open space has a distinct and separate quality from that of the same set of actions taking place inside. There is, of course, some fairly obvious contextualisation in that the temperature is less controlled, the smell and sounds are quite different, which means that the experience is inevitably quite distinct. If one accepts the logic of this idea, whatever references are translated from nature into a synthetic environment, the translational process will of course de-naturalise and deconstruct, and the immersion in enclosure will, additionally, define a clear and altered experience. From a phenomenological viewpoint one could argue that there is another level of change. It is not just 'inside' and 'outside' but a hybridised environment where the linguistic notation is shared and the boundaries are blurred. A common example might be the threshold between conservatory and courtyard. The conservatory is an interior space but with visible signs of nature, while the courtyard is open space but with all the visible evidence of enclosure. If one begins to consider this model as the beginning of the translational journey, it is not only the hybridisation and translation of artefact but also the experiential consequences. Christophe Girot adds to the debate with a particular European perspective in that he identified two of the most important values in landscape: time and place:

Landscape is the historical result of the different uses made of a place, its climate and its topography. It is also the cradle of the history of the human species. (Girot 2000)

Alan Tate, in his essay 'Making Places Different', states that one of the most important values of landscape is 'creating places that provide utility with beauty' (Tate, in Harvey and Fieldhouse 2005). The ostensible difference between natural and synthetic space is that the first is dynamic and the second is permanent. Those that are concerned with the design and the custodianship of the land have to seek methods by which they can connect different times, conversely there is an implicit understanding that the architect works with the notion of completion. In fact, both situations have an inherent dynamic. The seasonal change of the land has to be managed and these processes are well understood; yet, is this cyclical form of attention appropriate for fixed space, where the interaction between occupant, time, weather and degradation could be choreographed and built into the process of design? This question may be considered too narrow in isolation as the wider context of social, economic and ecological influences must surely play a part.

The environmental psychologists Rachel and Stephen Kaplan (1989) argue forcibly for the restorative quality of nature, maintaining that the experience of open space and proximity to nature is there to counteract the stress induced by contemporary urban living. Leanne Rivlin (2006), who focuses on the 'loose fit environments' of leftover spaces, explores an alternative concept within the metropolitan context. However, in our increasingly regulated environment, the 'loose fit'

abandoned spaces of the post-war years are almost impossible to find. The virtue of such spaces was that they were landscapes of exploration with an added frisson of danger. These were spaces without formal cultivation or synthetic intervention; they were spaces of urban wilderness and spaces for the imagination. If there is a possibility of appropriating a language from nature, perhaps the argument for recreating an urban wilderness becomes a more compelling argument. There exist design cultures that can be loosely termed mechanically interventionist, those that mimic the natural, and others that manipulate nature to mimic the synthetic – and all sit alongside a broad interpretation of wilderness. The expressions of recreating 'nature' are seen in English landscape design (exemplified by the picturesque garden at Stourhead, produced in the late eighteenth century), in Asian rhetorical practice (at Ri-oanji Japan, designed in the late fifteenth century), and in European practice (as seen in the geometrically ordered gardens of the Schoenbrun Palace, Vienna, designed in the mid-eighteenth century) and finally, the ontology of the pseudo-natural.

Europe is considered to have one of the most revered historic traditions of landscape and garden design from the English Romanticism of William Kent, 'Capability' Brown and Gertrude Jekyll through to the structured formalism of the French and Italian gardens of Mollet at the villa Montalto (Evelyns, in O'Malley and Wolschke-Bulmahn 1998).

Arguably of equal influence is the critical thinking that has emerged from the American arena in the last 20 years, which is remarkable given the short life of its 'landscape' culture. The impact of contemporary discourse on landscape urbanism may be fiercely questioned, yet within both the academic and practising community it has ignited a debate about the primacy of the land and the social, economic and iconographic value of the earth's surface. This debate is perhaps less surprising emerging from a background unencumbered with centuries of European landscape and garden design, harnessed to its culture, tradition and symbolism. One of the advantages of the American landscape designers is that they could gather to combine:

> great surges of collective energy. When architects, landscape architects, painters, sculptors, planners, engineers, social reformers, political leaders and others united they were able to accomplish some great manifestation of shared values. (Walker and Simo 1999)

The response to this statement is complex and must be understood as a series of overlapping conditions. Firstly, landscape architecture was an emergent profession, which unlike the European counterpart lacked the solidity of historic tradition. Landscape design began to emerge after two or three generations, yet the primacy of architecture as the object to be displayed initially reduced landscape to a subordinate role. The debates emerging in the United States were not the manifestos and dogmas of the European theorists and practitioners and it is for this reason it is fascinating that 'reasoned criticism did not follow, modern landscape slipped beyond even the peripheral vision of the art historians' (Walker and Simo 1999).

The emergence of landscape architecture in America came from people who worked the land, the farmers who understood the seasonal forces and the necessary planting regimes to make the land efficient.

From this historic, practical background emerged an understanding of the land, which, unlike the European model, was not quite so yoked to systems of status and privilege and in many ways their attitude to the social and environmental value of land has developed in a less synthetic way. However, it would be disingenuous to consider the development of the American landscape to be totally free from the influence of the European models, as many landscape architects were aware of the concepts of the Beaux Arts. For example, Frederic Law Olmstead (1822–1903), the acknowledged founder of the profession, had a broad understanding of the classical language of the great parks in Europe and the UK. Olmstead's design of Central Park showed influences from Europe, but like many pivotal figures that worked with the land, their work was still undeniably rooted in their own culture.

Olmstead offered a concept that the design of land should be considered both an art form but should also contribute to the social purpose of the community. These principles were to be highly influential for several generations, until the gradual emergence of scientific data positioned the landscape 'maker' as environmental custodian. One of the most articulate contemporary landscape architects, Lawrence Halprin (1916–2009), was one of the first to maintain the idea that land was part of an evolutionary process and was required to meet the social and economic needs of the time. Regardless of the political and economic imperatives, Halprin's desire to make space that was uplifting to the spirit never diminished.

The architectural importance of observing these designers whose palette was the land and nature lies in considering which principles might influence architectural thinking, particularly about surface, structure and articulation. The translation of linear language into a surface condition is normally a prosaic function, but concepts illustrated in another field can be the catalyst that changes a piece of architecture.

Olmstead was not only the first to place high value on the aesthetic composition of the land, but also to value the vernacular forms of space from which he took much of his inspiration. It is worth considering how these influences were translated. Both the architects and the landscape designers share notational language: the geometry of the whole, the adjacencies of objects and an understanding of spatial volume are all used in the developmental process of both professions. An awareness of material, surface and texture are additional shared components of the composition; these elements can be abstracted, assembled or deconstructed in whatever manner is decided.

At the beginning of the twentieth century there was influence that challenged the pre-eminence of the formal aesthetic language and the principles it embodied. The work of Ebenezer Howard and Patrick Geddes in the UK at the end of the nineteenth century, and later in the twentieth century the work of Lewis Mumford in the USA, brought about fundamental changes to the priorities embedded in designing the land. Socio-political influences emerged in an era of deprivation, and now the outer areas of the metropolis were envisioned as garden cities, where the spiritual and physical well-being of the individual was balanced with places of employment. These were radical, yet balanced, humanist views that produced a dramatic reform in the concept of the idealised (garden) city. The garden city movement in the USA and UK was driven by a strong ideology attempting to create a holistic place that was both environmentally and economically supportive. In this context the land was not considered or constructed as an artistic conceit, but as a commodity that had functional and social value, a fundamentally different approach to the rather didactic position adopted by architects of the modernist period. However, architecture was still considered to have primacy, and interstitial space was merely a secondary economic consideration.

The town plans of Radburn in the USA and of Welwyn and Letchworth in the UK were models of social and environmental responsibility; they demonstrated new relationships between road, land and building which were to have an ideological influence on the work of master planners, architects and landscape designers for future generations. However, the dynamics of historic events, the volatility of the economy, changes in technology and social structures meant that these ideological models were soon neither current nor affordable. Nonetheless, these ideas for community outside the city demonstrated the importance of the relationship of building/house to nature and offered an alternative way of living where the space outside was now of equal importance. An interesting model was also appearing in Germany at the early part of the twentieth century, but unlike the USA or the UK, this was a product of government-led ideology (Walker and Simo 1999).

Although there are few formal municipal records of the development of parkland during the period of the Werkbund in Germany (Burckhardt 1980), it was at this time that the political pressure for open space created the public parks. The different ideological positions within the Werkbund did little to cohere a strategic philosophy for design; open spaces eventually emerged with little conscious propaganda. Initially, attention had been given to the gardens of the 'middle class', where they were seen as an extension of the domestic space. Each quarter of the garden was functionally specific and was as deterministic as those within a building. By contrast the early attempts to transfer design ideology into public space created pseudo-aristocratic formalism, then waylaid by the political need to create open space for the masses, and the control of the government highlighted the growing politicisation of open space. From this era there were two distinct landscape models. The first was the emergence of the park as an open meadow with a minimum amount of pathway. These were areas for communal activity. The second, and perhaps more innovative, was the introduction of the working garden in the Siedlungen. The polemical writer and landscape architect Leberecht Migge was the principal instigator of these pioneering (sub) urban gardens, whose functions were ideologically the opposite of the bourgeois notion of aestheticised open space. The arable production of the Siedlung garden was closely linked to deprivation in the aftermath of the two wars, which saw a nation experience poverty unparalleled in history, yet it is still unclear from the records what ideological commitment the landscape gardeners of the Werkbund had to the political and social manifestos of the day.

Historically, the more modest attitude ascribed to landscape designers had immense value, for there were some who produced brilliant sensitive and sophisticated examples of design thinking well ahead of their time, there were inspirational lessons and examples that provided models that could be transported into the architectural lexicon. The importance of these examples, driven by the need to create a place of well-being, could also be seen against the work done by those:

> who had no formal training in landscape design but brought an interest in arts and science that led them to shape environments of extraordinary freshness, power, mystery and beauty. Whether haunting or exhilarating, these environments may seem to have been conceived with some fantastic imagination, unconstrained by tradition, precedent or utilitarian purpose. (Walker and Simo 1999)

The landscape architect Peter Walker exhorts the benefits of multiculturalism and multidisciplinary influences, and cites three landscape designers to illustrate this point: Roberto Burle Marx, Luis Barragan and Isamu Noguchi. These designers were amongst the first to demonstrate how to transcend the knowledge of other creative arts and science so that it could be drawn into the orbit of spatial design. The unifying characteristic that these designers shared was that although they all worked at various times in the USA, they brought to their work the unique and powerful influence of their indigenous cultures. All three brought different forms of expression, not only nurtured by social and cultural tradition but also an educated awareness of the forces of modernisation. One can debate just how much awareness of the artistic ferment elsewhere in the world influenced their thinking, but it was indisputable that all three had a refined interest in film, theatre, dance and art, and certainly some of the more contrived aspects of their work strongly reflected the influence of other creative art forms.

Born in Brazil, Burle Marx trained as a painter and botanist producing work that influenced generations. Burle Marx began by challenging the fashion for using Mediterranean plants, preferring those of his native Brazil, and, by observing the natural order of the tropical plant environment, he was able to understand both the hierarchical and parasitical order that allowed vegetation in these latitudes to reach enormous heights. Much of his work was the result of re-introducing the bromeliaceous and saxicole species that could grow in crevices and on granite surfaces and this work, with its sensuous vibrancy and bold heroic geometries, suited the sub-tropical flora of Brazil. His gardens were huge, bold, painterly statements where the concerns were of colour, structure, harmony, volume and expression. These landscapes were a mixture of metaphorical statement and context, often incorporating fragments of local material such as stone, wood and the discarded fragments of old buildings. If one looks at the plans of his gardens, they show clear similarities between the geometric language of constructivist and cubist paintings and some of the formal geometries evident in modernist planning beautifully illustrated in the garden of the house designed by Reno Levi in 1947. These semi-tropical environments were immersive paintings and it took three decades before the work of Burle Marx made an indisputable imprint on architects of the post-modernist period, with groups such as Archigram creating radical scenarios that bore the signs of his influence. Burle Marx was one of the first to understand the significance of the plane and, by placing objects on the surface, he emphasised the plane rather than the object; in doing so, he became perhaps one of the first landscape modernists.

Luis Barragan, a native of Mexico, also used dramatic colour and the sparse materials of his surroundings to create spaces of serenity that recalled the austere nature of his local wild landscape. The constructions he created were of walls, planes, rills, water-spouts, environments of brilliant colour and absolute calm. The landscapes he produced were often surreal, recalling images of Chirico or Magritte, images of emptiness and desolation.

At a Carnival Ball in Rio; and in the great sweep of the Botafogo gardens that gives human scale to Rio's sublime urban shore. Barragan offered refuge, a quiet space, walled against the assaults of modern civilization: the noise, the crowds, the pollution, the soulless buildings, the telephone. (Walker and Simo 1999)

Japanese American landscape architect Isamo Naguchi echoed aspects of his Japanese ancestry in capturing the essence of myth, reality, performance and theatre. These poetic qualities are deeply embedded in Japanese culture; traces are found in the great gardens of Japan (Katsura, Ryoan-ji, Daigoji). The language of these traditional gardens uses minimal material and presents a picture where each formal gesture represents part of a poetic narrative, where the landscape language is one of metaphor and great subtlety. His education as a sculptor influenced an intuitive inclination to command space through three-dimensional form: there is, of course, an intrinsic paradox in that the sculpture could so easily have become the object in space rather than the space itself. Naguchi was able to work comfortably in the commercial world, his precise attitude aligning easily with corporate thinking, where he was masterful in controlling external space and creating a dialogue with the architecture. The forms and materials he used were always part of the architectural palette: stone, timber, concrete, grass, gravel. The open spaces he created used few plants and were, in essence, open rooms. The courtyard garden at CIGNA 1957, designed by Gordon Bunschaft of SOM, is minimal, flat and sculptural, using a restrained palette that completely harmonises with the language of the building. Noguchi worked with Bunschaft again to create the sunken court at the Beinecke Rare Books Library at Yale in 1963. This was a masterly composition in polished marble – inaccessible, yet visible through the glass walls of the library. The sculptural forms created a frozen theatre whose dramatic story can only be created in the mind of the onlooker. The building creates a realm of monastic study and this aura of quiet reflection is brilliantly captured and reflected in its external space. Noguchi was one of the ultimate minimalists, requiring the observer to construct the meaning of each space.

Burle Marx, Barragan and Noguchi were following in the tradition of those designers who sought inspiration beyond the natural functionality of the ground. Although some of the earlier designers, such as Eckbo, Royston and Williams, closely observed the work of artists such as Kandinsky, Moholy-Nagy and Naum Gabo, this trio drew directly from the creative work of others. One of the compelling characteristics of these early landscape architects is the importance they give to the inextricable linkage of land and human experience, a corollary of which was that often the users of the space became involved in the creative process. In their work one can see influences ebb and flow between the disciplines, yet for as many

landscape architects that are inspired by painters and sculptors, the land has also been a critical source of inspiration for painters, writers and filmmakers.

At the same time, in twentieth-century Europe, the pursuit of landscape design was undertaken in a profoundly different context, where the influence of historic polemic was difficult to escape. One designer who radically challenged the focus of discussion was the French landscape artist Bernard Lassus (Conan 2007).

He used all aspects of his art training to direct a radical form of enquiry and used his skills and influence to raise awareness of the value of municipal and abandoned urban space. Born in 1929, Lassus trained as a painter at the national School of Beaux Arts, where he was strongly influenced by Fernand Léger, and ultimately became responsible for the creation of the Landscape School at Versailles (1976–1985). Lassus was the Director of the 'Workshop Charles Riviere Dufresny', where he taught landscape painting, promoting a phenomenological approach that advocated a multi-sensorial relationship between man and nature. His work was not easily categorised, and unusually he applied his expertise to undertake what were at the time radical studies for the Ministry of Research and the Ministry of Culture. Lassus was responsible for an exhaustive study of the aesthetics of the suburban garden and, through this work, developed a position of landscape democratisation; he maintained a strong position whereby liberty for the individual allowed horticulture to be used as a means of self-expression, this was absolutely antithetical to the unyielding theories of modernist architects. In 1977 he produced *Jardins Imaginaires, Les Habitantes-Paysagistes*, a critical study of landscape integration that advocated that buildings in the landscape should be imperceptible, guidelines that are still being used by conservationists and planners today. Lassus undertook unfashionable landscape projects of substantial scale, such as modifying the appearance of 15,000 housing units without disrupting the inhabiting community. It was this work that led him to develop a concept of 'critical landscape', where inhabitants are able to contribute and critique their own environment. He pioneered community involvement but also raised political awareness of the value of urban open space. Lassus was, interestingly, the under-publicised co-winner of the Parc de la Villette competition in Paris that Bernard Tschumi finally built. He was unusual in that he was a landscape artist who turned his attention to the very spaces that urbanists had abandoned, and for which there were no visible design strategies. The projects for toll roads, motorway verges and the borders of agricultural land all ameliorated the impact of major roads on the countryside. He championed the environmental rehabilitation of industrial landscape (for example around the Emscher River in Germany) and introduced the idea that archaeological research should underpin his proposal for the maintenance and renewal of the historic Tuilleries garden in Paris. In all his projects he advocated a phenomenological approach to reveal and continue the historic palimpsest of design with a contemporary interpretations. Lassus was significant in that he was one of the few artists of the twentieth century to understand and exploit the political importance of landscape. If one reflects on the idea of land being the signifier of social status and power, Lassus' work creates a rebalanced symmetry with the role illustrated in the eighteenth-century landscape painting.

Architecture has, with some exceptions, a conservative mantle: where, despite the advances of technology, it rarely challenges the status quo, whereby buildings still have fixed boundaries and a clear definition of internal and external space. The more radical developments in contemporary landscape by designers such as Martha Schwartz, Adriaan Geuze, Claude Cormier, Andrew Cao and Xavier Perrot, have questioned the idea that landscape design needs to be horticultural and the work of this contemporary group presents a challenging model to spatial designers. They confidently appropriate materials used in other forms of production, whether it is concrete, rubber or crystals, to create dramatic installations that question the omnipresence of horticulture. It is within this arena that the worlds of landscape design, sculpture, architecture and narrative overlap. Examples of their work – Central Garden at Gifu (2001) (Schwartz and Richardson 2004), Schouwburgplein (1996) by Adriaan Geuze of West 8 (Loosma 2000), The Blue Stick Garden (2000) by Cormier (2010), Cloud Terrace (2012) by Cao and Perrot – challenge the central precept that gardens must exhort the virtues of nature.

There are, however, a small number of architects whose work is equally radical and closely linked to nature, not only in a technical and ethical sense but viscerally, where nature plays such a potent force that it becomes difficult to disentangle whether the forms are fashioned by the functionally prosaic or natural force. Within the twentieth century there have certainly been architects who have gained inspiration from nature, but two architects from different continents with significantly different cultural backgrounds have illustrated the way that designers make a spiritual connection with the ground. Geoffrey Bawa in Sri Lanka and Sverre Fehn in Norway were architects of similar generations symbolising an engagement with nature and the land that was not pan-global but deeply rooted in the character and culture of their region. However, it would be wrong to consider their work parochial, as they not only brought their own cultural legacy but also the influence of a wider European education to bear on their work. Each had an immense sensitivity to the natural environment that avoided self-conscious reflection or pre-emptive narrative; the work was simply driven by a sense of poetry. The inevitability with which their work was acknowledged by successive generations is testament to its importance.

One of the great pioneers of modernism in the tropics, Geoffrey Bawa, established environmental principles that understood the pivotal role that nature played in both the concept and execution of design. As his clients made increasing demands to have their houses built closer to the centre of Sri Lanka's capital city, Colombo, the plot sizes reduced and the gardens were brought into the interior of the dwelling. The houses were, in essence, turned inside out and he created a model that had more affinity to the Muslim row house, or the European models of the Dutch courtyard house, and it was this arrangement that replaced the colonial bungalow. Through this model he explored ways of opening walls using screens to retain privacy. The need to accelerate ventilation in a climate where relative humidity is high meant that many of the design decisions were driven by functionality rather than by ideology. The house for Osmund and Ena de Silva (1960–62) (Bawa 2002) typified his approach,

where a series of linked pavilions and courtyards were connected around a large central courtyard or *meda midula*. Every aspect possible was viewed, the carefully crafted courts and linking corridors were designed as open frameworks that were harnessed to and disappeared into dense vegetation. The eclecticism of his references did nothing to deflect the overall impact of the natural flora that was the centrepiece of the design. This intimacy with nature is obviously achieved more easily in the tropics, where the scale and the pace of growth are overwhelming compared with the horticulture of more temperate zones. Response to nature was not only confined to the intimacy of courtyards but became dramatic once Bawa changed scale. He was responsible for some of the most architecturally memorable public buildings in Sri Lanka. The Kandalama Hotel at Dambulla, built against the sheer wall of a natural 'tank', is a celebration of nature first and secondly a feat of engineering. The building is immersed in the jungle, where boundaries between the synthetic and the natural dissolve it clings to the rock face, with the rooms vertiginously hung over a sheer drop. The entrance and the public spaces weave their way in and out of the natural rock, creating an almost parasitic relationship. The Triton Hotel at Ahungalla also demonstrates an unusual affinity between natural and constructed materials. Set in a landscape of slow contours, the grass banks have no further planting, and similar restraint is shown as the main lobby with its polished stone floor is situated at the same level as the pool and then the sea. The hotel demonstrates an impeccable understanding of topography and how materials can blend to create invisible edges and an uninterrupted panorama.

Bawa's cultural background provides some insight into his architecture:

> there is the central role of geography. His conception of a building, nearly all of his buildings, is strongly influenced by the character of the natural terrain, the vegetation, the potential for developing vistas, and hence light and shade: and of course the ever present aspect of climate … It is rare that his consideration of form will pre-empt the 'primordial importance of the natural surroundings, either by their scale, use of material or siting'. (Taylor 1986)

Bawa was acutely aware of placement, and the framing of nature integrated in such a way that physical boundaries de-materialised. His own house at Lunuganga remodelled the existing rubber plantation and lake to become a series of pictorial components of the dwelling. The journey through the gardens shares some characteristics of the grand European and English landscape, where romantic pictorialisation developed a portfolio of Arcadian views. Each view successively presented a series of rooms with artful frames of planting that might be designed in sequence or as solitary objects. The understanding of such space is of enclosure, but these enclosures had no walls.

There are of course other Asian traditions where landscape is an inextricable part of an architectural concept, in both the Japanese and Chinese traditions, the level of control demonstrates unapologetic intervention. However, the importance and interest of Bawa's architecture, though exactly planned, by contrast, shows the primacy of nature.

The philosophical and literal concept of boundaries in the tropical model offers a more comfortable translation, where delineation is often only a figment of the imagination. Such permeability is not possible in the northern hemisphere, where environmental protection is critical. However, there are certain principles about the primacy of nature that are considered by those who design in much colder climates, and the challenge for them is how to translate the poetry of nature into another setting.

Sverre Fehn worked in a different hemisphere, in the dramatic yet often reductive landscape of Norway. The two men overlapped in time and both shared educational influences in the principles of modernism, but what set them both apart was a cultural awareness and a sensitivity that the context of the ground, whether in the tropics or the tundra, could be lyrical. The historian and critic Francesco Dal Co illuminates the complex puzzle in the work of Fehn, in that his recurring theme of conflicting forces of nature symbolised by land and water are both poetically compelling and somehow elusive.

> The land tilled and cultivated by man reveals the sharp lines that render visible determined subdivision … The sea, on the other hand, does not allow a clear unity of space and law, of order and location … they assert the immeasurable distances that separate the dreams of freedom conveyed by the agile vessels and the reality of building that must conform to the stillness of the land. (Norberg-Schutz and Postiglione 1997)

Despite the conceptual schism that arose through awareness of the intertwined poetic characteristics of the land and the sea, Fehn's initial gestures have been described as 'unitary', as he began fusing the organic functionalism of programme with the order of nature. Embedded in his writing is a fascination with horizon, the meeting point between the earth and the sky. The terrain he considers could not be more different from that of Bawa. For the architect in the tropics, the challenge was to embrace a landscape whose characteristics were so vigorous they engulfed architectural space yet for Fehn, the landscape was dominated by solitude, where the only connection was between the land and the sky. In Fehn's architecture he 'tries to dissolve vertical elements – including façades – and to confront the dwellers of his construction with a radical opposition of the fundamental horizontal limits: the plane upon which things rest and that light penetrates' (Norberg-Schutz and Postiglione 1997).

'In the dark depths of the earth, objects speak,' said Fehn, 'When unearthed they are brought into the light of solitude.' (Norberg-Schutz and Postiglione 1997)

An intriguing aspect of Fehn's approach is his search for geographic position, his desire to capture its essence and describe the land. At the Archbishopric Museum at Hamar (1967–69), fragments of restoration are combined with the ruin to create the barest enclosure; a minimal aerial ramp separates the visitor from the archaeological floor. History contained in the monastery had been reduced over time to fragments and Fehn now saw those fragments at one with the soil. The primordial nature of the cycle from life to decay was the central piece of theatre, with the architectural shell a supporting and protective player. Much of his attitude towards the placement of building involves establishing conditions where the topography of the site and the building can engage in dialogue with the memories contained within the earth. Not only the ground, but all natural surfaces were vessels containing stories that needed to be recalled.

Fehn's view was that buildings had a primary role in revealing the secrets of the past and making those secrets understandable. His lectures often referred to a preoccupation with Nordic mythology, where the cyclical stories recalling the beginning and the end of life were both symbolised and contained by the 'ground'. The art gallery at Hovikodden (1963) breaks all anticipated rules. Where such buildings were generally characterised by top-lit neutrality, Fehn designed five glass fingers set into the landscape, all with glass walls. The objects on display were seen against the courtyards and the landscape, a naturally contextualised backdrop that was completely removed from the abstraction of a traditional gallery. However, this building still had the ability to create a contrapuntal form that withstood the immense power of the elements. The Church at Honningsvag (1965), the last inhabited town before the Northern Cape, was built in absolute wilderness. Verdens Ende (1988) literally means 'the end of the earth' and this simple gallery inserted into a granite formation required little other than a surface to provide shelter. Much of his work illustrates a proud respect for the land and its cultural importance, to such an extent that the architectural heroism, often muscular and overt, becomes a magnifying lens through which a partnership between the tectonic and the natural take on an increased majesty.

'What can you see?' he asked the audience at the Architectural Association in 1992. The audience looked at the image on the screen of a mist-shrouded glacier somewhere in the western fjords of Norway (Fjaerland). The picture of this great natural drama was so powerful it would always overwhelm any object placed in its shadow. Fehn's design of the Norwegian Glacier Museum (1991) was to acknowledge the natural magnitude and to prepare the visitor for the power of the vista. The central focus is a staircase on axis, on which the visitor could stand and contemplate the view with no other physical distraction; the principle piece of theatre was the glacier and the sky. The role of the building was subordinate; it was no more than a vehicle to observe and celebrate nature.

In literature and art the ground is perceived as a horizontal surface to which is attached a vast referencing system. The agriculturalists, horticulturalists, gardeners, planners, landscape architects and land artists have all worked with a datum that has been horizontal. Yet we should also consider how the complex nature of the ground surface has been transported into the vertical plane, both naturally and synthetically. The concept of the vertical garden has existed since biblical times, and throughout history there has been a glossary of examples, most of which exploit the horticultural characteristic of upward movement in order to photosynthesise. The technical concepts for the walls of natural planting were derived from an understanding of the epiphytes and parasites that were not dependent on soil. One of the early, contemporary designers to understand these principles was Burle Marx. Marx combined his painterly eye with botanical expertise, but a partnership with the ecologist Jose Lutzenberger worked less well in the pioneering concepts of Guarita Park. Although both were botanically literate, Marx's extravagant plans overwhelmed the delicate ecology of the site and finally, due to spiralling costs, the project was given exclusively to the environmentalist Lutzenberger, whose modest itinerary simply nurtured the natural flora of this coastline area.

The project developed by the ecologist Jose Lutzenberger for Guarita Park (1973–78) located on a rocky cliff face overlooking the sea near Torres, Brazil, combined on vertical surfaces certain plant species that need only the small amount of nourishment found in rock crevices and sea mist (Lambertini 2007).

Architects such as SITE, Co-op Himmelblau, Antfarm, Gianni Pettena, Emilio Ambasz and Peter Cook have all produced conceptual projects for the urban 'vertical garden'. Practitioners of vertical horticulture exist on both sides of the hemisphere, with acutely different environmental issues to address. The theoretical concept of the green wall has often been linked to the notion that organic matter has a dynamic that eludes and eventually overcomes synthetic structure, thereby claiming supremacy. The reality of the green wall is less adversarial and is often complementary where it brings a powerful potential for concealing boundaries. Vertical grass surface can also have a fragility and temporality that should be measured against the apparent permanence of the building; this alignment is often read as comparative measure of time highlighting the seasonal changes of the plants against the unchanging face of the building. The work of Heather Ackroyd and Dan Harvey at the Clare College Mission at Dilston Grove (2003) (Lambertini 2007) used a natural grass surface on an existing ruin to produce an ephemeral event that created poetic tension between the natural and the manmade in order to articulate the concept of transience.

Patrick Blanc (Lambertini 2007), one of the masters of natural texture and colour planting, has a catalogue of projects in Europe, the USA and the Far

East involving skilful displays of the contemporary green wall. Another pioneer of the vertically planted landscape is Teronobu Fujimori (Lambertini 2007), who, whilst building his own house, Grass House (1995), challenged the modernist manifesto of geometric purity by breaking lines with natural planting to create a house that suggested a closer relationship to humanist ideals. Fujimori is part of a wider Japanese culture that places great importance on the sanctity of the land, architects such as Hasegawa and Ando have also negotiated the complex relationship between synthetic and natural space. Hasegawa's Busshoji Elementary School, Himi (2006), claims the surface of the ground as an extension of the building, and Tadeo Ando's Museum at Naoshima (1996) (Ando 2007) relinquishes the spaces to the enveloping control of the ground.

Spaces that have a working relationship with nature are often those with an independently influenced language. The frames of Kew, Kibble Palace, the greenhouse at Chatsworth, the Palmenhaus Vienna, Schloss Schwetzingen and the Botanical Gardens at Karlsruhe are fragile structural extensions of the landscape, yet the engineering syntax does not conflict with nature nor resort to mimicry. The advent of the Industrial Revolution brought about the introduction of cast iron and the ability to form metal into immensely thin structural sections that were necessary for the construction of glasshouses, allowing for the maximum amount of glass and therefore light to penetrate. With this nineteenth-century technical innovation came the ability to raise plants outside their native territory. The construction of these delicate and ornate buildings is impressive and, although technology has progressed since the introduction of cast iron, these evocative structures still echo the sinuous forms of the plants they protect. The remains of the cast iron structure of the Winter Garden at the Botanical Gardens at Karlsruhe are testament to a seductive sculptural charm, despite the original building being no longer intact. The authority of this skeletal language is also remembered in more contemporary structures such as the MFO park in Zurich, 'the largest garden arbor in the world' (Aellen and Kienast 2005). There is a compelling quality to structures where enclosures are suggested and surfaces are physically absent, and this, of course, requires a formal structural presence that not only performs a technical function but also provokes the imagination. There are other forms of contemporary landscape minimalism that use a different syntax, such as Hentrup Heyers Furhmann's re-modelling of Station Square (Benitez 2009) in Aachen, Germany. This uses an elliptical concrete carpet to signify the entrance to the town. The only focal points included in the proposal are two high, brightly lit towers, a concrete bench and the use of two different textures on the surface.

As previously noted some of the most important commentary and theoretical perspectives followed Charles Waldheim's Symposium on Landscape Urbanism. This event and subsequent publication was to recognise many of the significant academic positions that existed. While this chapter does not attempt to probe the depths of this extensive polemic, the central critique is of some relevance in this context as the issues focus on the failure of urbanists, both designers and policy-makers, to create a city environment that satisfies the needs of the populace. It is argued that the mechanics of creating the city are regimented and rigid, conceived and constructed in a linear manner. The institutionalised nature of the profession supports unitary positions and therefore the argument for disciplinary interaction is clearly articulated. The complex model of an ecological dynamic is hypothecated and the established rule system was challenged. The arguments are many and varied and only limited observations are relevant in this context.

James Corner's essay 'Terra Fluxus' argues that 'landscape urbanism is the understanding of horizontal surface', conceiving of surfaces, whether synthetic or natural, as indistinguishable and with an almost infinite capacity to store information. The description alludes to an almost archaeological quality, where surfaces are not only read as a physical construct but are also able to show the 'trajectories of shifting demographics'. The ground surface is described as a staging ground 'for both uncertainty and promise' and he continues to acknowledge the imagination as a critical component without which none of the processes or principles can be achieved (Corner, in Waldheim 2006). The land is unique in being able to adapt almost infinitely to temporal change and it is both its abundant characteristics and ability to mutate that offer the possibility of some sort of interaction through design.

In her essay 'Constructed Ground', Linda Pollack identifies size as a critical component of how we understand the ground, yet in contrast to popular discourse where the land is commonly presented as strategically scaled, or described in terms of what she calls 'bigness', smaller incidents can be equally important. She maintains that the tradition of the figured ground diagram perpetuates the role

of external space being of negligible value, where it is understood as merely space between buildings. 'Yet to build landscape you have to see it, and the inability to do so continues to permeate design culture' (Pollack, in Waldheim 2006).

The commentary about scale also relates to the human condition, and one might consider land to have a 'vastness' that offers a relationship to terrain and 'smallness' that engages the individual. Pollack maintains that 'scale is an issue inherent in all urban landscapes and is barely addressed in design theory or practice' (Pollack, in Waldheim 2006). There are implicit established relationships (those between the architect and the site, the planners and urban area, the landscape architect and the garden) that acknowledge the scale differences of the components of urban landscape, yet a tradition exists within the professions where each group remains cordoned together with their own fixed boundaries of scale. These scales need not be fixed: the hierarchies are simply a product of cultural practice. The strategies of professional disconnection produce sterility, and therefore one must ask whether an analytical understanding of scalar language and a subsequent attempt at translation could be a tactic to enrich spatial propositions. The field, the road, the path and the room might have an interchangeability that could alter our strict notational and physical demarcation. If scale were to be altered, or at least cross understood, both detail and function could have a fluidity and boundlessness that is normally difficult to achieve. Immanuel Kant maintained that a tension exists in our perception of the sublime that beautifully challenges the concept of scale, claiming that 'the sublime can be found in an object' (Pollack, in Waldheim 2006). This has the duality of being both boundless and a totality: to what extent can spatial proposals achieve multiple recognition of scale? Perhaps one of the most successful examples is Alvaro Siza's Leca de Palmeira Pool (1961), which engages at the scale of the human body, the landscape, the sea and the horizon, 'the project intensifies existing forces by weaving different scales of activity into an existing site' (Pollack, in Waldheim 2006).

Yet the concept of ground scale has relative values as divisions of space have different geographic tempi; the undulating hills of Europe represent no more than a mound in the context of the major continents. Scale and space are not only a visual construct but also a component of time. To travel through the vast terrain of desert or prairie landscape involves duration and almost indiscernible changes of feature; topographic incident in these landscapes bear no relation to human scale and the incidents are mere scratches. It is in this context that the rule of measure begins to change and the description of A to B is not by length but duration. Our value system becomes one that is much closer to the experiential and less associated with the measurable. One might therefore consider the notion of space, particularly 'largeness', as both quantifiably visual and also experientially understood. Time is a dimension that is rarely integrated into design thinking as traditionally the architectural model is a unified static idea.

There are those, usually outside architecture, whose work exalts scale in such a way as to disengage with the everyday and to force attention to the universal power of nature. James Turrell, Richard Serra, Olafur Elliason and Walter de la Maria have used the land as the most powerful canvas available. Their work both celebrates human achievement and provides a glimpse of the universe. Robert Smithson's 'Spiral Jetty' created the largest land art spiral on earth, yet the scale of its backdrop at Salt Lake, Utah, dwarfs this human construction. Whatever determination forges these interventions, they remind us of the fragility of humanity. In a very different way, Jarman's photographs of his Dungeness garden symbolises the solitary, situated like a small dot on the unending stretch of empty beach.

Filmmakers such as Kiarostami use large expanses of land and water to document time and the rhythmic nature of the sea's occupation of the screen. Contemporary and classic literature uses the scale of the land as an evocative tool and a device by which to situate the individual. Thomas Hardy's Wessex landscapes, Willa Cather's prairie and Peter Høeg's endless horizons of snow are literary depictions of the natural majesty and scale of the land, used as a lens to magnify the isolation of the individual. Canvases as vast as the prairies can illustrate subtle changes of colour and light, the arctic wilderness is characterised by nuanced shadow and the English countryside bears the traces of generations. In these examples land is used as a dramatic tool to implicitly describe elements of the story. There is an affinity that draws artists and filmmakers to the land, and through a range of representative images and text we begin to understand that natural geography can be read in innumerable ways. Whatever the complexity of the story, the portrayal of surface is crucial, as it is through translation that metaphorical equivalents can become part of another lexicon.

The English countryside, the gardens at Chatsworth, Fiesole, Versailles, Alhambra, all portray a highly disciplined narrative with inexorable incident. In some ways one might relate the discipline of the European garden to that of the city plan, where the adjacencies and proportional rules have some degree of symmetry. The power and detail of the small scale does not exclusively reside with the West, as the gardens of Japan demonstrate an intricate cultural narrative executed with disciplined attention to detail. In Europe, there are distinct compositional languages – the narrative is embedded in sequences of historic or mythological incident – whereas the tightly knit concepts seen in the gardens of Japan use a higher degree of abstraction to symbolise forces of nature and the universal primacy of natural order. It is, however, the Japanese garden that is renowned in raising consciousness of the abstract concept of time and interstice. The Japanese word *ma* describes the space between a notional threshold, the space between two stepping-stones, a space through which we travel. Within the culture of the West it is a term that is harder to define. The language of the land, particularly in Japan, demonstrates that not only are the events important but also their relationship to each other. When one considers how the process of translation might occur, it becomes important that the lexicographers identify the building blocks. To describe and reflect on the quality of each element brings the process of translation nearer. Although many of the architectural projects illustrated in the book are conceptually connected to the land, the relationships have often been oblique and associational. However, in order to establish some form of methodological strategy, an elemental analysis of landscape characteristics has been created. Part of this lexicon is literal in that it describes absolute physicality, yet the description is subjective rather than objective and dictionary led, other characteristics are less tangible and attempt to evoke character. There is no syntactical analysis more an understanding of phenomena or character that will emerge through the ebb and flow of conversation, but the following headings have repeatedly been used as references and a springboard for ideas. It is important to state that most of this book relates to the ideas exchanged with others and through the process of reflection, development and iteration have bypassed forensic examination. The process of design is not the same as scientific research and production in that it uses an intellectual process in a much more lateral way, interweaving fact, fiction, association and deep knowledge in a way that is difficult to untangle.

The following headings are contextual and serve only as *aide-mémoire* of certain principles that might occur in the developmental process.

MATERIALITY

Material substance is commonly viewed as a form maker. It provides texture and colour and delivers typologies of surface. The architectural palette is predictable and the materials used by the architect have remained largely unchanged for thousands of years. There are usually clear distinctions between ground and the built object; however, there are intriguing examples that use organic language, where the materiality of the ground is blended into the surface of the building. Buildings of the ground are rooted in many cultures; some notable examples include Raimund Pietilla's Union building at the

University of Helsinki, Gunther Domenig's Stone House, Arthur Quarmby's House in Huddersfield, the Truli houses of southern Italy and the troglodytic houses of Capadocia. Herzog and de Meuron's Dominus winery in the Napa Valley uses a more sophisticated technique to dissolve into the landscape by constructing the façade from gabions as the local basalt rock provides a façade that becomes part of the local terrain.

There are contemporary and historic examples of architecture becoming at one with the land, where no clear boundaries distinguish the borders of the object from its context. Conceptually these buildings become extensions of the landscape.

MATERIALITY AND DISPLACEMENT

Lapena and Torres' project for the gardens of the Villa Cecelia (1986) in Barcelona uses materiality to create contrapuntal tableaux, where the re-arranged Renaissance garden exists alongside interventions of the twentieth century. A narrative unfolds about materiality and threshold, where the surreal juxtaposition of the Renaissance motif and the twentieth-century object creates an expression of the garden as non-garden. Pseudo-vegetation made of metal, walls with wire hair and ponds with collapsed statues are all deliberate contradictions and, on occasion, disrupt all sense of anticipation and comfort. Olafur Elliason's installation in the Kunsthalle in Bregenz (1967) transports nature into an architectural chamber to create a paradox, a living installation inside a synthetic environment. There are living organisms in water, and fog in the upper chamber which need light and air movement to fully dramatise their presence. The constructed environment within the Kunsthalle is devoid of any detail that distracts from the dramatic perversity of its presence. Once the installation is completely removed from a natural context, the fragile and often elusive quality of nature becomes much more vital. Hill's installation *Crucifix* (1993) relies on the observer inhabiting the conceptual physique of the disembodied filmmaker. The quadripartite screens transport the audience into a phenomenological, woodland walk. The sense of displacement is articulated by an awareness of the gallery context. This is not the world of total virtual immersion but a tour of nature as a distinct spectacle in a constructed arena.

SCALE AND SYNTHETIC OBJECTS IN NATURE

The most obvious synthetic intrusion into nature is architecture itself; however, there is once again an interesting issue of scale attached to those objects that have an environmental or engineering function, such as wind-powered generators, sewage and solar farms. The functionality of these operations relies on a scale that is so large that the normal architectural references that relate to human scale are invalid. Normally relationship to human scale is a prerequisite to understanding objects in space, but these objects, more importantly need to work with the geology of the terrain, harness the impact of surface geometry and atmosphere to produce their own micro-climates. The Solar Furnace at Barstow California (*Concentrating Solar Power: Energy from Mirrors*) (Mohave solar project 2001) is so vast that it appears as a giant mechanical garden in the Sierra Nevada. These objects are constructed to fulfil a technical function and must be specifically located in order to work. Their functionality makes them the antithesis of artwork built into the land, yet their scale gives them an abstraction that allows them a similar aesthetic status. The work of Richard Serra, Walter de la Marea, Robert Smithson and James Turrell create metaphorical relationships that offer a cultural critique, yet one could argue that large pieces of environmental engineering could present in a similar manner, philosophical questions about the nature of human intervention.

THE VISIBLE SURFACE

Open ground in an urban context is varied, and its situation and typology influence behavioural activity. The grassed surface, for example, has both a pictorial and functional purpose. An awareness of the environmental benefits of natural surface is largely part of contemporary consciousness, whereas the historic perception of a grassed area was that its role was subservient to buildings. The quadrangles at Oxbridge colleges offer space that both defines the planning of the building but also gives a necessary distance from which the buildings can be fully appreciated. This arrangement, through cultural consciousness, offers implicit levels of control that have no need of physical barriers. A more contemporary example is Kathryn Gustavson's landscape of the Shell Headquarters at Rueil Malmaison (Amidon 2004), which subtly covers the difficult terrain around the headquarters with immense constraint. The results are a sensuous blanket that envelops the austerity of the architecture, providing less of a garden and more of a backdrop. Steven Holl's landscape at the extension to the Nelson Atkins Museum, Kansas City (Holl 2007), respects the geometric precision of the original gardens and uses this to orientate a series of organic grass cascades that form the accessible roof of the new extension. This building is a masterpiece of landscape integration – not only does it fit seamlessly into the context, but also creates underground galleries where the visitor is hardly aware of their subterranean location. The design has as much to do with a sophisticated technical vocabulary that brings natural light into the interior as a masterly exploitation of section to create fluidity with the ground that renders the boundaries seamless. Holl also created an intimate relationship with nature in the Knut Hamsen Center at Hameroy, Norway (Broome 2012), reflecting the tradition of the Norwegian turfed roof while echoing the linear geometry of the pine forests in the bamboo roof garden. Each of the corporate, municipal and private examples illustrates that unadorned grass (or simulacra) has the visual potency of the most intricate of landscape designs.

THE CONCEALED SURFACE

Geomorphological surface is a planar phenomenon, presenting itself in the horizontal or vertical state and concealing all that lies beneath. The surface hides a three dimensionality that discreetly contains a myriad of invisible and critical networks. The surface can be construed as a mask that hides a vast supply of synthetic and natural infrastructure that transports, drains and supplies. Increasingly necessary for contemporary urban living, major systems of hydrology, power, movement and connectivity exist below the surface of the ground. Networks have little visible definition, and as they are not seen, they create no conscious boundaries. These 'sub-surface scapes' attract little attention from architectural designers, as they are not visible and the public rarely scrutinise their functionality.

These subterranean complexes are described by Elizabeth Mossop in her essay 'Landscape of Infrastructure' (2006) as 'shadow' cities 'inhabited only by default' (Mossop 2006). Over the last three decades there has been gathering momentum behind the concepts pioneered by Ian McHarg, where infrastructural systems had to embrace issues of sustainability and reinforce the cultural context and a sense of place. Mossop's 'shadow cities' are slowly emerging into the light as a growing awareness amongst both environmentalists and public acknowledge the efficiency of this unseen world as it plays a central part in how we engage and control the supply of resources.

LIQUID SURFACE

The use of water in landscape has a long and complex history. Its functional status as a means of irrigation has global importance, but water has philosophical and religious symbolism that is culture-specific. Water is a highly valued natural commodity and its inclusion in a landscape or architectural composition obviously has affirmative significance. The scarcity and value of water, particularly in hot climates, is demonstrated in the gardens of the Alhambra in southern Spain. The Moorish palace that sits at the heart of the complex was developed over six centuries, and each successive generation devised ways in which water could be used to portray themes of philosophical importance. In these climates water was also used to create micro- climates to increase greater personal comfort. The pools that reflect, the fast-flowing streams and the fountains all create an environment not only of greater comfort but also one of visual delight. The fascination with water in the land was not the exclusive reserve of gardeners;

it was architect engineers such as Alberto Galvani who constructed the technology behind the immense water strategy for the seventeenth-century Villa d'Este, introducing a dynamic element into an otherwise tranquil landscape. Water plays an essential part in different cultural settings: the classic Royal Palace gardens in Japan, the Alcaza in Seville, the cascade at Chatsworth and the Fort Worth Water Gardens. The inclusion of water into landscape for non-functional purposes creates an aesthetic range of infinite possibilities where the dynamic and static states produce qualities that are both highly dramatic and sublimely peaceful. Water is a source of latent energy and movement; any water mass has the potential to transport, lift and activate. The physical state is a paradox in that its perception can be of 'surface' but the actuality is volumetric, meaning it has a greater invisible geometric reality and an undeclared relationship to architectural space. Conceptually, water is capable of being contained and organised not as surface but as an architectural volume.

NEGATIVE SURFACE

The introduction of negative landscape (excavated ground) was first found in the deer parks of the Norman era in Britain and then formally recognised in the eighteenth-century gardens of Europe and the UK. The negative landscape enabled the owners of a country house to view their immaculately manicured gardens but also the grazing land beyond. There was an immediate appeal in the creation of illusion where vistas appeared to be endless. This historic moment witnessed the emergence of economic land value, and the status of the eighteenth-century landowner was inextricably linked to the size of his estate. Illusory uninterrupted panoramas viewed from the house necessitated the design of an unfenced garden and a restriction that prevented the grazing cattle in the pastures beyond from accessing the lawn. A simple solution was the creation of the 'ha-ha', a deep ditch that kept the cattle at bay and provided no visual interruption at the end of the cultivated surface. Horace Walpole was credited with the invention of the ha-ha, yet it was Charles Bridgeman who implemented the idea. These techniques of negative form were found in the gardens laid out with William Kent (Williamson 1998) and it was here that they brought their artistry from concept to reality, synthesising formal and informal landscapes. However, it should be remembered that although these three critical figures are credited with introduction and implementation, the landowners had much greater influence in the development of these gardens than is usually credited. The formal geometries of the landscaped garden contrasted with the soft and natural planting arrangement of the park beyond. However, it was the swept views of Capability Brown that are most associated with this piece of essential practicality.

SURFACE AND ISOLATION

In the uncultivated and undeveloped strips of land areas that create a boundary condition between the sea and road, the virtue of borderland flora lies in maintaining the fundamental structural integrity of the surface. Despite a Victorian enthusiasm for building coastal resorts in England, the historically abandoned dune-scapes have now acquired a status and beauty previously ignored. Derek Jarman, filmmaker and photographer, was one of the first to

celebrate and popularise these solitary landscapes. The beach and the dunes at Dungeness are cold and windswept and offer little more than the view of one of the UK's earliest nuclear power stations; perhaps the mythological potential for catastrophe ensures that this piece of southern English beach remains empty.

The concept of isolation requires scale. Isolation is not only related to physicality but also to the absence of human life. Geography is a powerful and evocative tool, capable of exerting its authority over human achievement. There are a group of artists who work with the land at this scale and have accepted the challenge that this presents. The solitary plains of New Mexico provide compelling isolation for Walter de la Marea's 'The Lightning Fields' (1977). Turrell's most significant recent piece of work, the Roden Crater (1979–2011), transforms the land into a massive naked eye observatory. In order to magnify the act of intervention, these pieces need the remoteness and lack of human association to make their interventions all the more remarkable. These projects are fascinating in that they represent the hitherto insurmountable scale needed to create a moment of significance that reminds the onlooker of the vast power of open ground.

There exist landscapes in the Americas, China, India, Africa, Australia and the two Arctic regions that are characteristically different from landscapes in Europe by virtue of human habitation being sparse and their almost unimaginable endlessness. Topographic incident in these settings has no relation to human activity, but is rather the product of nature. What would be considered major civil engineering in any other context is simply dwarfed by landmass. Roads, bridges, dams and even isolated buildings are mere surface traces. In literature, art and film there is the paradox of romanticism that draws people to these inhospitable environments, with an attendant desire to show examples of fortitude and heroism.

The solitary landscape is not always dramatically extreme or geographically remote. The vast cultivated prairies of the American Midwest, immortalised by such authors as Willa Cather and filmmaker Paul Tomkowicz, are characterised by subtle undulation that carries the eye as far as one can see. Cather's description of the Nebraskan prairie in *My Antonia* is characterised by a nuanced description of the colour gold as the sun passes over the endless cornfields. Change in colour is only visible to the keen and knowing eye that understands the minute folds in the ground that in turn adjusts the way in which the corn lies. These are forms of measure in a landscape where each minute variation in land level is as significant as a hill or mountain to the European eye: 'the painterly image is constructed of blocks of colour, yellow, gold, brown and blue it is a picture of big brush strokes with no detail' (Cather 1995).

In *Miss Smilla's Liking for Snow*, the Danish novelist, Peter Høeg, describes a very different, still isolated environment of the tundra, where vast grey landscapes present shades of grey ground against a grey sky. There is no vegetation and simply a description of one grey against another. Video artist and filmmaker Bill Viola brings a distinctive perspective to the concept of empty land, observing landscape as part of life's solitary experience. The contemporary artists Elliason and Goldsworthy's best-known work focuses on images of emptiness. One of the few small buildings that has a particular

relationship with large space is Stanley Seitowitz's Brebnor House, which uses a materiality and geometry that are contrapuntal to the language of the Transvaal so that the object becomes uniquely distinctive against the enormity of the backdrop.

There is of course a compelling allure about these over-scaled landmasses where synthetic interventions have a drama and resonance that cannot be created in a more visually noisy environment. There is a high level of potency in the scale of context, the extent of the canvas and the impact of any intervention.

Europe by contrast is a landmass of pocketed nations that have developed cultural and physical characteristics that are reflected in the way the land is managed, used, aestheticised and boundaried. The scale and utility of each marked area of ground is governed by cultural understanding developed over generations.

THE HEATH

Land connected to an urban environment is inevitably adjusted in scale and therefore commands a different level of appreciation. The heath is defined as a wide uncultivated piece of ground within an inner city, originally destined for the gathering of large crowds and where a range of outdoor pursuits could be undertaken. The land has no restrictions of access and provides the nearest simulacrum of the countryside for the urban dweller.

THE PARK

A park is a designed, often enclosed space that can be formally or informally constructed and offers the visitor a range of scenic experience. Olmstead and Nash typify designers whose 'natural' space offered the city dweller a healthy and aesthetic experience. The park is a natural island that offers tranquil seclusion from the city and the design understood that generational needs were different. Movement could be dynamic, graceful, energetic or non-existent and the scale of the park was clearly understood to accommodate formal and informal landscape, waterscape and wilderness. The park encapsulated a microcosm of nature. How far did carefully judged scale allow the individual's imagination to escape the city? The answer will be different for each person, but the intention was certainly there.

Asplund and Leverund's park at the crematorium in Stockholm (Skogskyrkogaden 2012) prepares the visitor for another type of experience. The space offers a calm open landscape in which to sit and reflect and to this end it is a park of minimal distraction, allowing for the mourners to connect with their memories. The history of the design is less than benign as the two architects quite literally fought for the high ground. Both designers endlessly reconfigured the Elysian ground-scape of gently rolling hills in order to obscure each other's buildings and vistas, though there is little that now remains as a reminder of this caustic history. The design maintains a reductive quality that is fit for its purpose and exudes a sense of calm unlike the ebullient activity of Olmstead's design for Central Park.

THE PICTURESQUE

Normally attached to a grand country house, this type of open space often mediated between domestic gardens and farmland. European examples tend to be more self-contained, but notable examples in the UK provided an aesthetic interlude between the parts of the house that command grand views and the farmland beyond. There is a clear social ordering system attached to such spaces and representation in art often confines the illustration of the owners to an Arcadian garden context, implicitly conveying an understanding of wealth and influence. The gardens at Chatsworth and Sissinghurst demonstrate an English taste for the picturesque; there is also a quintessential illustration in the gardens at Stourhead designed by Henry Hoare in the mid-eighteenth century. A garden of illusory artifice, laid out to introduce nature to the visitor, Stourhead was actually meticulously contrived to create the simulacra of Elysian pastures. The gardens, arranged around an artificial lake, use pathways to create a journey of cinematic revelations. The tableaux are intended to evoke the Trojan hero Aenaes' descent into the underworld, achieved by presenting a sequence of figures and monuments all depicting epic passages in this mythological tale. To the casual observer the journey reveals scenic views of an apparently natural landscape, yet the land has been artfully constructed; the scale, colour and texture of planting chosen to display both contrast, harmony and composition. The foliage is positioned to control the sequenced views, creating a mnemonic construction which through fragmented glimpses deliberately creates a sense of anticipation and finally of theatre, when the ultimate picture is revealed. Chatsworth is perhaps a more typical garden attached to the residence of the Cavendish family. The initial garden first established by William Cavendish in the sixteenth century was very much smaller than the current landscape, whose most notable designer was Capability Brown, who in the eighteenth century blended the formal garden into a pseudo-naturalistic landscape that continued to the park and woodland beyond. However, it was a young Joseph Paxton who proved to be the most innovative gardener together with Decimus Burton he was responsible for Chatsworth's most notable architectural features: the Great Conservatory and the 'Conservative Wall' (1844). This garden is an extraordinary amalgam of objects and plants that illustrates the capacity to dynamically change over time. However, the landscape is not merely an accumulation of design gestures. The garden has been edited to reflect the changing priorities of each successive owner. This garden presents a canvas that was to be endlessly adaptable, leaving the archaeological traces of each generation.

The experience of the journey appears to have had equal importance to horticultural decisions and this seemingly freeform parkland exerts much greater control over movement and spatial comprehension than many of the more formally constructed gardens. Issues of movement, time, control and comprehension are techniques found in filmmaking and literature, but the permanence and determinacy of building does little to encourage understanding of different modalities. Critical issues are raised by examples of the eighteenth-century 'picturesque' that concern the management of journey and how this might be translated through architectural space where the human body creates a dynamic, offering a different perspective of spatial understanding.

THE FORMAL GARDEN

The use of the clear, uncompromising geometry of the formal garden has historic influences from Persia, first seen in Europe in the fifteenth century in Italy.

The Italian Renaissance Gardens, the Villa d'Este, Boboli and the Villa Lante were to have a lasting influence on generations of landscape designers. However, the gardener Claude Mollet (1564–1649) was one of the first to introduce formal linguistics into French gardens, and he was the beginning of a dynasty of gardeners who developed formalism into an art form throughout the eighteenth century and began to construct landscape through conceptual narrative. The landscape designers were not working in isolation, however, and the theorists of the day, Jacques Boyceau and Joseph Antoine Dezalier d'Argenville (MacDougall 1974), undoubtedly exerted an influence on these horticulturalists whose work, until now, had been merely a prosaic technical pursuit. The intellectual partnership between horticulturalists and theorists whose texts reflected the conceptual and philosophical illustrates one of the great historic examples of linguistic assimilation. Notions of no physical substance yet great philosophical and symbolic value are matched and translated into physical metaphor. The indirect yet powerfully influential *Plato's Theory of Forms* (Ross 1951), which expounded the Platonic axiom that art should imitate nature, served as a cultural subtext to much of this design. These natural constructions of the formal garden are much closer to the architectural lexicon where the promenades, arbours, loggias, parterres and praeneste developed an illusion of enclosure, with clear architectural similes. The emergence of controlled platonic geometries during the eighteenth century was a conscious reaction to the excesses of the Baroque and Romantic period and now there was a consideration of optics, perspective, light, shade, texture and colour, all of which are primary constituents in the development of spatial design. The alchemy of theoretical concept and interpretive physicality was to establish the introduction of landscape design as an academic discipline. The most substantial formal garden was constituted from ten distinct elements, ranging from the parterres to architectural monuments; the garden as an accompaniment of the stately home requires the complexity and scale that is absent in the domestic house.

THE MOORISH GARDEN

Pre-dating the European formal garden were the gardens of the Alhambra Palace, built for the last Muslim Emirs in Spain outside Grenada. These gardens were strongly influenced by the real and theoretical Persian gardens (4000 BC) whose qualities were intended to embody paradise on earth. As previously discussed, water was celebrated in the gardens, not only as the most vital of horticultural necessities but also as a source of sensual pleasure. In an inner courtyard of the palace the watercourse is diverted to create a cascade and create subtle background noise. Lines of fountains cool the air, the water plumes rising to exactly the right level to cool the women as they strolled within this private sanctum of the female garden. The stillness of the water in the patio de la Alberca created a mirror to reflect the sky and some say to reflect the soul. Water not only had an acknowledged value but remarkable technology was developed to keep it flowing and, even in the fifteenth century, baths, hot and cold running water and pressurised showers were all in existence, well in advance of such technological developments elsewhere in Europe.

Seville boasted the gardens of the Alcazar Palace, reflecting a similar Moorish influence, where water provided several critical foci for the four independently themed areas contained within the walled compound. The original gardens, planted in the fifteenth century, became an accretion of different stylistic expressions, each reflecting successive generational interests. One generation would herald the introduction of exotic plants and the next would celebrate all that was indigenous. Over the centuries the amalgam of ideas created a garden of extraordinary breadth and complexity. In both of these Moorish gardens the vegetation was fed from a central tank that not only watered the visible features of the landscape but also provided a technically ingenious underground network to supply and support the humidifying systems. One of the important aspects of gardens in this part of Europe was their susceptibility to exceptionally high temperatures during the summer months and it was therefore through their mastery of hydro-technology and the ability to create microclimates that provided some respite for both vegetation and humans Little is mentioned in the designs of gardens of northern Europe about the need to create comfort, and while in theory this may be an ideological statement, its real importance lies in physical reality. Comfort, in the north European garden, is the need to provide shade, which is both basic and simple, and this, by contrast, highlights the subtlety and imagination of the Moorish medievalists who produced models that can still inspire today.

THE COMBINED GARDEN

There are few gardens that combine the features of orthogonal formality and wilful organic exuberance better than the garden at Schwetzingen near Baden

Wurtenberg in Germany. The landscape is cleanly divided into the recognisable sequences of the formal garden, yet an alternative parallel route leads the visitor along a meandering rill, past grottoes and monuments of mythology. This bucolic scenery provides a theatrical contrast to the un-negotiable order of its formal counterpart. There are many examples of English garden design, particularly in the eighteenth century, that combine elements of formality with landscape, but almost none that demonstrate the consciously stylised counterpoint seen in the gardens at Schwetzingen.

THE DOMESTIC GARDEN

This domain is cultivated to produce anything from the pictorial that is saccharine sweet or wildly absurd, to one where the owners have abandoned all interest. The British are not the only Europeans to revel in the absurd – shell-gardens and personalised topiary, gnomic characters and faux display – the rule systems happily give way to personalisation in all cultures. The use of the absurd accompanies a reduction in scale, as the rules of parterre and open landscaping only remain in the province of grand scale. The domestic garden shows a consideration to the control of scale and an understanding that this space has different territorial status. The suburban house with a front garden displays territory that is neither public nor private, accessed by visitor and owner alike, whereas the land to the rear of the house has the status of privacy. Therefore the positional relationship to the house determines both the nature of access and levels of privacy. The nature and planning of these spaces varies, and what might appear to be manicured precision at the front can be a mask that gives way to a wilderness at the back.

The domestic garden is still seen by many as a form of personal expression for public view in a way that the interior of the house can never be, and this tool of exhibitionism expresses individuality, which is possibly essential in the midst of built homogeneity.

THE KITCHEN GARDEN

The origins of growing edible plants domestically may have developed from the 'physic garden' of the Elizabethan period, where herbs were cultivated for colour as well as medicinal purposes. During and after the two world wars the scarcity of food put particular pressure on families to become more self-sufficient and encouraged the establishment of kitchen gardens. The use of cultivated public wasteland is now seen as more essential, as scientific data indicate the perils of climate change, rampant urbanisation and the political necessity to increase food production. Speculative urban proposals now use as a form of forecasting the suggestion that integration of urban land and agrarian function will become less surprising in the future. Grassed or planted surface can be found in a range of scales that have different functions, status and ownership and one might argue that these conditions might be used as metaphoric models within constructed space.

If the categories already mentioned are the words of the lexicon, there are also individual letters. These forms of articulation denote ownership, allow movement and create barriers.

BOUNDARY AND THRESHOLD

The French landscape designer and author Bernard Lassus in his writing on the suburban garden poses the question: at what point does a threshold occur and does it exist as a finite line? The most obvious example is the main door into a domestic house; however, the definition of threshold becomes less clear if one assumes the journey from the public domain to privacy starts at the front gate. This is visible and accessible to the public, as is the garden, yet it is in private ownership. The threshold occurs once the visitor has opened the gate; physical enclosure is therefore not necessary, but a cultural understanding of ownership is required. The threshold could be described as the front garden and therefore the journey through this unenclosed area represents a moment of transition where the visitor is gradually moving away from the public towards the private realm.

Alvaro Siza's Leca Swimming Pools is a definitive example of blurred threshold, where the pools cut into a retaining wall and the rocky edge of the shore, providing no clear distinction between the natural and the synthetic and the municipal and private ownership. The pools fill and empty according to the tide to create a dynamic rhythm of multiple edge conditions that have no one single contour.

Enrique Miralles and Carma Pinos' Cemetry at Igualada and the Archery Range for the 1992 Olympics at Barcelona (Miralles 1996) have inextricable relationships to the earth where multiple thresholds blend sacred and common space. The rough-hewn sepulchres at Igualada recede into the earth to establish a network of chambers that overlap, and where status is deliberately inexplicit. Both the visitor and the buried descend into the earth through a constructed excavation. The site evokes the mythological narrative of life returning to the soil, and the boundaries between life and death are symbolically marginal. The immersion into an excavated landscape draws the visitor into an awareness of the cyclical rhythm of life where the thresholds between each become indistinct.

THE ROUTE

At the largest of scales in Europe are the motorways and within the context of the major continental landscape they are mere ribbons that criss-cross the continent. These pieces of engineering are both symbols of and the reality of connectivity. They are forms of expedience that allow people and goods to be moved, and they have come to exemplify speed and time. At an urban scale the road and street support similar functions, but they are slower and more intrusive. Although one cannot draw direct architectural comparisons, speed and efficiency are mechanistic concepts that were associated with the models of Buckminster Fuller, the metaphors of living immortalised by Corbusier and analysed by Peter Reyner Banham (Banham 1960). This was a blatant ideology that drew parallels with the production techniques of industrial components. The main highway into Tokyo presents an anomaly – an elevated motorway built for efficiency and speed yet compromised as the sheer volume of traffic has slowed levels of movement down to, at times, almost walking pace. The experience of approaching the city was not considered an aesthetic experience, it was designed to produce an efficient piece of transportation; paradoxically, the aesthetic experience is an unforeseen consequence of increased motorisation and the long, detailed views of industrial rooftops are perhaps not the gateway into the city that the urban designers originally envisaged. This form of functionality for arterial roads was not the principal purpose of the grand city plans of Europe, where formalised geometries were concerned with vista and the framing of civic monuments. These avenues were to be experienced at walking pace and are much closer experientially to pedestrian boulevards and the park promenades.

More discreet are the grand drives of the palazzos, villas and country houses. With the buildings invariably hidden from public view, the drives were designed to take the owner or the visitor on a journey that culminates with the final vista of the house. This type of route has two purposes, one explicit and one implicit. The first is that the drives are sufficiently long to afford the owners both privacy and security and the second is to raise levels of anticipation before the ultimate denouement. Similar strategies are used to design the routes in the great parks of Stourhead and Chatsworth, which formed part of an 'arcadian' tradition, whereas the formal vistas at gardens such as Versailles were intended to dramatise the object, to frame and aggrandise. In both cases the buildings cannot change but our perception can, inevitably influenced by human movement through space and theatrical control.

THE PATH

The path, on a smaller scale and running across a surface with little or no engineering, its longevity is compromised, yet this may be the subtlest of ground markings as erosion then becomes an associate of memory, the scale of ground lines will define purpose, efficiency and pleasure. Some will act as lines of demarcation and others will simply offer archaeological traces.

Arata Isozaki has used the concept of path as the central idea in the Contemporary Art Museum at Gunma, Japan (*Arata Isozaki Architecture 1960–1990*) (1991), where the circuitous path in the landscape that reveals vistas episodically has been recreated internally to take the visitor on a journey through to the centre of the building. The ramp is designed to allow the visitor repeated, partial glimpses into the central gallery space. These views, caught through a sequence of non-orthogonal apertures, are cubist in concept to enable fragmented glimpses to be made comprehensible on arrival at the core of the building, where the entire gallery can be seen.

THE WALL

Conventionally used as a means of territorial demarcation, used within the context of the building the principal purpose of the wall is environmental control and functional division – but within landscape its language becomes less clear. Culturally the wall can be read in a number of different ways; the wall around the Stone Garden at Ryoan-ji is not simply a line of curtilage but an indicator of history, of wealth and of status. The wall in landscape may be natural, cultivated or synthetic – in summary, the manner of expression is, if not limitless, much wider than its architectural equivalent.

THE INCIDENT

There are many ways of achieving foci within the construct of an arranged landscape. It can be reductive, as in the eighteenth-century 'ha-ha' – a ditch between the manicured garden and agricultural land. Water is used to great effect in the Villa d'Este and Chatsworth and in more ethereal form in the fog gardens of Fujiko Nakaya (1990).

LAND AND TEXT

In the representation of land through text, the nuances of a highly developed and abstracted language have an inordinate number of constructed variables. Each word can be interpreted historically and culturally with different nuance, from the Phoenician pictogram and biblical narrative to the writing of Rabelais, and Olivier de Serre. Serres' *Le Theatre de d'Agriculture*. in the seventeenth century not only made clear references to the production of edible crops but also introduced the idea of 'parterre' or patterning, where a preconceived geometric construction would have a particular purpose and a secondary level of implication.

The writings in the seventeenth century of Andre Mollet, originally royal gardener to Queen Christina of Sweden and later to Charles I, were amongst the most formative and informative of their time (*Le Jardin de Plaisir*).

Contemporary writing can evoke images that are more abstract than the functional and figurative quality of much historic text, where descriptions of surface, plane, height, light and shadow create more suggestive relationships and words have an alignment rather than numeric precision. Gabrielle Garcia Marques' surrealist essay 'Light is like Water' describes a spatial landscape where the cataclysmic drowning of a group of children is described by the transposition of words used as metaphor. The place, the children and the game that they play are all illusory, yet the story creates a vivid image of a tragedy that is inevitable. The transposition of words where all that describes light is used to describe metaphorical water, for example light *filled* the room, light *flowed* out of the windows; this highlights both the subtlety and the fluidity of syntax that allows understanding to be radically changed and complement Marques' pictorial landscape of the imagination.

LAND, MEMORY AND RISK

The urban environment is structured predictably and a corollary of this formalism is our ability to recognise urban signage and iconography so that an implicit and explicit understanding of geographic position is relatively easy, the ability to navigate is therefore assisted by physical predictability. This fixed system of navigation is not present in open landscape, which is more vulnerable to seasonal change and can dramatically alter in extreme weather. There is a hidden yet inherent danger in navigating on open ground as predictability is not a given attribute. An argument could be made that the characteristics of the natural surface with its hidden formative language and relationship to climate systems might offer principles of risk that could be translated in synthetic design. Contemporary designers perform in a world that is risk-averse yet should we ask what is the value of unpredictability.

MEASUREMENT AND THE NATURE OF REPRESENTATION

The act of measurement has a simple physical reality, correlating areas with a determined set of linear scales whereby a synoptic outline of space can be established. The translation of form into numbers and line is usually introduced by the act of miniaturisation, and representation commonly uses these two forms of abstraction. Both the map and the plan serve to offer a qualitative and quantifiable summary of topographical information. This codified language communicates physical statistics, for example the position of a wall, road, railway, river, incline and forest. The map crudely imitates form through contour, but this linear precision is incapable of conveying the rounded variations of reality. The plan uses code to position and measure and is often augmented by written and numerical information offering a greatly reduced description of space. The function of the map and the plan is to impose systems of order and consistency, and to convey anything more experiential or nuanced is too complex to execute. These systems of communication lack subtlety and cultural reference and are incapable of describing the types and nature of activity within a building in a particular location. As this form of synoptic representation has evolved historically, one could assume that the limitation of expression might undermine both breadth of imagination and original thinking. Analytically synoptic representation simply does not have the ability to project nuance, In order to convey the qualities of light, sound, silence, shadow or wind, the line drawing would fail and a part of the exploration has been to search for other methods of representation. The relentless logic of rectilinear geometry should be challenged by the dendritic geometry of nature.

GIFU
RECONSTRUCTION
PROJECT

2.1   Gifu, north elevation at night
photograph by Tomio Ohashi

Arata Izozaki had been requested by the Japan Central Government and the Prefecture of Gifu to initiate a programme to reconsider the model of post-war social housing in Japan. This project was offered to four teams of female architects, two from Japan, one from the USA and one from the UK. There was a presumption that, despite identical briefs, cultural differences would emerge in the proposals each team produced.

Post-Second World War housing in Japan was a rapid response by the government to the immense damage inflicted on the built infrastructure, housing in particular, that rendered whole communities homeless. As an acknowledgement of the urgency of the situation, the speed of delivery was lauded; however, the model used for both speed of construction and economy had inherent problems, which became more serious over time. Traditional Japanese housing was small, low-density, constructed from wooden frames with little internal subdivision except for lightweight sliding screens. This typology had been used for generations and had evolved to accommodate the extended family, where more than one generation could live. The principles were simple and effective, with minimum space and maximum flexibility. The spaces could be used communally during the day and then be subdivided at night to provide appropriate levels of privacy. To facilitate this arrangement furniture was at best small and retractable (futons) or non-existent (tatami mats), storage had some premium but little else was required. The accoutrements associated with the development in the West could not have been embraced if the minimal finesse of the traditional house were to survive. There were other aspects of this traditional construction that were

critical and that was the materials used, all of which were natural, and each house had a configuration that allowed as much natural ventilation as possible. Communities were built with these small domestic dwellings organised along narrow streets, with some houses containing discreet internal courtyards and others owning small parcels of arable land on the perimeter of the town. This basic formula was repeated on both a modest and grand scale, where constructional and planning simplicity were prized, as was the relationship to natural space. For those families that had an internal courtyard garden, both the arrangement and ornamentation were meticulously planned. These houses were built with external sliding walls that slid away to enable the inner floor plan and the outer courtyard to be one continuous space. In a society where the scale of domestic space was so tiny, this extension into the open yet still within the domestic curtilage was a luxury. There is complex mythology and symbolism attached to Japanese shrubs, trees and mosses and the placement, orientation, size and seasonal rotation were as carefully organised as any aspect of design within the house.

The Japanese government quickly realised how vulnerable this housing was, particularly after the onslaught of the Allies during the raids at the end of the war and, with accelerated effort to accommodate those rendered homeless, they looked at Western models of apartments, particularly from the USA. During the inter-war years there was a subtle yet perceptible shift away from the model of the traditional extended family and a slow but noticeable acknowledgement that the younger generations were beginning to adopt some aspects of western lifestyle. The introduction of small apartments built from concrete and organised around a Western cellular plan was greeted positively, it was only after the novelty waned and the reality of living in this way, in a geographic part of the world with distinct climatic features, that the problems slowly began to emerge.

Culturally space had always been at a premium and historically reflected the history of feudal ownership; the government in its reconstruction programme was therefore only prepared to allow the same area per family unit that had existed under the system of traditional housing. The floor plans were now either on one or two levels, not the usual one storey of the traditional house. Concrete walls were now used to create a compartmentalised and diminished usable floor plan. For those that chose to still furnish their homes traditionally with futons and tatami mats, the spaces were barely workable; for those that chose the Western commodities of chairs, tables and beds, the apartments were totally impractical. The introduction of the washing machine perhaps exemplified the spatial problems, as most were situated on the tiny balconies where the machines froze in the winter and the exterior of the buildings were permanently festooned with washing and futons. Whatever level of consumables the family owned, all activity – even the most basic function – within the home was uncomfortable. The government's Department of Housing, responsible for the regeneration, were beguiled by the statistics of economy and speed of construction, but they ignored how people occupied space. There were additional problems with the post-war blocks where the lack of through ventilation became a serious technical problem. In areas where there are hot summers with very high levels of humidity, the

concrete was unable to dry out and the resulting condensation gave rise to material decay, fungal growth and structural damage. In summary the apartments over a 50-year period became unhealthy and unsafe. The fundamental problems were created by an imported planning template and construction materials ill-suited to the climate.

Four practices with international experience were invited to reconsider the template for social housing and create a model that could be used in the future. Initially introduction to the programme was deliberately disconnected from the site, the existing social context and the influences of legislative constraint and cost. The ambition was to create an environment where the designers were as liberated as possible. The situation obviously had an inherent paradox in that subliminal constraints were impossible to totally ignore. Isozaki was responsible for the master plan and each practice was given a perimeter strip of land each with different characteristics. However, all the practices had identical briefs to produce the same number of units (107) with the same typological mix. It was only in hindsight that we saw that the cultural and experiential diversity of the practices produced markedly contrasting results.

The site was on the periphery of Gifu, a town historically at the centre of the textile industry. The city was relatively compact, with most buildings built post-Second World War. The town was geographically situated in a wide river plain with the river running to the south-east, and the regional propaganda for the areas was focused on its landscape, the river and the Arcadian quality of the local open spaces. There was a communal and corporate understanding that the qualitative aspect

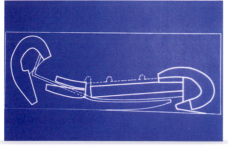
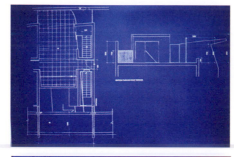

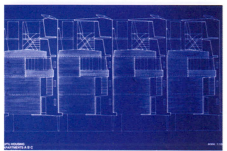
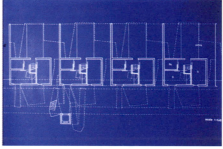
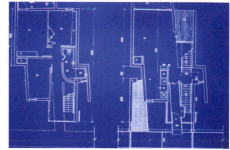

of this area lay in the surrounding nature and what it had to offer, not in the city. The area beyond the town was sporadically dotted with buildings interspersed with small parcels of arable land; there was little that gave the area any cohesion and it was at the periphery of this suburban development that the site for redevelopment was located. It had already been developed just after the war with a series of typical two- and four-storey blocks laid out with relentless municipal uniformity. The community that was originally housed there had been decanted and they were to be part of the community to be re-housed in this new development.

This brief offered the architects an opportunity to consult both with the local housing department and also with a group who were to be the new tenants. It became clear that their priorities were not only to do with the practicality of the apartments but also how they could access open space, if not physically, then visually. The post-war master plan of the estate had been organised with military regularity into a series of parallel blocks with alternating roads. One presumes that at the time of construction anything other than basic shelter was considered an extravagance. There was now a need to offer some form of contact to nature and to create a sense of space that belied the minimal nature of the apartments.

The site did not have the advantage of being situated in an urban context where the relevance of history or issues of adjacency would provide the usual sources of references. In this location there was nothing that was built that was worth referring to except the ground, the vista and Gifu's proximity to open landscape as a venue for recreation. In many ways this town had the characteristics of a typical mid-region conurbations, where there was little contemporary culture and its relationship to open space became critically important. The region had a significant medieval military history, where the local warlords trained and used soldiers to engage in covert operations to carry information to critical outposts. Throughout this period, military envoys would travel throughout the night and in order to navigate were dependent on an intimate knowledge of the landscape. The land became a critical point of reference as it had a historic resonance, contemporary importance and a qualitative value to those who lived locally. There was one final and practically critical aspect of the ground that none of us could ignore: a fault line ran through this area; the ground and its substrate had the ability to collapse. The initial studies were simple and introduced the idea of ground and open space making simple references to the geometry of the site and the internal courtyards found in some traditional houses.

The position on the site was pre-determined and we were allocated the south-west corner with a particularly unique geometric complexity. The initial sketches explored a range of geometries that could negotiate a 90-degree bend and still maintain an organic line rather than use Pythagorean geometry. The forms were varied and interchangeable and the simplicity allowed a degree of graphic freedom. The group was then asked to design in parallel an 'idealised' dwelling or dwellings and again these initial proposals were naïve as the intention was not constrained by programmatic issues. Early drawings show a series of arrangements all utilising the traditional principles of the sliding screen and flexible space. The drawings also illustrated ideas of internal space and how on at least some arrangements there was the ability to slide back screens to create a boundary-less plane between inside and outside space.

The façades developed a variation of screen motif with a suggestion that the elements might be made of slatted bamboo. This was in essence a European interpretation of the critical components of the traditional Japanese dwelling. A three-dimensional model constructeded in parallel began to incorporate some additional information about massing and height and explore how the means of access could be a fragile counterpoint to the solidity of the block. These exercises were not completely wasted in that they offered an opportunity to explore the translation of ideas as principles. The possibility of designing in a void is a rare and luxurious event where exploration of critical concepts need not be compromised by practicality. This process was unusual in that value traditionally lay in speed and economy, not concept. The design had established two principles: the first was that both the basic and more intricate aspects of the development needed to be aware of the character of external space and location; the second principle was to create a sense of space despite the guideline restrictions on size and volume. The detail of density, typology and cost were gradually fed into the equation and throughout each iteration some form of spatial negotiation was made. One of the most striking characteristics of the post-war blocks was their relentless uniformity; no matter where they were located throughout Japan and no matter what their scale, they all looked identical. This was due to the use of standardised templates but even these had been manipulated so that any difference in scale was erased. Perhaps our view about the importance of identity and recognition was a European characteristic, but it became a major goal to incorporate within our initial concepts.

2.8   North elevation detail

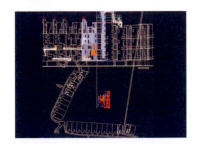

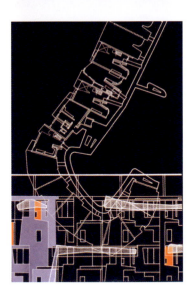

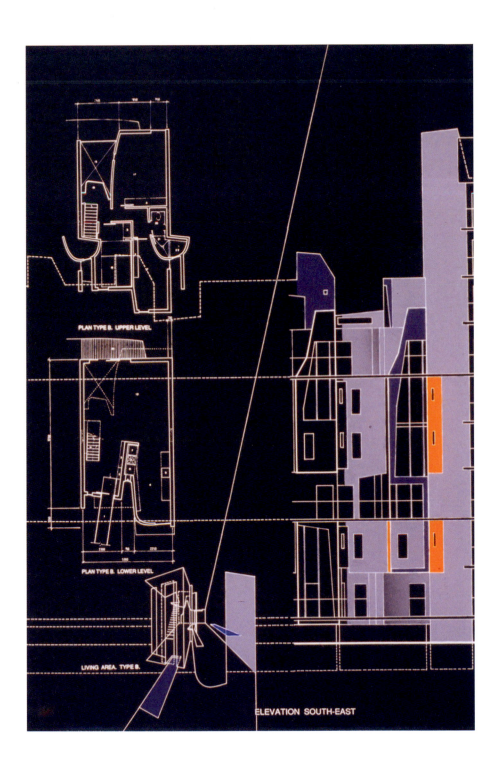

2.9   Painted detail of south façade

2.10   Sketch plan and elevation

2.11   Sketch detail of plan and elevation

2.12   Sketch detail of elevation plans and interior

2.13   North façade and garden

2.14   Early computer model of duplex interior

A matrix of seven different units were required, which were organised into five different volumetric arrangements. The majority of apartments were arranged over two floors to achieve both the volumes and density required on the allocated site plan.

By configuring and reconfiguring the different volumes, the external face of the building was able to have local variations. Throughout the design process there were inevitable digressions that tested the emerging form against restricting criteria. The principle of identity and how the building maintained a relationship with the ground plane and open space was to become increasingly important.

There were a number of different techniques of representation – which were neither purely technical nor figurative – that were used as tools of exploration; simple computerised images were abstracted from the conventional forms of expression in order to maintain our focus on principles. A small physical model was constructed to establish the aesthetic and structural relationship and means of access within the main block. The housing would be a solid construction and therefore the stairs and external corridors were designed to be a lightweight steel assembly using attenuated geometric form that was both hung and cantilevered. This was a lesson in cultural sensitivities as our structural advice was to design a structure that was as flexible as possible to accommodate ground tremors. However, whatever technically proven logic existed, the popular perception of what reassured was that structure had to be substantial, solid and rigid (this had proved disastrous at Kobe). After we produced the first set of drawings for the executive architects in Japan to consider, the scheme was completely remodelled and the entire building now sat within a substantial framed box; the design was unrecognisable. Both the concept and the developing aesthetic language had disappeared completely.

There now began a long and eventually productive relationship where the learning curve between our office and that of the executive architects Sunny Sekai was mutual. Schematic computer images were produced to try to understand the volumetric relationships and learn whether by manipulating the vertical space we could give a greater sense of openness. Finally a series of paintings was produced that took the geometric form of the building's footprint and lifted it vertically so that it could be painted onto the façade of the building. This was an attempt at creating a notational system that captured the signature of the ground on which the building was situated. Compositionally the motif was added to the lexicon and eventually contributed to the building's identity. In part, this exercise was a graphic exploration, using painterly techniques to applied to a spatial solution.

During the development of the plans it became evident that the non-linear geometry of the perimeter would inevitably influence the formal planning of the apartments. The principle had been established that the typologies would form an interlocking volumetric matrix, but if the plans

had a cross wall construction, interlocking on plan was also necessary to give the building structural integrity to counter earth tremors. The planning was emerging as a series of alternating and interlocking volumes, both vertically and on plan.

The centre of the site was landscaped, offering the residents a view of the garden. The position of our block on the south-west corner of the site allowed the occupants at the upper levels an uninterrupted view of the wider landscape and the hills beyond. The verticality of the apartments and the use of double-height space allowed more expansive views, and the top-level duplexes and triplexes had external

2.15   View towards interlinking staircase

93

terraces echoing the early attraction of traditional internal courtyards. Early ideas about flexibility were much more difficult to achieve; all the lower floors were open plan with windows arranged to encourage cross-ventilation horizontally and the double-height entrance encouraged air acceleration vertically. This arrangement addressed some of the environmental problems created by the over-compartmentalisation of the post-war houses. The upper floor of each apartment were bedrooms and bathrooms and these did not have the flexibility of the traditional family house as the rooms were required to have permanent privacy; however, all had sliding screen doors so the ability to create partial open space was greater than in a traditional post-war layout.

Throughout the design process legislative and economic information was incorporated that repeatedly changed aspects of the design. It is salutary to look at the early naïve sketches, with ideas created in a relative vacuum, and ask how many early concepts had been preserved.

2.16   Entrance detail

2.17   View down access corridor

2.18   Access corridor on north elevation

2.19   Double-height entrance

2.20   Access bridge

2.21   Staircase detail

2.22   Detail of canopy on top floor

PFAFFENBERG MUSEUM, AUSTRIA

WITH PETER COOK

The proposal was developed as a result of a limited competition to provide an extension to the existing Museum at Bad Deutsch Altenburg that housed a collection of Roman remains from Carnuntum and its surrounding region of Pfaffenberg. Carnuntum was the Roman military fort, strategically positioned in Lower Austria close to the border of Bratislava. The encampment was the largest military fort outside Rome and provided the strategic base necessary to move into northern Europe. The base was not only a garrison but also a market and trading post for those bringing merchandise from southern Europe. It existed from 6 AD and was conquered and destroyed by an invading German army 400 years later. It is arguably one of the most important sites in northern Europe, with both architectural and artefact remains that offer a unique and detailed picture of not only military but also civilian roman life. The area the base occupied was approximately 10 kilometres in diameter and although the existing museum displayed a definitive collection, the archival store was unable to accommodate any further artefacts that were continuing to be excavated.

The programme therefore demanded a solution not only to display more archival material but also to consider the importance of the ongoing archaeological work. One aspect of museum display that denies the impact of time is the process of reconstruction; a more authentic strategy would be to accept the process of decomposition and to understand how the by-products of a civilisation once destroyed return to the ground. The removal of artefacts from their original site serve to undermine our understanding as the objects become de-contextualised, the ground and

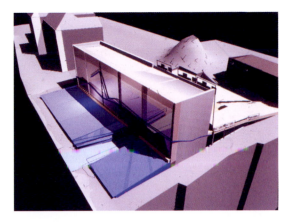

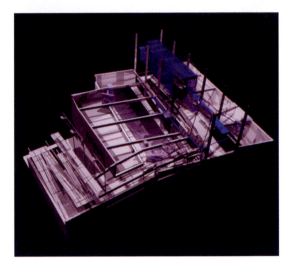

the position in which the objects were situated therefore became critically important. An obvious response to the programme would have been be to extend the existing museum; however, limited site space and the scale of the required display made a building extension impractical. A composite response was developed; the first part was to build a modest entrance pavilion adjacent and linked to the existing museum, to serve as an introduction to

2.23   Museum exterior view

2.24   Skeletal view of interior

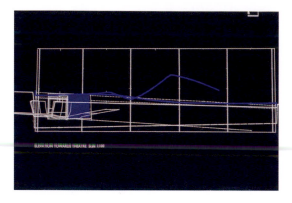

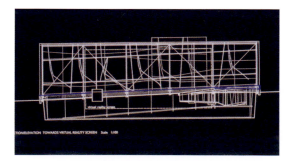

2.25   Detail of front façade

2.26   Plan of sunken exhibition space

2.27   View of internal structure

a journey out into the landscape where the artefacts were to be displayed. This offered the double benefit of minimising the scale of any new building in a town where the scale was restricted and also allowing the display of objects in the positions in which they were originally found. The conventional view of museologists is that found objects need to be restored, if necessary reconstructed and preserved in a state of artifice that destroys the evidence of time.

The design incorporated four distinct parts: the entrance pavilion, an amphitheatre, a subterranean exhibition vitrine and a belvedere. Copies of Roman maps gave sufficient information for one of the many archaic routes to be traced and it was along this route, often close to points of previous excavation, that the pavilions were placed. The intention was to take the visitor on a journey that not only displayed the artefacts of another historic era but also gave them geographical and topographical understanding of the encampment. As the historic terrain had changed very little over time the journey was used to describe why the Romans had settled in particular locations and what impact the context had on the military and civil community.

The journey began at the entrance pavilion, and although it had a bridge link to the original museum, it could still be understood as the beginning of an autonomous museological journey. The adjacency to the original building built as a faux Roman villa was designed as a neutral counterpoint. The outer shell was aluminium with one rail on which the sliding entrance door hung. The metal rail was twisted into the form of the lower Danube, the river that skirted the perimeter of the town, reminding the visitor of two facts: the first was its geographic location,

critical in the siting of a military encampment; and the second was the importance of the town as a spa, which was the other determining factor in establishing the Roman settlement. The choice of visual language to both express the importance of geographic location and physical characteristics of place was a highly reductive form, a line.

The interior of the entrance pavilion had a ramp that led upwards to a small meeting room and downwards past introductory objects to the entrance of the garden. The land to the rear of the existing museum contained a large rock and initially this was a major obstacle in planning the route.

The original concept celebrated the land as the primary form of context therefore we logically made the decision to incorporate the rock into the entrance sequence and garden. Conceptually the boundary between synthetically constructed and open space was deliberately blurred as the route continued into an archaeological garden. Here, environmentally controlled vitrines displayed some of the larger archived objects as close to their original excavated position as possible. The route continued into open land arriving at a naturally formed hollowed embankment that created a base for a small amphitheatre. The architectural components were minimal – an elemental stage and frame to cover a retractable backdrop. This area was envisaged as a point to pause and listen to lectures and discussions outside the formality of the museum.

The route continued to the most elaborate architectural pavilion, an exhibition space constructed below ground; the roof was made of structurally reinforced glass, allowing the visitor to walk over the structure and see the exhibits beneath. The artefacts displayed were repositioned where they were originally excavated, once again echoing the importance of location. The glass roof of the sunken pavilion was etched with both a contemporary and a Roman maps positioning objects in both a wider historic and geographic context. The importance of the land and its geographic location for the Roman military was appreciated once the journey was concluded at the arrival of a belvedere. The belvedere used the miniaturised elevation of the entrance pavilion as a mnemonic to form a seat positioned at the top of a major escarpment chosen by the romans specifically for defence.

Throughout the attenuated journey the principle objective was to heighten an awareness that a Roman community existed and also how the land had been used both in the act of preservation and decay.

2.28   Model of entrance detail

2.29   Model of glass viewing floor for sunken exhibition space

2.30   Model of belvedere

AALBORG AQUATIC CENTRE

2.31   Detail through water mat

WITH CJ LIM

There are few opportunities where the deliberate objective is to design an architecture that remains unseen; to design space underground is in economic terms very costly and in human terms environmentally oppressive. There are arguments attached to environmental control and contextual sensitivity that supported the reasons for the Aquatic Centre at Aalborg in Denmark to be designed as a subterranean structure. The topography of the Netherlands is uniformly flat; this is a country that has little articulated ground surface. The picturesque tradition of the English garden or the grand geometries of the European tradition are not visible; this was a geographic location more visually memorable for its flat agricultural land.

The aquatic programme for the centre was predictable in that there was a requirement for a main and subsidiary pool, a diving area together with the usual supplementary facilities of spas, sauna and restaurant. The brief was perfunctory and unimaginative, with little to distinguish the description of this potential building from any other leisure centre.

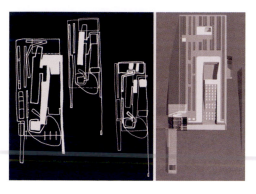
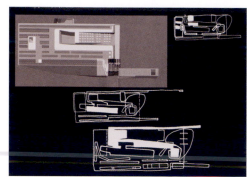
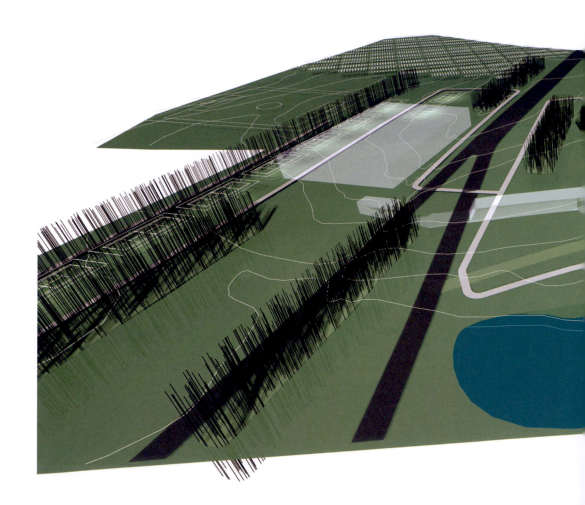

2.32　Sketch pool plans

2.33　Sketch pool and roof plans

2.34　Site plan

2.35　Aalborg Aquatic Centre view
of landscape

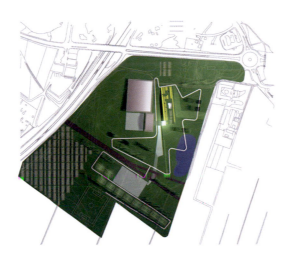

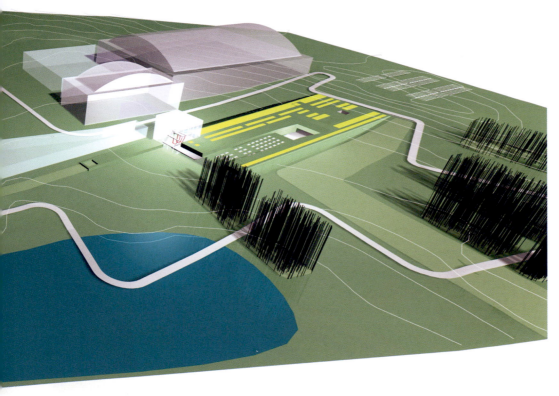

LIVERPOOL JOHN MOORES UNIVERSITY
LEARNING SERVICES

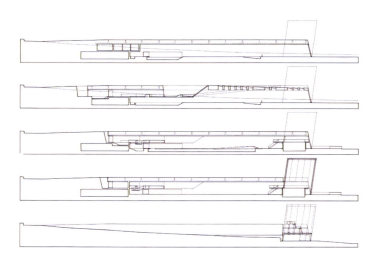

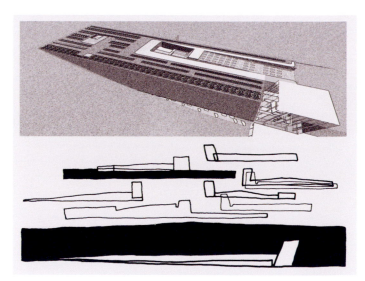

2.36   Sketch of landscape

2.37   Sketch section through pool and diving
tower

2.38   Sketch showing relationship of
landscape to pool and ground

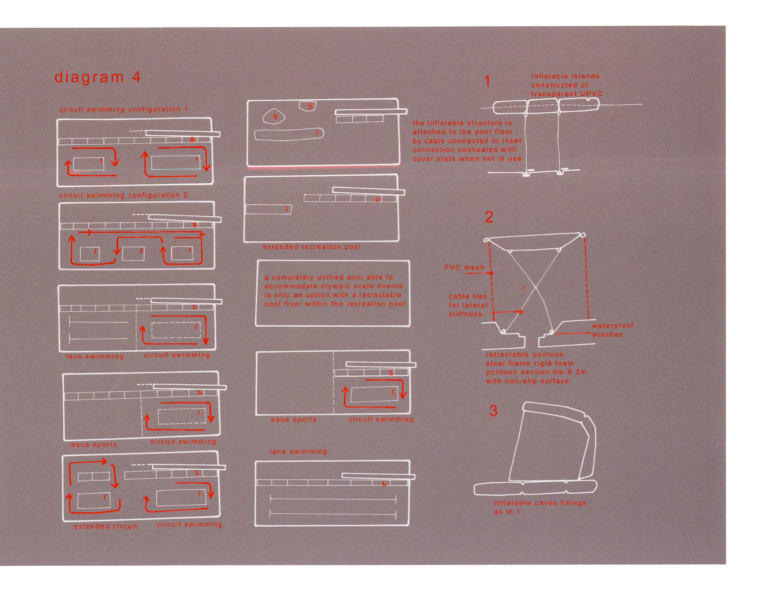

diagram 4

circuit swimming configuration 1

circuit swimming configuration 2

lane swimming   circuit swimming

aqua sports   circuit swimming

extended circuit   circuit swimming

extended recreation pool

a completely unified pool able to
accommodate olympic scale events
is only an option with a retractable
pool floor within the recreation pool

aqua sports   circuit swimming

lane swimming

1   inflatable islands
constructed of
transparent UPVC

the inflatable structure is
attached to the pool floor
by cable connected to inset
connection concealed with
cover plate when not in use

2

PVC mesh

cable ties
for lateral
stiffness

waterproof
winches

retractable pontoon
steel frame rigid foam
pontoon section 5m X 2m
with non-slip surface

3

inflatable caves fixings
as in 1

These expensively run public facilities often become desultory and worn; the brief needed an alternative approach. If the basic functions were largely non-negotiable, attention needed to focus on the site. At the edge of Aalborg the town drifted into semi-industrial neutrality with no definable places for the public. Aquatic leisure facilities are extremely costly to run almost always due to high energy costs. The first issues that influenced initial thinking were practical: how to conserve energy and whether there were opportunities to create supplementary amenities. These amenities needed to augment the facilities of the pool and raise levels of attendance. Water leisure centres are by definition immersive; they support one set of functions and obviously do not cater for those who do not like water.

The ground not only offered a practical opportunity to address the issue of long-term running costs but also it could be used to create a park appealing to those who failed to be lured by the indoor facility. Natural landscape is never far from the edge of Aalborg; one might argue that this could be a reason why no tradition of the grand city park had been established and the project therefore developed a cultivated landscape, not adjacent but over the aquatic centre. The historic tradition of public building as icon was challenged, as all the amenities with the exception of the diving tower were to be buried beneath the ground and the ground surface was to become as important as the building in providing the facilities of an urban park in the classic tradition.

The organisation and geometry of aquatic centres has been subverted over the last three decades as organic forms heralded the introduction of play rather than exercise. Once an organic or non-linear shape defines a pool, its ability to be used for aerobic training is compromised. This proposal maintained the orthodoxy of a linear formation, providing for both sport and non-sport activity. The plan included minor organically shaped counterpoints in the plan of the restaurant and the spa facilities and also included a water pillow for children's play.

The pool was sunk 10 metres below ground level and the ground/roof structure was a 450-millimetre concrete slab with a trough profile, planted with both long and short rooted plants. A tubular heat exchange system was embedded in the structure together with a system for rainwater collection. This passive technology augmented the pool's heating system and also provided supplementary grey water, thereby minimising the use of fresh water. The insulation value of the earth together with the composition of the roof provided a stable thermal environment, protecting the building from excess heat in the summer and the sharp drop in temperature in the winter. The functionality of the ground was not only environmental but also economic as the additional cost of excavation was mitigated by the absence of an external envelope.

The overriding geometry, both spatially and technically, became critical in establishing the planting regime for the landscape. The organisation of planting was intended to echo the formality of commercial planting seen throughout the Netherlands and the use of colour was organised in blocks reminiscent of commercial flower growing rather than the more informal arrangements seen in picturesque landscapes. The formality of the planting arrangement also echoed the linearity of the internal space. The surface was carved to allow both light to penetrate the interior and for the park users to gain oblique glimpses of the pool. With the exception of the diving tower, conceived as a dynamic projection, the architecture had all but disappeared; the visibility of the public building was non-existent and only the ground surface prevailed as a testament to a public facility. Compositionally and conceptually the representation was stark and in the nature of northern open space there was the search for the quality of emptiness.

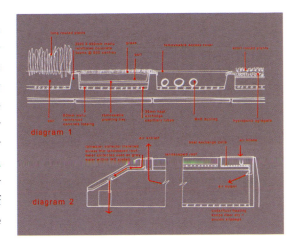

diagram 1

diagram 2

2.40   Detail through landscaped roof
construction

PANGYO HOUSING, KOREA

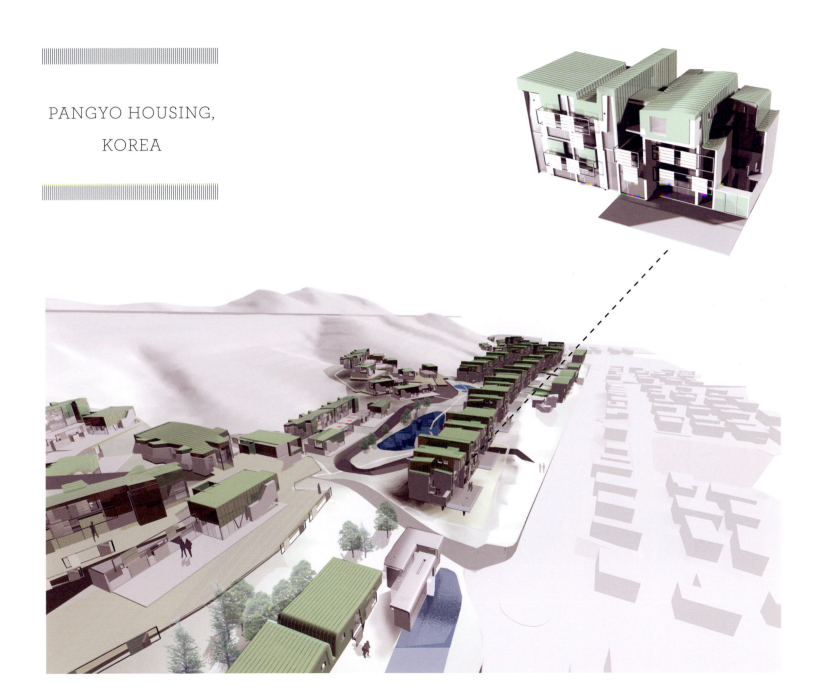

2.41   Interlocking models showing units a to d

2.42   View across landscape

WITH ANDREW PORTER

The site south of Seoul was topographically typical, on the edge of a city surrounded by hills; a 2-kilometre strip that undulated from east to west and also had a 23-metre drop from north to south. The nature of the terrain presented a unique challenge, in particular how 1,000 units of housing were to meet the ground. The vista from the site was sparse, with no visual contact to the city and no discernible landmarks; therefore predictable points of references could not be used. At the top of the site on the northern edge there was a natural spring and so, together with the dramatic contours, the conceptual references were established. There was no rhythm or continuity in the gradients; the terrain was neither vertiginous to be cliff like nor evenly stepped to be a terrace or smooth enough to create undulating hills. The obvious and most expedient response would have been to excavate and backfill to rationalise the surfaces, but this approach seemed to deny the very character of the site. If the terrain had highly variable contours, the response would have to be an architectural map that mirrored the natural surface. Conceptually the nature of the land dictated not only the architectural response but also the way in which individual structure navigated contact with the ground.

The narrative was additionally developed both through the need to provide external shelter using indigenous plants and to consider how public spaces, each with their own character, might be designed to provide locational foci. The technique of harnessing longitudinal vistas was impossible as the terrain was too uneven, and the gambit of creating one enclosure after another too repetitive over such a long distance. The Louden concept of the land as a 'recognisable work of art' seemed impractical as perception and understanding had to be clearly navigable. Horace Walpole's sentiment that the land was to be laid out along the principles of

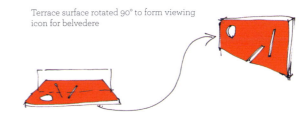

Terrace surface rotated 90° to form viewing icon for belvedere

Social Centre icon

Roof icon

Icon

Landscape icon

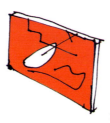

Fitness Centre icon

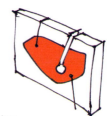

Reservoir icon

2.44   Indicative signs in the landscape (a, b, c, d, e, f, g)

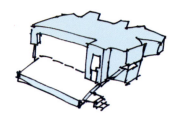

Unit type g   stepped terrace

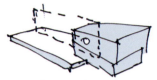

Unit type f1   stepped terrace

Unit type f2   stepped terrace

Unit type e   ribbon development

Landscape between buildings with tree lined vista

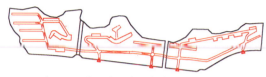

Access roads to carparking (mainly under buildings)

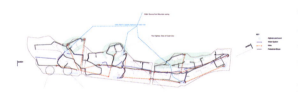

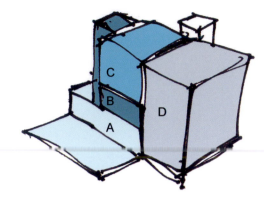

'natural picturesque beauty' was perhaps an approximation of the strategy used. The architectural response needed to be conceived within a landscape strategy and the landscape in turn needed to be developed in tandem with the architectural proposal. The two components were completely harnessed, with the land as the primary constituent.

The housing was organised with a north-east, south-west orientation so that as many as possible were to have uninterrupted views. Ten typologies were developed, with no single unit being allowed above four storeys. This dictated a very low-density

and consistent site coverage, thereby negating any major focal point for public open space. The housing was organised along three avenues, each one being higher than the previous, allowing all the units to have views with no overshadowing. The apartments ranged from the most typologically and geometrically complex, with six interlocking volumetric units, incorporating studios to four-bedroom apartments. All had windows on the public elevation, with sliding shutters to control sun penetration, and the apartments on the upper level had internal courtyards. The distinguishing characteristics of this housing block were the ground plane, where a varying relationship to the ground level was necessary where some units floated above and others rested on the surface. This structural necessity subsequently influenced the form of the roof profile, where the distinctively undulating curves created a metaphor for the terrain on which they were situated.

All the roofs were constructed from insulated bent copper and the valley gutters acted as collection channels for surplus rainwater directed into the grey water system running throughout

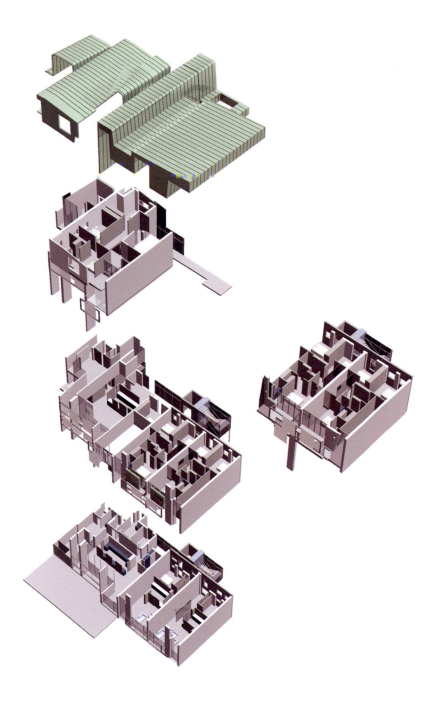

2.53   Exploded view of interlocking units

each of the blocks. The motif of the roofs followed the same basic principles throughout the site. There was a range of intermediate units ranging from the most complex six-apartment block, to large single-family houses at the rear and upper level of the site. Most of the units were dual aspect and incorporated stack principled air-cooling to mitigate the need to be solely dependent on artificial environmental control. Some of the larger houses had accompanying terraces where the narrative and sequence of landscaping was etched into its hard landscaping. Much of the building floated above the level of the land, but where necessary the structure could form a terrace both onto and into the ground.

The landscape was seen as a subtle geometric counterpoint to the linear nature of the development, with semi-discreet pockets of space characterised either by botanical groups of indigenous shrubs and trees or, where appropriate, using gravity-fed diverted water from the natural spring to form aquatic channels. At certain junctures the water route was punctuated with large ponds that provided habitats for both local bird and aquatic life. The sequences of spaces were linked both laterally and horizontally in order to create, if not unifying vistas, then pockets of related space.

The development was divided into three zones; attached to each was a community facility, a cultural centre, sports club and library, and these were positioned as autonomous objects in the landscape.

Principles of eighteenth-century landscape influenced the planning where the pavilions in the landscape provide a long-distance focal point and a near-distance means of realigning sightlines; however, this tactic shares its origins not only in the West but also in the structured form of the Asian garden.

Interlocking block 1:300
Types A, B, C & D

fourth floor plan

Ribbon block 1:300
Type E

Stepped Terrace 1:300
Type G

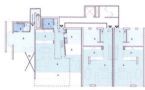

third floor plan

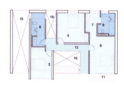

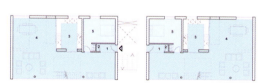

second floor plan

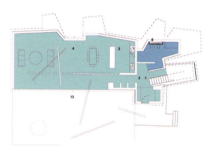

second floor plan

second floor plan

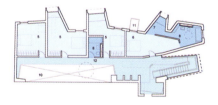

first floor plan

first floor plan

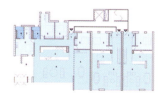

first floor plan

2.54   Interlocking blocks a, b, c, d plans

2.55   Ribbon block plans

2.56   Stepped terrace plans type g

each of the blocks. The motif of the roofs followed the same basic principles throughout the site. There was a range of intermediate units ranging from the most complex six-apartment block, to large single-family houses at the rear and upper level of the site. Most of the units were dual aspect and incorporated stack principled air-cooling to mitigate the need to be solely dependent on artificial environmental control. Some of the larger houses had accompanying terraces where the narrative and sequence of landscaping was etched into its hard landscaping. Much of the building floated above the level of the land, but where necessary the structure could form a terrace both onto and into the ground.

The landscape was seen as a subtle geometric counterpoint to the linear nature of the development, with semi-discreet pockets of space characterised either by botanical groups of indigenous shrubs and trees or, where appropriate, using gravity-fed diverted water from the natural spring to form aquatic channels. At certain junctures the water route was punctuated with large ponds that provided habitats for both local bird and aquatic life. The sequences of spaces were linked both laterally and horizontally in order to create, if not unifying vistas, then pockets of related space.

The development was divided into three zones; attached to each was a community facility, a cultural centre, sports club and library, and these were positioned as autonomous objects in the landscape.

Principles of eighteenth-century landscape influenced the planning where the pavilions in the landscape provide a long-distance focal point and a near-distance means of realigning sightlines; however, this tactic shares its origins not only in the West but also in the structured form of the Asian garden.

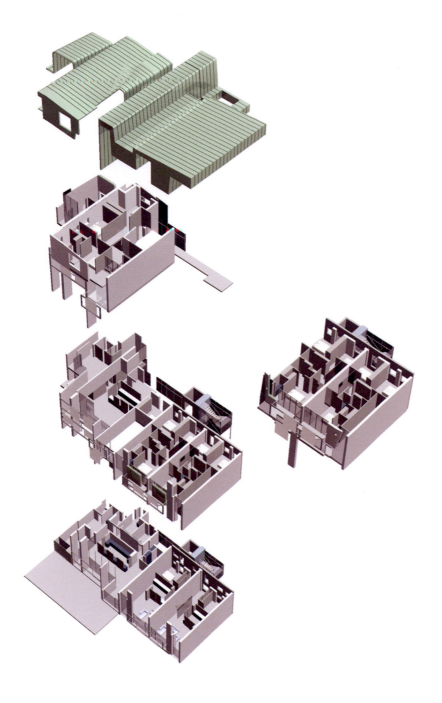

2.53   Exploded view of interlocking units

Interlocking block 1:300
Types A, B, C & D

Stepped Terrace 1:300
Type G

fourth floor plan

Ribbon block 1:300
Type E

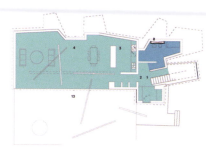

third floor plan

second floor plan

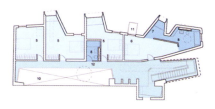

second floor plan

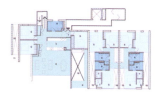

second floor plan

first floor plan

first floor plan

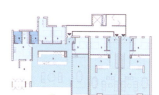

first floor plan

2.54   Interlocking blocks a, b, c, d plans

2.55   Ribbon block plans

2.56   Stepped terrace plans type g

In each landscaped area the small community buildings were accompanied by a series of stones tablets, on each was a carved symbol characterising the area often making reference to the historic principle of the cultivated landscape by using both visual metaphor and mnemonic.

As the scale of the land and the complexity of its topography were so dominant, the architectural scheme was driven both tactically and in detail by these contextual factors. There is always an underlying desire to capture some of the qualities found in other methods of representation and perhaps in some small detail there may be an association with the use of planting and colour depicted in the images created by Yimou and Doyle; the difficulty of capturing poetic moments in the same way is regrettably difficult. There were too many overwhelming demands to satisfy technical criteria that ultimately undermined the ability to create a visual environment that had sufficient poetic force.

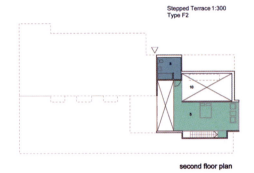

Stepped Terrace 1:300
Type F2

second floor plan

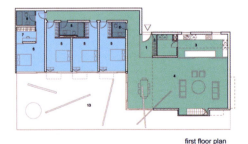

first floor plan

2.57   Stepped terrace plans type f2

SHANGHAI REDEVELOPMENT PLAN

2.58   Model plan of water and landscape

The contrast in scale to a European planning proposal suggested a focus on ground strategy rather than the detail of the architecture. The competition brief offered a site of 30 hectares and a requirement to accommodate 10,000 units of housing. There was little context other than an arterial road on the eastern edge, a rail line and station on the western edge and a river on the southern edge. The site was triangulated and at its northern point the peri-urban edge pointed towards the city of Shanghai. Within a planning culture that conspicuously lacks any sensibility, there was no contextual information of any type. The architectural proposals were to be treated quite generically and the site and ground organisation were the strategic focus of the proposal.

The organisational strategy needed to be clear and simple; the site would be divided into four corridors of mid-rise housing running north–south and the density would be achieved by the addition of three towers of housing in each corner of the site. The physical presence of structure was therefore dealt with in a very rudimentary fashion.

2.59   Model view of hard landscape

The more fundamental question was how, on a site of this scale, could you not only provide the infrastructure, but, more importantly, how could you provide any vestigial trace of identity and neighbourhood in a development that was destined to become a vast faceless ghetto?

This project was developed in 1990, in advance of the highly publicised data and discussion on sustainability, and it is somewhat ironic that it was the Chinese tradition of non-vehicular travel that became the primary influence on the system of transportation. The site's scale necessitated a movement programme; a network of cycle lanes orientated east–west carried people to the key points of entry and exit and this system was supplemented by a parallel network of footpaths that threaded north–south into the housing corridors. A bus route ringed the site, with spurs off to the key points of embarkation. Both the cycle and bus routes were designed to be at different levels, thereby separating the pedestrians from all other moving traffic.

The objective was to create a system whereby travelling over the site completely excluded cars. There is of course an irony in this proposal in that over the last decade China has become one of the biggest car producers and users, creating some of the most polluted environments in the world.

To address the challenge of how to try and break down the scale of the development and give the communities some identity, each housing corridor had a particular landscape and different function, offering a range of environments and facilities in localised areas; the edges of the site were seen as a neutral zone that carried pathway links. The first corridor was constructed as a hard landscape that provided for a range of outdoor sporting activity; the surface was marked for small-scale team sport and landscaped to provide areas for individual and collective shelter. The second avenue provided a marked and punctured surface for a temporary de-mountable market facility. Although most of the activity in this area relied on temporary infrastructure, a permanently supported canopy provided an awning for shelter during the hot summer months. The third avenue was landscaped with planting and a waterscape, designed to be the public park for the community. The final area, less an avenue and more a zone to the east of the site, was provided with a more substantial sports area where large field team sport could be played.

The ground surface provided the focus to the development's identity; not only was it a surface across which people moved, but also a surface that had been scored and marked to suggest and determine a range of activity.

Central to any housing proposal must be the accommodation, but this study offered an opportunity to consider how a contribution could be made to the identity and cohesion of a community, and looked almost exclusively at the way in which the ground could not only be used but also symbolically understood.

OSAKA STATION,
NORTH OSAKA

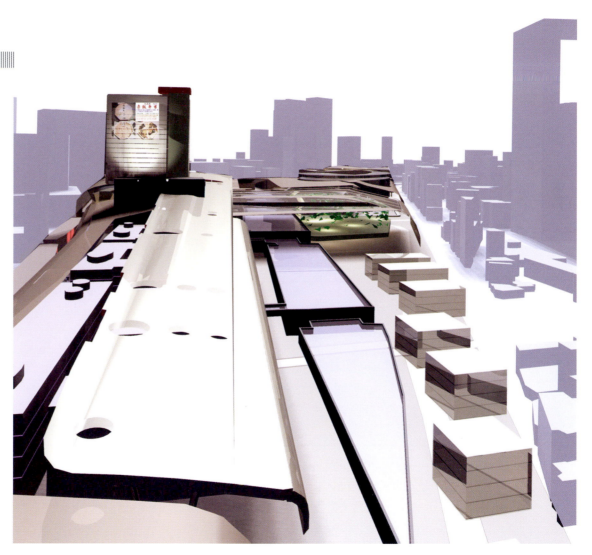

2.60   Overview over roof and landscape

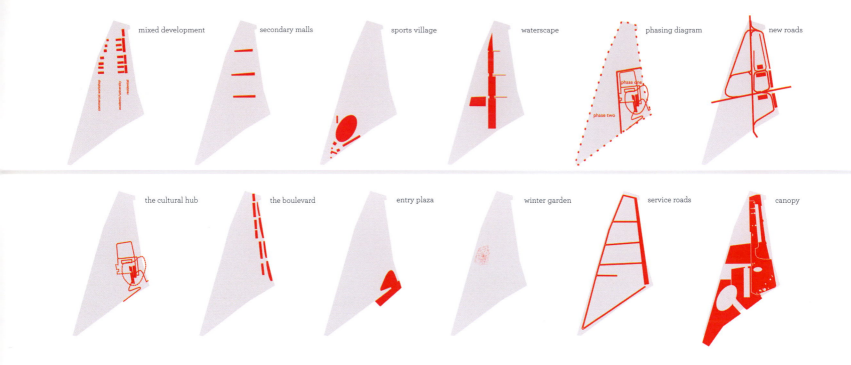

mixed development   secondary malls   sports village   waterscape   phasing diagram   new roads

the cultural hub   the boulevard   entry plaza   winter garden   service roads   canopy

2.61   Organisational diagrams

WITH ANDREW PORTER

Osaka, situated at the mouth of the Yodo River on Osaka Bay, is the third largest city in Japan. Historically it was the commercial centre of the country and currently functions as one of the command centres for the Japanese economy. Originally the historic centre for trading rice during the Edo period and more recently the first to create a futures exchange market. It is a vibrant commercial centre with an exceptionally large commuter population to support its commercial industries. The transport network, particularly the rail network, is very heavily used and the main stations carry millions of commuters each day. North Osaka station serves commuters working in the university district to the north, the cultural quarter of the city to the east and west and to the south, the main commercial centre of the city. Situated to the north of the station lies a derelict site bounded on two sides by major arterial roads and on the southern edge of the triangular piece of land lies the entrance to North Osaka Station (arranged on three levels).

The proposal incorporated activities that directly complemented the diverse functions of the adjacent areas and provided an urban facility that would be unique to Osaka. The area was designed to attract international visitors while also providing a resource for the local community.

The strategy deliberately rejected the traditional street and block structure and chose to organise the design around a series of activity nodes in a quasi-natural landscape. Although Osaka has public parks, most are formally arranged with perhaps one or two municipal facilities.

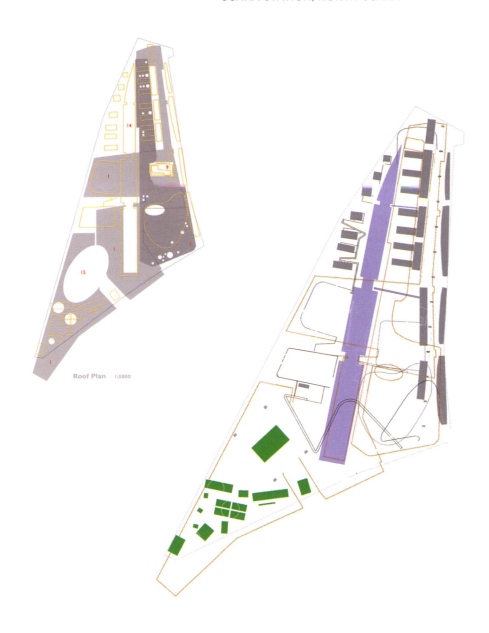

Roof Plan   1:5000

This area was conceived as a loose association of buildings and open space where the visitor could experience undifferentiated boundaries between internal and external space. The density of the city and proportionally minimal open space suggested that the design could be thought of conceptually as a park and that it needed not only to benefit the area environmentally but also attract a demographically wide range of visitor. As the rail and vehicle thoroughfare needed to be maintained, the park with its facilities was raised on a plinth to allow all rail and vehicular traffic to move underneath, pedestrians could then move through the site in a safe environment, experiencing the minimum of environmental pollution. The surrounding area has a recognisable urban grid typical of post-war Japanese development influenced by the American city model. This inherent rigidity of city plan was balanced by the relaxed arrangement of buildings in the park, this may have been a countercultural move in a country that values not only the cost of land but also its functional efficiency. The argument used was qualitatively based, where the design attempted to dissolve the rigid boundaries between work and leisure.

2.62   Roof diagram

2.63   Overall plan

2.64   Roof canopy

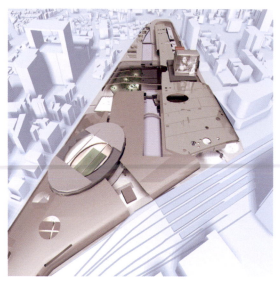

The development is divided into two phases: the cultural complex and retail boulevard, in phase one is seen as the gateway to the development. The entry point is via a public podium with connections to the station below; the scale of the site required secondary entry points distributed around the site at ground level. Movement throughout was wholly pedestrianised with strategically placed travelators to assist movement where necessary. The urban form and route network defined the location as a safe car-free public space where both the physical facilities and the park-scape could be appreciated in a calm and unpolluted environment. It was critical that the concept of a quiet landscape be developed as a counterpoint to the busy and heavily used transport interchange that lay beneath. The area also aspired to be an urban oasis where the possibility of solitude could act as an antidote to the frenetic pace of the city. The most striking aspect of Japanese urbanism is its speed and energy and

the seemingly impossible intensity of activity; therefore the concept and perhaps the reality of repose was attractive. Although this was a large development, the use of nature to act as a foil to the city became increasingly important. If there are references to the portrayal of nature in text or film that have been used in this project, they are those that refer and understand scale. Abbas Kiarostami's *Five* shows the solitude of the seashore with the act of observation as a central activity. Willa Mather's description of the Nebraskan plains understands the land at a totally different scale, but both the film and the book share one characteristic in that the audience is required to consider the land as the central subject.

The first phase centred on the cultural complex; the main entry point is at the station podium and flanked by bars and restaurants. This acted as a point of orientation for the facilities and events, from civic exhibitions to performance. This area is a

2.65   Roof model
2.66   Model situated in urban context

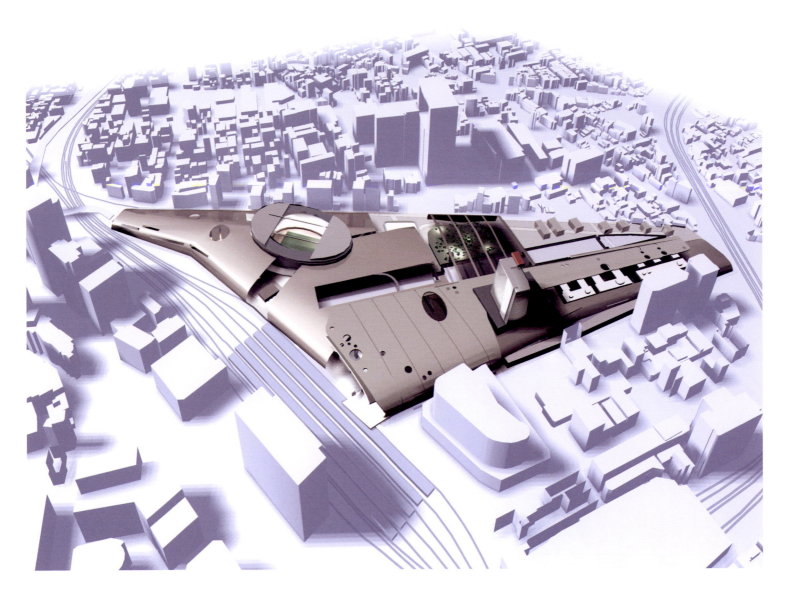

2.67 Model viewed from the south

pivotal part of the proposal where visitors can relax or be directed to another part of the development; in particular it acts as the gateway into the park. All the major public spaces at this point are positioned to have views over the parkland; the visual unification of both ground and building is considered crucial.

The podium leads into a covered arcade at higher level and the entrance to the Congress Hall, exhibition space, theatre and hotel. The Congress Hall is seen as the architectural landmark of the development; the building occupies a key position on the site and has the most commanding views

125

over the city and the adjacent park and waterscape. Along the northern edge is a retail boulevard; this is envisaged as a lively sheltered promenade, providing focus for both commercial activity and also a place for experiencing street life. The major boulevard runs north–south; subsidiary routes run east–west, offering facilities more appropriate to local needs.

In the tradition of a European and perhaps more directly English landscape design, the concept of an object in the landscape (usually belvedere) was translated into a larger scale and a series of freestanding buildings were placed in substantial open space, therebye consciously challenging the idea of high-density development.

The landscape, which provided the backdrop for the project, was both natural and synthetic and offered sheltered and open space, optimising its use throughout the year. The intention was to develop a planting regime in two stages, with mature vegetation being introduced as both plants and saplings and the second stage introduced seedlings cultivated through to maturity. An emphasis was placed on indigenous plants, both aquatic and land based, that had a symbolic association with the area and the same principle was used with the aquatic and bird life. The structured biodiversity was consciously introduced to magnify the benefits of nature in the city to the visitor.

The individual facilities provided were a sports arena and sports village, with both indoor and outdoor amenities, a culture factory containing workshops, library and exhibition spaces, and an academic and industrial research park that extended the facilities of the nearby university and allowed researchers to co-locate with their industrial partners.

The compositional arrangement of the central spine of the park and waterscape echoed the geometric formality of the city and acted as a formal contrast to the more organic outlying spaces. The water was divided into three sections, each with a different aspect of plant and aquatic life. Each pond was at a different level, allowing oxygenation to take place through the natural movement of water. The water contained Acheiloghathus longipinnis, a locally protected species, together with funa and ayu, water lily and a water chrysanthemum, which were used to balance the aquatic environment. On land the planting was organised according to the seasons and included trees such as plum and gingko and plants such as iris and primula.

Although much of the site was open, there were secluded spaces that acted as a buffer between the private development of the north and the predominantly public zone of the south; quiet sheltered gardens were created with a perimeter of shrubs. A canopy containing a variety of panel types provided shelter ranging from an open pergola to complete cover. The intention was to create micro-environments that would optimise the use of the site.

In summary the development was a series of mutually supporting functions built at low density to enable an urban park to provide a safe non-polluted environment that was a qualitative addition to the city.

HAKKA CULTURAL CENTRE, HEYUNG CITY

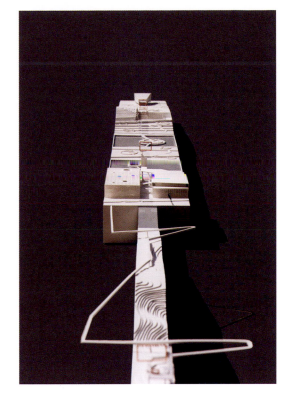

WITH METAMODE (ASHTON PORTER AND MOYANG YANG)

Every ten years a grant is awarded by the central government in China for a city to celebrate the historic achievements of one of the myriad of ethnic groups that populate China. In 2007 Heyung City was awarded a grant to celebrate the history and culture of the Hakka clan, one of the largest and most nomadic groups within the Chinese continent. An international competition was organised, ultimately in two separate stages, which we won.

The requirements were to provide a range of facilities both temporary and permanent to celebrate all aspects of Hakka culture, from language to writing and from music to commercial trading. These aspects of Hakka life were to be housed in three main pavilions containing a library, gallery, museum and conference facility. The site offered for this complex was on the periphery of Heyung City and was one kilometre long and half a kilometre wide. By the standards of European development, the scale of the site was immense.

To establish a narrative that had some resonance, it was not only critical to look at the history of the Hakka people but also to understand the importance of the scale of the site. The competition had two different juries: the first an international group and the second constituted from local officials.

2.68   Hakka development model viewed from the south

2.69   Hakka development model viewed from the north

2.70 Entrance pavilion and connecting frame

Culturally this was critical; as non-Chinese participants it was impossible to enter with an erudite knowledge of local mores, therefore we could only make assumptions about concepts and principle rather than reflections of fact; this was a critical factor in the second stage of the competition.

The Hakka (a sub-group of the Han Chinese) are amongst the largest cultural group, emanating originally from the central plains of China. They currently number around 80 million and are the largest and most consistent diaspora. Their nomadic lifestyles led them to originally move from the northern to the central plains and finally to the southern provinces; they were amongst the earliest to leave and establish colonies outside China. The majority of Chinese communities established in other countries are almost exclusively of Hakka origin.

The land was not only important to them as a source of food (they were primarily a farming community), but they also used the land opportunistically as they moved from one area of grazing and cultivation to the next. The Hakka were not originally conquistadors but over time they needed to defend the territory they occupied. As their movement across China became more military, travel and the land were inextricably linked and their folkloric culture contains many references to the significance of the terrain they passed through and occupied. One of the iconic land geometries associated with the Hakka is the ubiquitous terracing primarily used in the cultivation of rice; the most iconic architectural form, not only of the Hakka but also of a period of Chinese civilisation, is the circular Hakka house (Toulou). These were structures varying in size housing anything up to 60 families and always organised in the same stratified manner. The lowest level was for sheltering livestock, the second level for the storage of grain and the third (and sometimes fourth) was living accommodation for the families. The circular form of the structure encompassed a central courtyard, sometimes left empty, and in others a cluster of

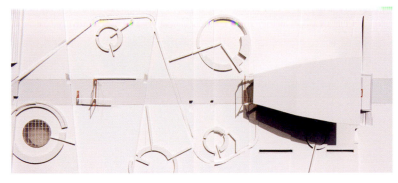

2.71   Early landscape model to show the re-contouring of landscape to accommodate a sunken gallery

2.72   Model showing landscape references to the formal geometry of the Hakka houses, the scale of the geographic diaspora and the dials indicating the geographic location of the settlements

2.73   First stage competition, entry pavilion

communal buildings; the central space was always used for communal gatherings. The design of these houses was made to resemble fortresses with only one point of access at ground level and minimal openings at higher level as a form of defence. The houses were always made from materials available locally, usually rammed earth and timber; the land gave them the means not only to survive but also to construct shelter.

When initially considering the critical factors to be incorporated in the narrative of the design, not only was the site itself important but also the conceptual representation of its significance in Hakka history.

The entire site was conceived as a journey across the landscape from one pavilion to the next; it was a symbolic representation of the Hakka journeys that had taken them across the world. The site itself was hilly and so the introduction of gradual terracing not only made the terrain more navigable but also served as a reminder of the Hakka's agrarian past. The circular form of the Hakka house was to be used as it was the most potent symbol and needed no further explanation. The statistics showed that there are currently 26 areas in the world where there are settlements of over 5,000 people originating from the Hakka clan. The most important design principle was not connected to the buildings *per se* but to the manner in which the land was negotiated. A continuous route was established that ran from the south to the northern end of the site, meandering from east to west to offer the largest viewable area. A number of circular vantage points were situated along the route; each one had a proportional size that corresponded to the size of each global settlement and a cursor within the circle pointed to

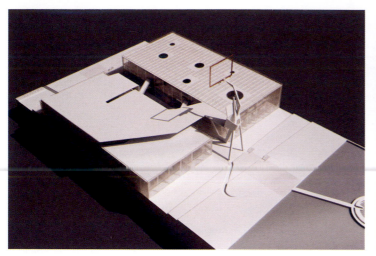

the geographic location of each diaspora. As one made the journey to each building and through the site, these circular interventions would offer modest facilities, such as seating and shelter, and also inform the visitor of something of the Hakka's historic journeys.

Each of the buildings is situated on a line that runs at the mid-point from south to north. From each building there is a clear view to the next and the penultimate building (the library and conference centre is bifurcated to enable an uninterrupted view to the final belvedere). Positioned at the highest point of the site is the belvedere, a viewing platform from which the observer can look back over the three main buildings, the landscape and the city beyond. Each building, including the belvedere, had a viewing frame positioned to visually link one building to the next and to allow the observer the opportunity to contextualise not only the individual pieces of architecture but also their

sequence within the landscape. In order for the viewing frames to connect to all the buildings, including the belvedere, part of the gallery was sunk below the level of the ground; this both maintained the line of sight but also augmented environmental control in an area where there was large seasonal temperature and humidity fluctuation. The architectural language was kept deliberately simple, as the focus of the experience was to be the journey through the landscape.

This initial proposal had some resonance with the international jurors but very little with the local dignitaries, who would finally finance the scheme. It became clear as a non-Chinese participant how insubstantial our cultural understanding was and how much we needed to understand the attitudes of our eventual client.

The first and the most critical issue was the apparent lack of reference to a traditional Chinese architectural lexicon. The use of abstract references was wasted; the suggestion that part

2.74   First stage competition, model of library

2.75   First stage competition, model of sunken exhibition space

130

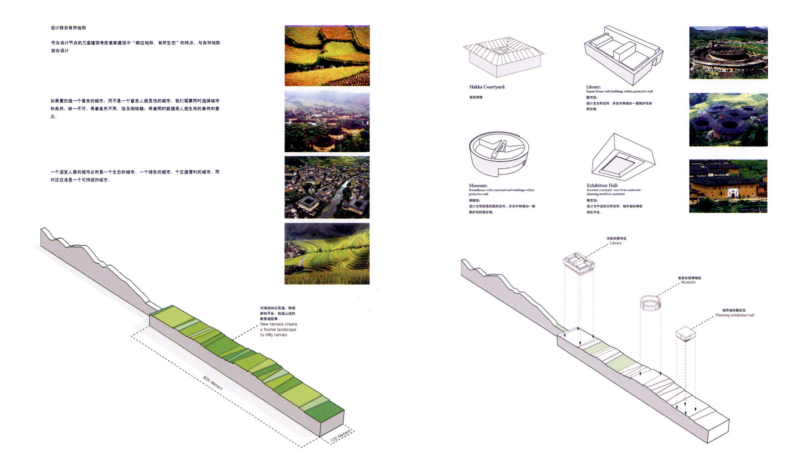

of the architectural proposition could be beneath ground level and therefore energy-efficient had no impact; the team were told unequivocally that all buildings had to be both visible and to be an ostentatious celebration of both status and wealth, which we failed to deliver.

The conflict between the result of the original adjudication panel and the final clients created an impasse and a second stage was organised to address the concerns of the local dignitaries.

Whatever knowledge architects might use to address issues of sustainability, there needed to be a cultural awareness of the differences in both perception and in terms of priority. The competition's concern to keep the architecture both understated and to some extent hidden did not strike a chord with the local funders of the development. There was a need to make the next iteration celebratory with reference to local cultural history. The dilemma for any non-local architect was that references to localism could degenerate into naïve stylistic pastiche; therefore a judgement needed to be made about how the introduction of reference could avoid this problem.

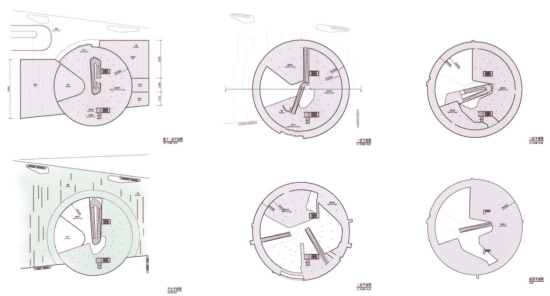

2.78   Hakka museum, view in the landscape

2.79   Museum plans (a, b, c)

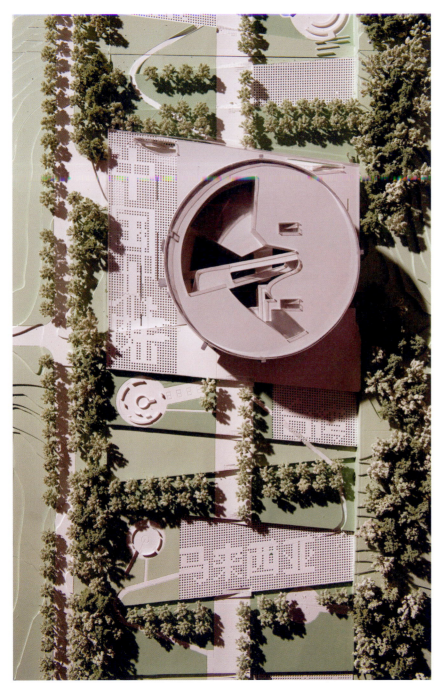

2.80   Museum model, aerial view

Fortunately the landscape strategy was retained as it was still appreciated as the focal point of this scheme. All the buildings were now positioned at ground level and the entrance pavilion situated to allow the obligatory cavalcade to arrive, the dignitaries to process and speeches to be made. The viewing frames were still kept in this and all the buildings, as they were included as a unique link between the architecture and the vistas of the land.

The second building, the exhibition and museum space, was now designed as a circular structure, a homage to the form of the Hakka houses (Toulou), and although the form of the envelope was a clear reflection of the historic icon, the internal arrangement rejected the traditional geometric organisation that relied so heavily on subsuming to radial geometry. The building referenced traditional defence by having only one opening for the entrance, and a series of small apertures that pierced the outer skin. Internally a micro route mirrored the paths through the landscape and at each change of direction a platform and aperture offered views across the landscape and the city, allowing a different scale of contextual relationship to be understood.

The central core of the space was a void with light penetrating from above and as the route ascended it finally emerged on a rooftop platform allowing the visitor a panoramic view and the opportunity to reconcile the fragmentary vistas of the journey. The building was constructed with two skins, the inner wall constructed in traditional fashion from rammed earth and the outer skin a light metal foil onto which was printed examples of linguistic notation to express the language and dialect that existed across the Hakka nation.

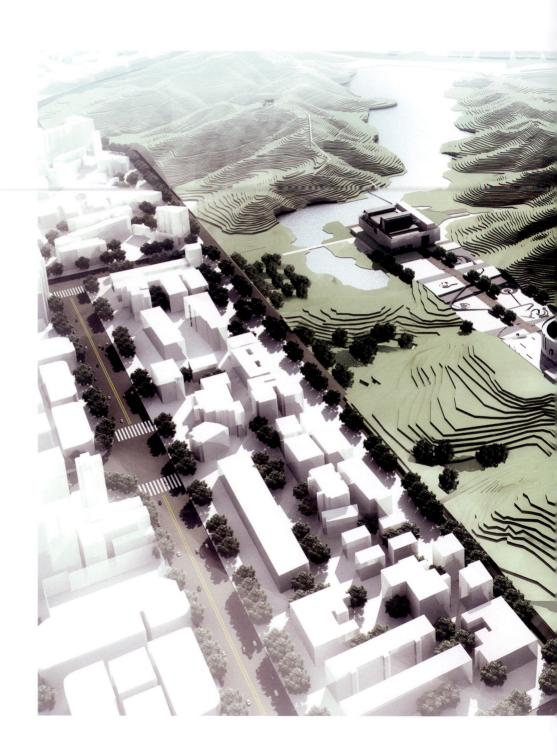

2.81   Final model: exhibition, museum and
library building

2.82   Aerial view of landscape at night

This technique was repeated in the first and third building and became a simple motif that referenced different aspects of linguistic culture. The symbols were printed at a scale that could only be read at a distance and became deliberately abstract at close quarters.

This double skin construction with the outer perforated layer allowed interstitial lighting to be used at night, and enabled the cultural centre to have a visual presence at night and also to have surfaces that could be read mnemonically. The final building in the sequence, the library, was divided into a local exhibition space, the library and administration. The building repeated thematically the notion of glimpses, views and layers, with the final being a framed view of the belvedere. Throughout the development the buildings and the landscape were read as an interdependent relationship where the buildings and their context provided the opportunity to reflect on a complex and sophisticated culture.

HAMBURG DOCKS
REDEVELOPMENT

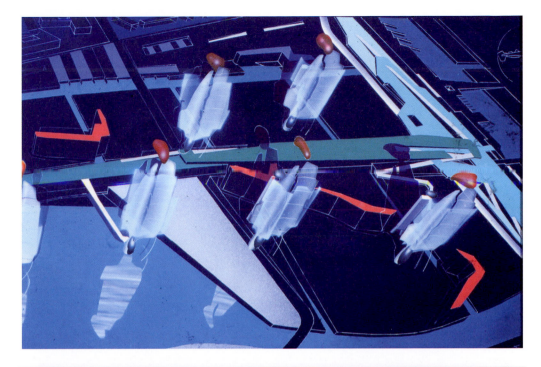

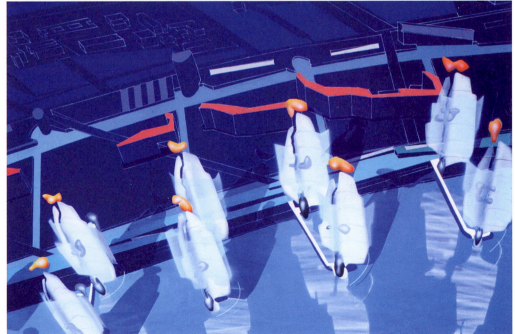

2.83a   Hamburg docks redevelopment

2.83b   Accommodation towers, detail

ROME CONGRESS

CENTRE

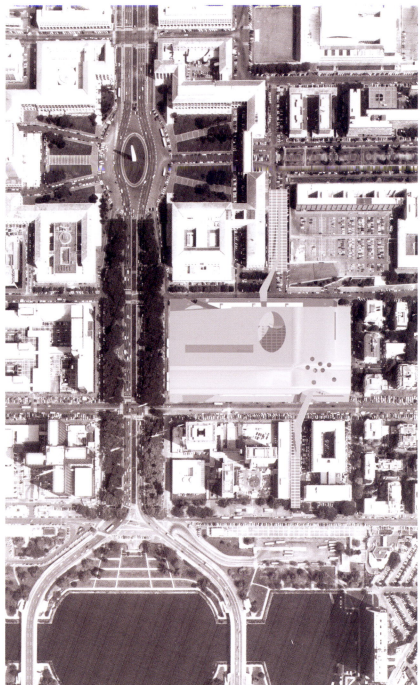

2.84   Rome Congress Centre

2.85   Rome Congress Centre location plan

EMVS HOUSING,
MADRID

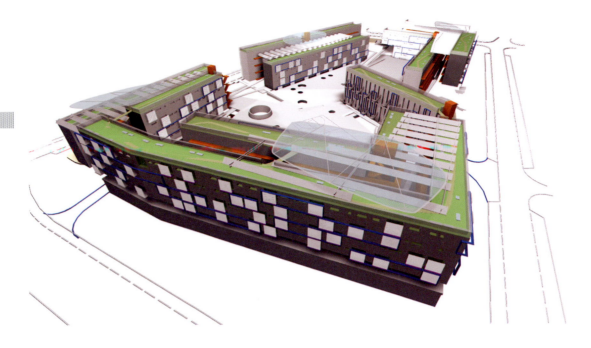

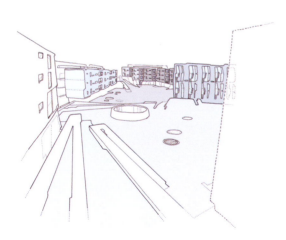

2.86   Aerial view of housing and internal
landscape

2.87   Sketch view of central courtyard

2.88   Sketch of arcade entrance

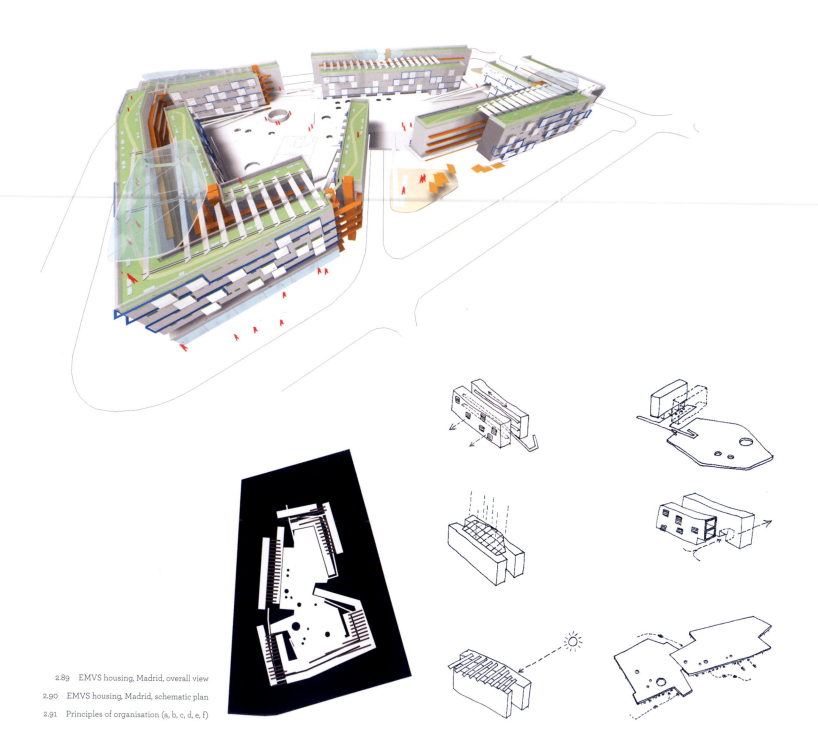

2.89   EMVS housing, Madrid, overall view

2.90   EMVS housing, Madrid, schematic plan

2.91   Principles of organisation (a, b, c, d, e, f)

MOCAPE
CULTURAL CENTRE,
SHENZHEN

2.92   Mocape exhibition halls and planning offices for Shenzhen, China

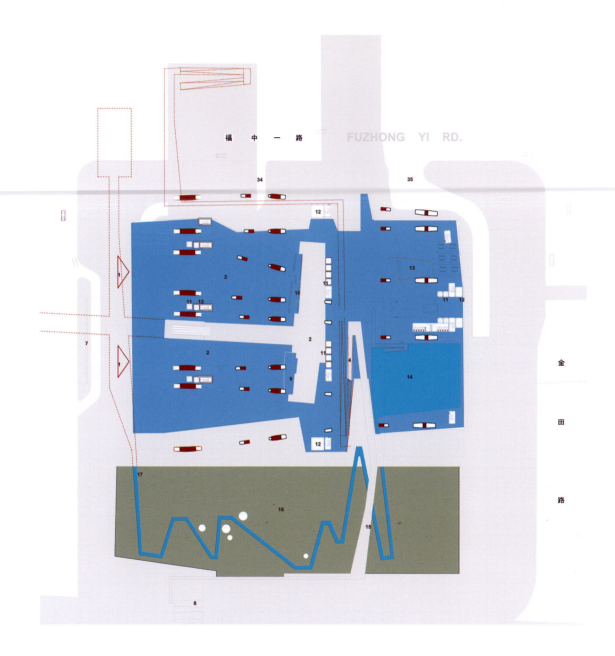

福　中　一　路　　FUZHONG YI RD.

2.93　Schematic plan

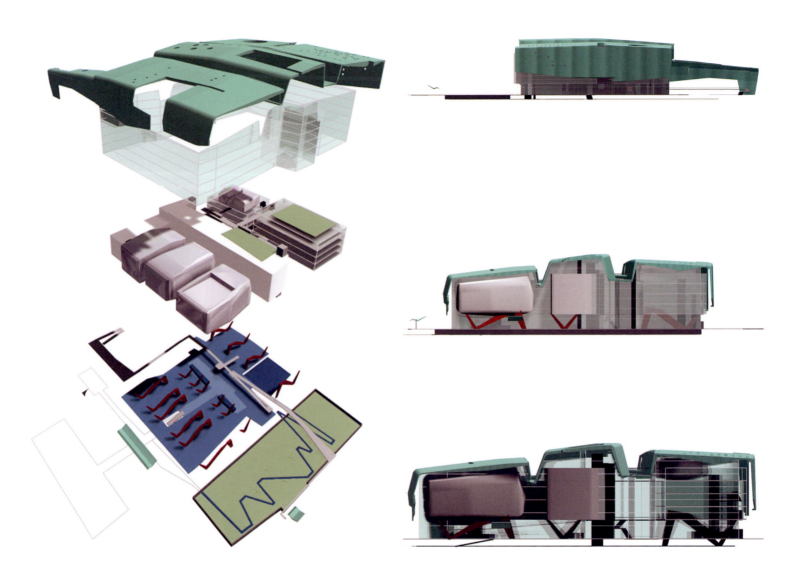

2.94   Exploded view showing ground plaza,
exhibition galleries, planning offices and
roofscape

2.95   East elevation

2.96   South elevation

2.97   North elevation

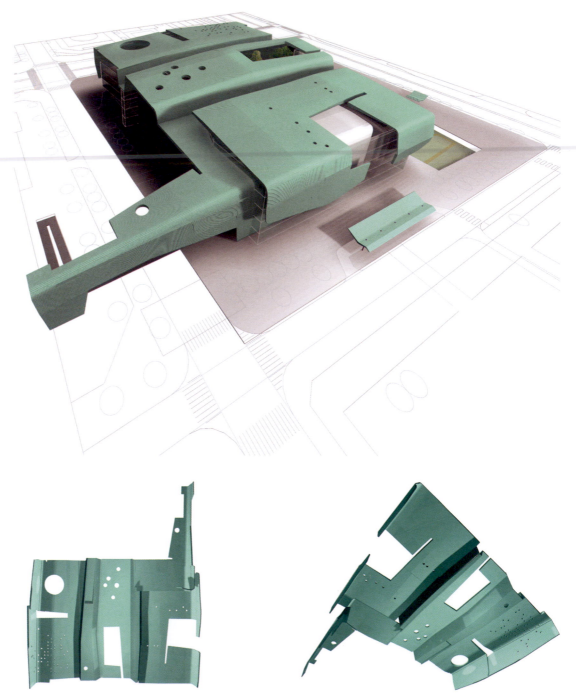

2.98   Rooftop profile

2.99a   Roof detail viewed from below

2.99b   Roof detail oblique view from below

2.100   Interior view from public plaza towards
exhibition galleries

Shadows and Lines

Forms of representation within architecture are both intriguing and perplexing. The drawing, the primary tool by which spatial ideas are developed, illustrates information with precision. There is a paradox in that within architectural drawings two conflicting conditions emerge. Within the technical drawing, communication is precise, but in the conceptual realm the boundaries of definition are limitless. There has always been a quality of spatial experience sought by designers, but in most cases the search is elusive; these ambitions have less to do with function but rather seek to express a form of poetic dream. The ideas are enigmatic or suggestive, existing in the imagination rather than in reality, and are notoriously difficult to capture. Each generation of architects has searched for elusive ideals through the abstracted language of drawing, yet the limitations of graphic representation fail to capture the illusory/the power of suggestion and the nature of ambiguity yet the technical tools of other creative genres have often been more successful in expressing the insubstantial. This chapter examines conditions of representation considering line and shadow as both principles and polarised expression of space; it attempts to explore aspects of the philosophical and functional process to examine whether there are ways of re-interpreting or re-evaluating certain techniques of representation, through observing visual work that is created outside architecture.

Enigmatic space exists more comfortably in the realms of historic and contemporary art, text and film than in architecture and this dreamlike quality is more easily constructed in a language that lacks physicality. Genre-specific language that capture dreamlike ideas are notoriously difficult to reproduce

as spatial conjecture, unless it remains within the conceptual realm. There is little of the intellectual process that emerges into the physical world as the architect struggles to manage the transformation of poetic idea into constructed reality. Is it therefore possible to re-think the status of the architectural drawing and use it more as a tool of implication than a description of specificity? This chapter will reflect on more than just the architectural drawing or graphic methods of representation; it will also consider how line, critical to the architectural drawing and shadow embedded in the product of physicality, can be used as symbols of enigma. The elasticity found in other forms of representation might be transposed or they might remain little more than a subliminal influence. This chapter explores some of the techniques evident in other genres and considers the possibilities of translation and reflects on whether a borrowed language could have architectural credibility.

First, the understanding of line as a dominant and ubiquitous graphic expression must be challenged. Line applied to paper, or the digital equivalent, describes a precise boundary. There is an explicit understanding of demarcation, a clear separation of one space from another; however, the word 'boundary' as a linguistic term in other genres is often legitimately compromised. Within the family of linear representation, the cartographic line has the closest abstracted similarities to the notational system used in architecture as it describes boundary, surface and object. However, this synoptic mode of language is still interpreted and the judgement of the viewer determines how this unconstructed reality is understood. Whether the maps are geographic or cosmological, they are ultimately a fiction, denying the richness and the nuance of reality (Corner and MacLean 1996). Unlike architectural drawings, these cartographic lines are an abstract expression that describe a historic rather than futuristic interpretation. The paradox exists in the fact that line is both explicit and inexact. Precision is derived from the line that gives an absolute position, together with the numerical codes that give coordinated locations, in some ways cartography also has similarities with the language of engineering. Yet cartographic information together with iconic nomenclature only describes terrain in a quantitative manner. Within these descriptions there is a lack of pictorialisation, history, human activity and the poetic sense of the environment; the references give neither a sense of physical reality nor information about what lies between the lines. The cartographer's map is also time-related in that all information is retrospective and can be precisely dated to the time of survey, whereas the architectural drawing has no such reference point in time, whether the drawing is conceptual or technical.

Robin Evans noted that 'drawing is the principle locus in architecture' (Evans 1997) and that drawing technique can be both a facilitator and an inhibitor to conceptualisation. If the reductive nature of the line and the limitations of its linguistic range curtail conceptual potential, this will be even more evident of the limits of sciagraphy. Architecture offers a technical framework of references, which, though not unique, limits the range of communication. Therefore we might consider line and shadow in other media and how this has been used to create a less constrained form of expression. Through simple observation one might discover possibilities for linguistic translation in particular those techniques that create subtlety, ambiguity and mystery. Translation is not the transposition of concept; it is more about uncovering ways of thinking that are unorthodox and inspirational. The challenge might also be to find a borrowed language that through manipulation could be brought into the architectural realm., Of course, the transformative act might prove to be too difficult, yet by trying to understand relative values, the process itself could uncover unforeseen ways of thinking and making. There is both historic and contemporary evidence that critically challenges the traditions of representation and reference and this may prove valuable in providing a loose contextual framework.

Whatever the implied narrative architectural vocabulary used for construction is a linear and numeric notation, and this language denotes physicality and definition. The line is an abstraction on paper that through transmutation loses its coded meaning. One might argue that drawing a line can take many forms, just as the pencil held in the hand and rotated can create something on paper that changes from the merest whisper to a mark of aggressive definition. However, progressing into the realm of construction, this subtle arc of change is hardly possible. Evans noted that the difference between the visual representation of the artist and that of the architect is that the artist is working with the end result and the architect is working with a predetermined fiction that will never be realised until others intervene and manipulate the information (Evans 1997). This level of detachment is interesting in that it becomes a focus in its own right yet also serves to illustrates how deceptive and un-representational the architectural drawing can be.

It would be possible, I think, to write a history of Western architecture that would have little to do with either style or signification concentrating instead on the manner of working. A large part of history would be concerned with the gap between drawing and building. In it the drawing would be considered not so much a work of art or a truck for pushing ideas from place to place, but as the locale of subterfuges and evasions that one way or another get round the enormous weight of convention that has always been the architect's greatest security and at the same time its greatest liability. (Evans 1997)

The work of an artist, not an architect, may best illustrate the distance between indicative drawings and final product, and in a sense highlight the inadequacy of conventional technical line drawing. The work of James Turrell presents a clear illustration; it relies on the manipulation of light, space and surface and its impact can only be realised through physical experience (Sinnreich 2009). The diagram used to construct these installations uses a linear language, yet the intention of the installation is to appear with no edges and, using the physics of light, to totally erase boundaries. The construction relies on a balance of hidden light, the absence of shadow, surface and depth, generating as a result an experience of retinal distortion and disorientation. The understanding of distance and edge compounds this experience; these are in turn dependent on the observer's location within the installation. A conflation of space, light and shadow creates an illusion where the observer is tricked into thinking they understand the spatial relationships – but with a minute adjustment of position that confidence is shattered. This phenomenological experience is impossible to describe through a technical linear drawing and, in fact, the drawings that reveal the technology behind the magic are remarkable in their banality. These installations accurately demonstrate that an immersive three-dimensional experience can create optical illusions that are totally absent in the reductively linear language of the technical drawing. If interest does, however, lie in the penumbra and the areas around the shadow line, a different form of communication needs to develop. However, a paradox still exists, for all the precision and specificity of the line, Evans argues that 'the transmutation that occurs between drawing and building remains an enigma ... the experiential appears far more at risk and far more real than the indirect and abstract' (Evans 1997).

Maintaining that the experiential is a more ethical form of representation, the argument then presents a *prima facie* case for the architectural line drawing being a subordinate tool of material manifestation (Evans 1997). These comments were made at an interesting time between the 1980s and 1990s when the aggrandisement of the architectural drawing adopted new cultural definition; architectural drawings were then not merely tools of technical instruction, but commodities on the art market. At a time when the commoditisation of the architectural drawing was at its height, there was no other substantial critique of the status of drawing as a tool of communication, as interest had swung to the imbued value of collectible drawings. The subsequent emergence of digital media destroyed the commoditisation of the architectural drawing and the uniqueness of authorship. One could argue that the value of the architectural drawing lies not in a reflection of reality but more in a projection of the future.

The power of the line is therefore dependent on the reader's acquired understanding of depth, as the drawing depicts no more than a profile edge and a pattern of lines that suggest the building's volume. What we understand of materiality and depth is not depicted within the linear construct and it is only brought into focus by the observer's cultural and technical awareness. The drawing is therefore incomplete and presents nothing but an edited illusion. The development of orthographic projection in the fourteenth century defined an important moment in the genesis of linear drawing, where the concept of depth became petrified and defined in pseudo-relief with attempted sculptural definition. Unlike figurative representation found in art, these linear techniques were attempting to combine notions of reality through the synoptic language of technical line.

One can only speculate how much embedded knowledge was used in conjunction with these early technical drawings, as it is impossible to understand from only the drawing how lines could curve in more than one direction. Stereotomic drawings used conventions that depicted what was essential to know for fellow craftsmen and therefore assumptions of prior knowledge or practical experience predetermined how much editorial license was taken; these drawings were therefore defined just as much by the characteristics of omission than by those of inclusion. Contemporary digital tools currently illustrate the mathematical precision needed to construct such forms; one can only assume that the relationship that medieval masons had to the drawings was an understanding of their paradoxically implicit nature. Architectural text has relentlessly used language that tries to capture the moment of change. The prefix 'trans' can then be followed by an array of mutations – transport, transfer, translate – yet the journey through the cellular maze of the mind that activates a precise physiological response is still a mystery. How and why the hand might twist and turn to draw a line and what intellectual or visualised potential might interfere with the outcome is still a phenomenon about which we still know little. The architect classically adhered to a canon of mathematical proportion, the modernists to ideas of 'essentialism', but the reductive dogma that supposedly gave guidance, concealed hidden dangers in what had been depicted on a flat surface could become hideously distorted in the third dimension. For those who understood the concealed problems of the line, a mutation occurred within the journey from idea to object.

Piranesi's *Carceri d'Invezione* (1750–60) pictorially and spatially challenged the hegemony of classic linear or geometric representation. These images introduced a spatial discordance that defied geometric order and consecutive logic. The prints were images of underground vaults, vast staircases and machinery that had no obvious relationship to one another and although the images were portrayed in a manner we would understand to be realistic, contained what we understand to be realism, they were in fact surreal, an aberration of imagination. These were some of the earliest architectural drawings to resolutely defy classification and the normative role of linear drawing. They are unique in that they are perhaps the most fluent historic line drawings portraying multi-focal spaces, where spatial definition is an illusion. Produced in the eighteenth century, they still remain as enigmatic today as they were when they were first drawn. The allure of such illustration lies less with what is seen but more with what is suggested.

There is an expectation that the architectural image as an abstract language must describe volume; unlike the language used in abstract art, there is no such expectation. The architectural lexicon could be viewed as either a simple and accessible translational tool or a system that imposes impossible constraints. The function of the architect is to position the observer so that they might understand the content in such a way that avoids ambivalence; in one sense the function of conventional architectural drawing could be accused of deliberately lacking layer and nuance. Daniel Liebskind's *Chamber Works* are perhaps the best-known contemporary drawings that have attracted serious analytical criticism and raised fundamental questions about the status of the line and the way in which it should be understood. Evans describes the drawings as having a 'staid politeness', but this may have been attached to the orthodoxy of presentation within a prescribed frame. 'As one steps closer and the propriety of the frame disappears the lines acquired a "demonic energy"' (Evans 1997).

The lines assumed a status that was completely independent of and superior to the normally supportive role of spatial descriptor. The drawings remain a compelling enigma, providing the observer with an unending range of spatial possibilities. The author never offered a key to interpretation, yet the closest alignment was to the parallel creative force of music that was physical, aural and unseen. The corollary of these observations was to consider whether the line could be used as an exploratory rather than a translational tool. There is something compelling about the intense intricacy of Liebskind's work that demands repeated enquiry, yet it still never reveals its meaning. Perhaps this is part of the function of such pieces where ambiguity is fundamental. There are ways in which such drawings can be understood which relate to intensity, balance and variation, all of which are adjectively used in music but rarely within the classic notations of architectural language. It is easier to place these drawings within the context of modern art, but if left there, architectural practice would lose an essential catalyst with which to explore the mysterious edges of space where the use of non-material metaphor is applied to the qualities of space that are most difficult to describe. Only the work of Joseph Albers comes close to the realm of spatial ambiguity, but his work still resolutely resides in the world of art. Despite *Chamber Works* not alluding to any recognisable orthographic vocabulary, the observer is obliged construct an understanding neurologically despite the spatial relationships bearing no resemblance to the adjacencies we understand. The straight line is not the most obvious vehicle to illustrate movement, yet one sees in Liebskind's work the quality of dynamic which may come from the ferocity of repetition and the visual insistence of making similar lines move with minor adjustments of position and with relentless regularity. The linguistic force is repetitive and domineering. Embedded within the culture of making these drawings are the arguments made by the French structuralist philosophers such as Claude Levi Strauss and Jacques Lacan and the anti-philosophy of deconstruction embodied in the work of Jacques Derrida. This emerged in many creative art forms in politics, economics and in architecture, and the early work of Liebskind, amongst others, was exploring the ideas of disengaged space, where recognised associations are, if not deliberately broken then intuitively scrambled. Evans, amongst others, argues that this work is not de-constructivist as there is no recognisable unity from which it can emanate; this is perhaps philosophically pure but associatively inaccurate. This work does not support the mathematical correlations that dominate the classical canon or indeed the modernists of the twentieth century. What is the role of the drawing if it is not a vehicle of translation? It can, as *Chamber Works* illustrates, possibly be a potent force by which or through which alternative possibilities and potential might be considered. This idea constructs a new level of importance for the line, no longer a measure of abstraction but more a mark that has been liberated from its traditional associations. Constructed space, unlike art, music or literature, even theatre or film, is not transient, and this more than any other virtue, even cost, mitigates experiment. Therefore the only form of experimentation that can reasonably be tolerated is through the expression of linear form on paper.

In Europe in the 1960s and 1970s there was parallel interest emerging in how conventional forms of expression could be challenged by a group of architects and artists emerging from Austria and Germany. This group was more politically explicit than most of the profession and consciously attacked the inherent conservatism that was embedded in European culture and its messianic preservation of urban heritage. This pre-emptive work from Vienna emerged from art/architecture groups such as Haus Rucker, Gunther Domenig, Co-Op Himmelblau, Herman Nitsch, Valie Export and Peter Weibel, where action – expressionism – was inextricably linked to commentaries of the city. Their installations created a dialogue that challenged the status quo and the deep conservatism that underpinned the culture and conservation of the city. Through installations, text, art and architectural drawing, their illustrative work challenged the cultural understanding of linear linguistics. The body of work that emerged during this time – dramatically influenced young architects who were searching for forms of expression and liberated them from the reductive tyranny of the line. These ideas destroyed the barriers of conceptualism and combined techniques across the visual spectrum. Their embryonic themes were probably crystallised within the *Grazschule*, but Himmelb(l)au and Domenig were the architects whose drawings most publicly captured the zeitgeist and whose later built work had the technical sophistication to embody the spirit of those early drawings. Whether they were particularly conscious of the global debate about structuralism and de-construction is questionable, but the drawings were remarkable in that they captured a dynamic more readily perceived in the texts of J.G. Ballard than spatial images. The initial sketch for the Beach House at Santa Monica drawn by Wolf Prix of Co-Op Himmelb(l)au has become a seminal image of a visceral impulsive response to site. The sketch showed little more than a shell precariously perched on an inclined site. The compelling quality is the sense of tension that exists between object and context and the sinuous life that exists in the lines as they stretch over the page and in the imagination as the building hovers above the cliff edge like lines of force emerging as an expression of physical energy (Lerup 1989, Vidler 1990). Although the subject is far less ambiguous than Liebskind's *Chamber Works*, they share an intensity of energy largely due to the abstraction of dense directional line work. These drawings offer more than simply a technical outline of space – they allow you to look into the world of your own imagination.

Line is traditionally associated with the abstract form of expression on a planar surface; it is a code for edge, enclosure, boundary and threshold, but when removed from this context it acquires other qualities that escape the traditional relation of line on paper. Two different examples that show sculptural line can exist in such a way as to create a mnemonic and suggest the poetic are examples that are totally different in scale and function and transcend conventional understanding. The first is the engineered structure of the Brooklyn Bridge designed by John Augustus Roebling in 1883, and the second is a sculptural series entitled *Utsurohi* by the Japanese artist Aiko Miyawaki, produced over a 20-year period at the end of the twentieth century. The bridge is an expression of functionality, designed with absolute technical precision to transport traffic over the East River; the wire sculpture by Miyawaki, freed from pictorial or representational confines, search for the abstraction of concept. Both forms of constructed line share common characteristics. Konrad Wachsmann, the visionary engineer, was the first to comment that the catenary cables of the Brooklyn Bridge were perfect lines in space, a pure expression of function and a perfect definition of volume. The lines had precision yet physical volume was absent and, in his view, this was a faultless definition of volumetric envelope. It was a mnemonic, in that the volume was implied only to be completed in the mind.

Wachsmann's view was not formed by poetic ambiguity but through highly reductive thought that regarded minimalism as a form of technical superiority. Within the pantheon of iconographic drawings sits the diagrams of Wachsmann, who, in pursuit of a technical vision, created the drawing of the 'universal joint' that defies the normal rules of perspective and accurately captures the concept of 'endless space'. In this context, perhaps more interesting than his virtuoso engineering, was the alarming analytical simplicity he brought to the concept of spatial definition and in so doing immediately translated the abstraction of geometric linearity into constructed form. These images share some characteristics with Piranesi in that there is conjectural space beyond the drawing, imagined in the mind of the onlooker. Miyawaki's wire 'intermediaries' are also minimal and try to depict the concept of transience, a cerebral idea that has no fixed reality and is generated by the poetic idea of capturing concepts. Hiroshi Ichikawa describes the work as straightforward art with no hidden narrative, yet these vast, fluid cable structures are both interactive and dynamic, creating endless lines and forms of interpretation (Ichikawa 1986). The bridge and the sculptural installations are not models;, they have city and landscape scale and their dominance through size is an essential part of their impact. These examples explicitly challenge the notion of line being an abstract signifier, as they can quite clearly have a physical presence in the city and have the ability to control spatial volume and frame.

The distinct shift in scale enables the photographer (Gefeller 2010) to capture the allure of the aerial network of cables that are ubiquitous in Japanese cities. In a country that is culturally and materially fastidious, it is a surprise that the networking of digital services is so exposed. Normally these high-level knots of cables and transformers are considered visual chaos, but Gefeller has clearly understood that, viewed with a particular eye, they are objects of unintentionally constructed beauty. Both the proportion of line to solid is carefully composed in his photographs and it is this attenuated linearity that turns these everyday objects into both an object of beauty and a demarcation of space. These lines in the air create boundary and edge but also create an immensely complex web of virtual space. In the more serene context of Copenhagen, the street lighting system throughout the city is held on a fragile system of wires, which lie like a grid over the street, giving the city a barely visible cartographic order. On closer observation this delicate system creates an aerial ceiling to the city that in turn establishes and reinforces the city's unobtrusive scale.

Line can also acquire the role of signifier if painted onto the city surface and there is an obvious overlap between the minimalist form of 'urban writing' where marks have no more substance than the line itself. The codification of urban writing is often obscure, where the hidden language lays claim to territory only known to a socially defined collective. The paradox in this context is that line can be displayed in public yet only understood by those groups that share a 'street culture'. Both Wachsmann the engineer and Gefeller the artist understood the poetic 'substance' of 'line' and that its use offers another layer of complexity and richness that adds tension to the competing vocabulary of the city.

If our understanding of line lies in the comprehension of exactitude, the concept of shadow must offer the opposite, a substance that evokes a notion of mystery, menace and a condition where no one has a perception of edge. If line is a boundary that one might transgress, shadow is neither boundary nor surface. Shadow is part of our conventional visual lexicon without which there would be no understanding of depth and no visual articulation. Architects consciously manage light, yet shadow has always had a more circumstantial presence. It is essential in the understanding of three-dimensionality, yet it has no substance. It can have an ominous presence and can be a visual vacuum that fires the imagination, and most intriguingly it creates illusion. Shadow is an elusive fiction. The technical vocabulary which uses shadow to create illusion is more commonly found in photography, film and theatre, where the intention is to persuade the audience to suspend belief.

Moholy Nagy's *Light Space Modulator* (1922–30) and more recently Cornelia Parker's dramatic installation *Cold Dark Matter* (2010) – an exploded view – bridge the optical language of line and shadow and demonstrate that two forms, one physical and one non-physical, are completely interdependent. Both installations use shadow as an illusory technique and, more importantly, shadow then suggests a spatiality that goes beyond the realm of the physical object. The compelling quality of these pieces lies less in the central object than in the extended space of light and shadow that creates an extended three-dimensionality (Passuth 1985).

The architectural use of shadow is far more restrained, and in much design it becomes a by-product of surface articulation or a negative intrusion onto neighbouring property rather than a design tool. The visual shadow drama created by Nagy and Parker, however, was a highly considered part of the composition and this level of awareness of the potential of shadow should be a necessary part of architectural discussion.

Although architect Sverre Fehn acknowledges the importance of shadow as a component of the tectonic vocabulary in his work, this was still predictable and calculable (Giardiello, in Norberg-Schutz and Postiglione 1997). Shadow is rarely seen as a phenomenon with which one can experiment or use as a defining tool. Shadow is, of course, a critical consequence of the obstruction of light falling onto surface and, although less considered, it is of vital importance, creating the essence of three-dimensionality. An interesting additional dimension to this optical state is when the light rays are not interrupted but intercepted and refracted to create reflection, as in the myth of Narcissus, who explores the status of shadow, reflection and self. Architectural culture considers the phenomenon of shadow to have less importance than line; it is therefore interesting to consider its status within the context of art, film and literature, where compositionally there is a long history of intentional use.

The poetry of shadow lies in its characteristics of ambiguity and enigma; it is a reflection of the unknown, and philosophically has been depicted by the Egyptians as the human soul. The Egyptians attached a symbolic status to shadow, the essence of spiritual embodiment, and peripheral and deep shadow were each understood to have their own significance. Renaissance painters such as Masaccio depicted the apostle Peter with his shadow, illustrating the primitive myth that shadow was the expression of the soul. The art historian Ernst Gombrich (1997) presented a scholarly analysis of the use of shadow in painting and accords the significance of shadow as the origin of Western representation in art. Yet, architecture barely recognises its importance. The intriguing question is, why, as it forms an essential component of some visual genre and not of others?

The Plinyian and Platonic representations of shadow are cornerstones of our understanding but demonstrate critical differences. Plato conceives shadow as a mythic representation of truth, as in Plato's Cave, where he likens shadow painting to the idea of deception or magic, whereas Pliny describes shadow as the representation of the birth of Western art, as illustrated in his text.

> Eventually art differentiated itself (se ars ipsa distinxit), and discovered light and shade, contrasts of colours heightening their effect reciprocally. (Stoichita 1997)

Pliny showed within his treatise both knowledge of the metaphysics of shadow and also its relationship with death. What both the Plynian and Platonic texts share is the implication that shadow could be used as a mnemonic. Shadow was of 'the self but not the self' and therefore it required an imagination to capture detail. These classic texts also suggested that the use of intellectual mediation could create a sense of ambiguity. Although the scientific study of shadow was well understood during the medieval era, there was no depiction of it in paintings of the time and this may have been due to the ontological status of the image. It was only with the painters of the Renaissance, who discovered perspective, where shadow became a subject of serious study and indeed this became scientifically developed to be included in the requirements of the art academies.

Leonardo da Vinci was consistently preoccupied with the relationship between the notion of ambiguity and shadow, and this concept was embedded in the notion of light and shade being a fundamental asset of nature. He critically made the distinction between primary and secondary shadow and, by developing a theoretical observation, produced the painting technique of *sfumato*, one of the four canonical modes of painting of the Renaissance (Syson and Keith 2011). It is described as being 'without lines or borders, in the manner of smoke or beyond the focus plane' (Earls 1987).

The literal translation of *sfumato* is 'gone up in smoke'; this technique heralded one of the most significant painting styles and introduced a way of thinking that was 'borderless', where paradox and magic could co-exist. This was to liberate a conceptual process where the very notion of edge was challenged. The poetic qualities of shade extolled in art were depicted symbolically in many of the Renaissance and post-Renaissance paintings, where shadow was also used as an expression of power and autonomy. Adelbert von Chamisso's story of Peter Schlemihl selling his shadow to the devil illustrates the value of the shadow, as Schlemihl loses his soul forever. Jaques de Gheyn's 'Three Witches Looking for Buried Treasure' (1604) uses an exaggerated form of shadow to illustrate a demonic form (Stoichita 1997). An altogether more urban and contemporary representation of autonomous power is to be found in the metaphysical paintings of Giorgio de Chirico (1888–1978). Enormous arcades disappear into deep shadow, creating dysfunctional perspective and producing at one end of the spectrum a sense of enigma and at the other – in 'Melancholy and Mystery of a Street' (1914) – a sense of deep foreboding (Harrison and Wood 2003).

Edward Hopper used shadow as a mannerist technique that heightened the sense of melancholy and isolation; the dramatisation both of environment and content would be totally lost without the application of deep shadow, which is often the principle component of the composition (Wagstaff 2004).

Whether one considers the work of the Renaissance or twentieth-century artists, there has been a premeditated awareness of the poetic utility and iconic status of shadow that has simply not been employed with the same intellectual awareness in the making of architecture.

The conceptual expression of shadow in both painting and photography changed, influenced by the principles of *sfumato*, where 'blending' necessarily erased the edge and shadow was used as the indefinable connection between one surface and another. Early photography in the twentieth century became particularly conscious of the use of shadow as a defined component of narrative. Alfred Steiglitz's *Shadows on the Lake* (1916) was the first seminal example of shadow and reflection where the phenomenological technique dominated the figurative content. However, it was Man Ray (Emmanuel Radnitsky) and Lazlo Moholy Nagy who produced some of the most publicly acclaimed photographic work where shadow was the substantive component of each photograph. Photography was an embryonic technology in the early 1900s and was considered only as a rather facile means of reproduction and Man Ray was one of the earliest artists to challenge the concept that photography was a form of reproduction for failed artists. His cultural and personal contact with the Dada and Surrealist painters provided a background of cultural experimentalism that was open to the technical potential of the photograph rather than seeing it as a lesser form of figurative representation. Man Ray was prolific and his range unusually extensive, producing commercial work when necessary in parallel with creating the more experimental images that were eventually to define his status within the art community. These images were capable of dramatically demonstrating ideas and vision that were as strong as if not stronger than the work of his surrealist contemporaries. Unusually, he found a balance between the commercial and the more experimental and this co-existence of two distinct photographic typologies, commercial and conceptual, created a necessary tension that was to fuel his more radical work. Although he may have suffered a lack of confidence as a painter, he had an undisputable compositional eye and constructed his sets and subjects with absolute technical precision before any photography took place (de L'Ecotais and Sayag 1998).

Jean Cocteau sculpting his own head in wire, circa 1925 (de L'Ecotais and Sayag 1998) is a beautiful illustration of composition, light, line and shadow and the last three components were equally as important as the physical object. It was during the process of printing commercial work that he began to experiment in the darkroom and discovered a technical process that was to produce 'solarisation' and the 'photogram'. This critical discovery allowed Man Ray the chance to develop an experimental and visual language that gave him the artistic credibility

he lacked as a painter. In using this technique he produced images of stylistic rupture that challenged the cultural position of the Dada artists and poets. The level of technical manipulation he undertook produced images of such enigma and complexity that he created a form of surrealism. The illusions were often dependent on the use of shadow which rendered the recognisable, unrecognisable. He constructed the images he wanted with all the technical manipulation he needed at his disposal, he created images where boundaries became questionable and the static was represented as dynamic (de L'Ecotais and Sayag 1998). Although prior to Man Ray's dark room experiments scientists had understood the technique of solarisation, there was no one else who enthusiastically embraced the violation of the photographic process as a mark of creativity. These experiments produced images whose partial reversal of values created ghostly shadows of the physical subject. This ethereal quality appears to cast the objects into a mystical world where figuration is simply a memory. Some of the figures glowed with a haloed outline, others became disembodied; this, together with far more complex lighting arrangements, created an aura that was beyond reality.

An interesting phenomenon emerged within the early years of amateur photography where photographic technique was specifically used to capture the notion of corporeal spirit. Disembodied auras were seen in photographs that apparently illustrated the spiritual substance of a person. These pictures were created to demonstrate aspects of Victorian spiritualism, but whether this was a conscious reference to the classic definition of shadow as the representation of human spirit is debatable. The exhibition at Krems (1997), *Im Reich der Phantome Fotografie des Unsichtbaren*, displayed images of photographic manipulation to convince a technically uninformed audience that the spiritual world could be captured on paper. The photos, some beautiful and others comically deceptive, describe an abstract concept that uses the language of shadow to suggest a realm that exists in our imagination outside the borders of reality (Fischer and Loers 1998). Chronologically these photographs predate the work of Man Ray and one can only speculate as to whether these early photographers discovered the techniques of light manipulation and whether their work inspired his. Although Man Ray, unlike these early photographers, was not known to be interested in the occult, his techniques nonetheless rendered the suggestion of a phantom-like charisma. Images of *Lee Miller* (1930) and *Retour a la Raison* (1923) manipulate shadow cast over the human body to distort them, both figuratively and texturally. Undoubtedly the most enduring and alluring technique he pioneered was the photogram. He discovered that by simply placing objects onto light-sensitive paper, the interaction of the two created three levels of tone. The place of contact remains white, the shadow becomes grey and the untouched areas become black. There is no line, only shadow; with this technique he developed an important portfolio of work in 1931 for the Paris Electricity Board published as a limited addition of 500 copies entitled *Electricite: Integration of Shadows* (1919) and *L'Homme* (1920). These works demonstrate that shadow can, when created in appropriate light settings, be equally as sharp as a solid object. This illusory quality and the ability to create dissolving

boundaries address our notion of perception, which is rarely acknowledged in the constructed world.

Marcel Duchamp also experimented with the idea of painting with cast shadows and the irony of this work lay in the fact that the objects were isolated through shadow and created a visual barrier that disengaged the painted object from the painter. A more contemporary influence is seen in an exhibition produced by Andy Warhol called *Shadows* (1979) and later a series of self-portraits that depict shadow projections of his head, *The Shadow* (1981) and *Self Portrait* (1978) (Stoichita 1997).

Although much of the experimental surrealist photography was done decades before its publication, Roland Barthes' book *Camera Lucida* (1993) meditates on the authenticity of the photograph and its status. Philosophical and functional relationships were examined in the text to explore whether an understandable method of translation was possible. Barthes considered the associative nature of the subject within the photograph as a method of understanding the image. Throughout the book there is an analysis of how we interpret reality and what we understand as real. The importance of Barthes' text lies in his pursuit of how we look and how we understand what we see. His analysis could easily be used to understand or at least be more aware of how we comprehend the physical reality of the city.

The city is a physical construct we inhabit and use, and our perception is of an environment that is all-enveloping and has a physical presence that creates 'intellectual reality'. The relationship between the physicality of the city and the range of perceptions and readings it offers needs to be compared with what are generically termed synthetic representations. The painting, the print, the film and the photograph are all distillations of space and representations of substance mediated through a synthetic process, with secondary and often tertiary interventions that, in turn, has raised questions about relative authenticity. Opinions will never be reconciled as to the primacy and status of each genre, and this should be a considered when searching for how the language of one can be transposed or translated into another. It is easy to see that the shadow in a photograph is not constructed in the same way as a shadow on a building, but observing the phenomenon, from a tectonic perspective, the act of reconciliation from one medium to another could be achieved by using an imaginative bridge, as the translation of visual language has none of the formal transpositional framework of oral linguistics. As a corollary it is therefore interesting to consider the philosophical reflections in Barthes' essay about the authenticity of the photograph as he examines the themes of presence, absence and time whilst considering the nature of the photograph (and to a lesser extent, film). An obvious paradox is that a photograph is both the subject and the object and is not susceptible to conventional scientific taxonomy, unlike urban space, which can be quantified and analysed in a technical and historic manner. It is these differences that make the photograph fascinating, as both methodological engagement and assessment are necessarily much more subjective. Can these more intuitive processes influence ways of looking at architecture and urban space? Photography has traditionally been considered in a number of ways, either as a technical construct – the combined action of chemistry and physics, viewed as an instrument

to record social history – or as an aesthetic object. Barthes viewed the act of taking the photograph as a sterile process: 'photography is anything but subtle' (Barthes 1993). His comparison with the act of painting is interesting in that he assumes the portrait artist is able, over time, to capture subtlety through nuances and inflection that the photographer is unable to do. This is a limited and highly personal response that fails to consider the nature of the photographed object or how the photographer will interpret the image or manipulate the process. The important element that is obliquely alluded to is time; the understanding is that the photographic act is seamlessly quick while other acts of pictorial or physical representation are not. Therefore speed and technology, in his view, create unsophisticated mediators of image.

> The important thing is that the photograph possesses an evidence force, and that its testimony bears not on the object but on time. From the phenomenological viewpoint, in the Photograph, the power of authentication exceeds the power of representation. (Barthes 1993)

His concern about the process being simply mechanistic is neatly balanced by his personal reflections, where he classifies photographic content into two typologies: those of 'punctum' and 'studium'. Those regarded as 'studium' give rise to less anxious deliberation than those of 'punctum', where he searches for the reasons that certain images are emotionally impelling. There is little compositional analysis to support his preferences, more a commentary of historic associations or literary metaphors and their importance in his own personal calendar.

Barthes accesses an understanding by looking deep inside his own personality where the photographic image challenged his philosophical balance. He believed that the pictorial image could be appreciated through an associative process rather than scientific scrutiny and that it has for many a mnemonic role as a catalyst for deep-seated memory. One might therefore argue that the role of a particular space within the city could also be understood in a similar manner, not through a measurable lexicon, but through the associative language of memory. This would support a loose argument whereby an associative method of evaluation could be used in both modes of representation.

There is some indication that Barthes saw the photograph as a creative tool when observing how more advanced forms of photography could be used to construct implied narrative. This reflection is helpful in that it reminds us of the physiological and philosophical relationship we have with the primitive photograph. However, he ignores progress in both the technical and the intellectual goals of photography and film, which require a less deductive mind for their appreciation. He maintains that 'Photography is an uncertain act' (Barthes 1993).

Although Barthes' observations have little reference to the compositional value of visual imagery, his discussion of status and significance becomes more useful when trying to construct an appropriate transformative lexicon. It is easy to get swept away on a tide of visually sumptuous material without considering what its purpose may be and, if used as reference, whether there is a cultural reciprocity. In contrast there are two contemporary female photographers whose work has been regarded by the art-sensitive market,

nearly fifty years after they began, their photographs still use the negation of light to create enigma. In many ways the work of Dianne Arbus and Annie Liebowitz perpetuates the Bartheian puzzle of how to understand and relate to such work.

Arbus, over many decades, has presented an uncompromising black and white social catalogue of America. The absence of colour is critical in that it accentuates formidable characteristics that prevent an image of realism. The paradox in her portraiture is that the subject, through highly attuned lighting, acquires a blandness that is worryingly familiar. The portraits are exact at capturing the banality of a personal situation yet the subjects somehow appear to be not of this world. The brilliance of Arbus' work is in the lack of dramatic lighting. There is only the faintest use of shadow, which has the perverse effect of making the subjects far more ambiguous. These photographs serve to remind us of subliminal expectations where shadow plays an essential role in articulating three-dimensional form. Liebowitz by contrast shows images of sumptuous complexity, saturated in colour, where visual dramas are borrowed from a theatrical or cinematic tradition. The use of light and shadow is carefully staged to create hugely centred and dramatic foci. Many of the more renaissance compositions used in the production of *Pilgrimage* (2012) use the varying depths of shadow as the major visual component in order to dramatise the illumination of the focal point. Once again one is reminded of the da Vincian model of *sfumato*, which introduced an understanding of the varying depths of shadow now recreated or transposed into a photographic medium (Liebowitz 2011). Perhaps this is also too obvious a parallel, but in these images Barthes' 'punctum' is clearly evident.

Although this chapter has touched on Evans' view of Turrell (Evans 1997), and the gulf that exists between the technical drawings and the phenomenological experience, a wider reference is necessary. It is impossible to consider the nature of shadow with all its wealth of ambiguity and ability to erase definition without considering the other part of the asymmetry: light. Turrell is arguably the most significant light artist of this generation whose work is analysed predominantly through the physics and the experiential aspects of light. To reflect on the impact of this work, consider the context into which focal illuminations are set, the essay 'Geometry of Light' (Bohme, in Sinnreich 2009). Arthur Zajonc, in his book *Catching the Light* (1995), considers the concepts of light from physics to mythology. His essay 'The Entwined History of Light and Mind' describes an experiment that is constructed to demonstrate that light in its pure and unobstructed form cannot be seen by the naked eye. It is only when it falls onto and interacts with a surface that it becomes visible. What we register is brightness, and this cognitive recognition of calibration is always against the context of shadow. The easiest examples to understand the ways in which we register light are within cathedrals, where the light streams through stained glass windows, which is articulated by the relative darkness of the interior space.

Turrell dramatically uses shadow in a phenomenological manner. 'Night Light' (Bohme, in Sinnreich 2009) presents the viewer with a different conundrum, where the audience is led into an enclosed space of deep shadow. It takes some time for the eye to adjust and this usually gives rise to a familiar sense of anxiety due to the loss of visual control. However, it becomes apparent that there is a very low level of light and, once recognised, the relative position of the viewer in the space becomes comprehensible. Subdued light may have been a critical component in this installation, but deep shadow was the context in which the light was made legible. Without shadow these light levels would have been unreadable. Park (in Sinnreich 2009) has likened Turrell's work to Plato's Cave where the interleaving of light and dark poses the philosophical question of whether shadow represents reality. Perhaps this philosophical relationship is closer to the phenomenological experience of the installation, where the understanding of reality becomes the challenge, but on examining the construction and the physics, shadow has created an illusion.

The Third Breath (Sinnreich 2009) describes an immersive installation where the 'diffuse darkness' provides the room with a calculated symmetry that is needed for the circular disc of light, created by the *camera obscura*. This captured image of the sky becomes an overpowering, light-filled counterpoint, which without darkness would fail in creating its theatrical potential and subsequent impact.

A long association between cinema and architecture. has its historic roots in the 1920s in two organisations, CIAM (Congres Internationale d'Architecture Moderne) and CIC (International Congress of Independent Cinema), They were brought together at a meeting at La Sarraz in 1928 where each was claiming to speak for the spirit of the age and shared an agenda that characterised the *avant-garde*. However, there were others who pursued the representation of the city from a different perspective, emerging from the surrealist film genre with such works as Man Ray's *Les Mystères du Château de Dé* to the english documentary figures such as Grierson and Jennings. In their films the city was used to represent politically utopian ideals, surreal projection of time and space, and used the documentary style to create the neo-realist city (Penz and Thomas 1997). The relationship between film and architecture has been extensively documented with a formidable array of analytical texts that deconstruct the socio-political influences within film and also explore the technical detail involved in the making of an urban image. However, there is little that describes the composition of the image and how these momentary views present such potent influences.

Much of the imagery includes shadow saturation creating the emphatic and dramatised statement. Contemporary architects have often referred to the influence of filmmakers on their work. Jean Nouvel attributes much of his inspiration to the work of Wim Wenders, while Patrick Kieler extensively uses his architectural background to create some of the foremost contemporary studies of the city in film. The intuitive attraction to dynamic imagery is less well explained, yet there is no doubt that the compositional grammar of filmic image is a substantial force in building architectural narrative and architectural reality. There are, of course, some similarities between architectural production and that of film, where each is continually edited and refined to create a coherent end-product. Major distinctions are obvious in that architecture is not created to be ephemeral but literal and physical, and therefore the laws of nature and involvement of community are critical. The attraction of film for designers is that it is produced within a culture

that values the same imaginative and creative drive but without the same levels of social, legal and bureaucratic constraint. The use of shadow in film and video require much higher levels of dramatisation and accentuation than are usually visualised in architectural design, yet this attenuated characteristic is a compelling goal for those that create space with physical substance. If one considers film as a narrative platform, there is often a strong speculative dimension where the audience uses film as an interpretive tool creating a breadth of appreciation that architectural functionality ignores. The technological functions in filmmaking are strategically used to develop 'effect' and because scenes can be so carefully controlled, the audience must work with visual fragments, as conventional understanding of a total environment is deliberately absent.

Light and shadow are the classic devices that suggest suspense and the pioneers of this tool emerged in the development of *film noir*. If the dramatic black and white imagery of the *noir* genre was allied to image, the cinematographers were as much the 'auteurs' as the directors. Anthony Mann was one of the early film directors and cinematographers who brought high levels of sensitivity into the composition and context of each shot. His style of photographic construction was probably one of the most influential to this day, and his highly stylised black and white photography was critical to both the delivery of narrative and the implications of nuanced emotion. The lighting positions were important, but simply constructed to create an image that was often profiled and dramatised in shadow with little background detail. In contrast to much contemporary film that aspires to realism, the *noir* genre was minimalist and slow-paced. The use of shadow was one of its signatures and for the architectural observer the language of shadow in this film genre shows a larger and more consciously nuanced range. Within a constructed image both figure and object were often obliquely lit to conceal exposure and amplify profile, a simple theatrical trick that heightened the sense of drama.

One cannot consider architecture in film without acknowledging Fritz Lang's *Metropolis* (1925–26), still considered to be the seminal work that shows a metaphoric vision of a new urban age. Much of the imagery uses deep contrast to over-dramatise the city and reinforce a threatening narrative, but also to negate the reassurance of figurative pictorialisation. Similarly, the use of shadow is used to reflect a haunted darkness in the films *The Cabinet of Dr Caligari* (Wiene and Hameister 1919) and *Nosferatu* (Murnau 1922). Ominous dark relief in early expressionist cinema was possibly used to suggest an unacknowledged subtext, a reflection of the social and economic situation of the time and the effects of the capitalist society. 'If one notices a horizon at all, one usually sees symbolic and grotesque silhouettes, graphically bold images, which project the protagonists' feelings and fears' (Penz and Thomas 1997).

The most dramatised use of shadow is found in neo-expressionist films such as Paul Leni's *Hintertreppe* (1921), where the staging uses precise pools of light that gradually fade into a vast area of darkness. The visual focus is exact, but the context is deep shadow and, without this extreme form of tonal counterpoint, both the mood and the sense of the unknown would be absent. In these films the lighting uses chiaroscuro techniques to create the level of blend necessary to suggest another or extended spatiality. Throughout the film, the screen is dominated by darkness, with only tiny areas of illumination; therefore once again spatial understanding can only be constructed intellectually. Other expressionist films use flickering light and shimmering shadow as a central part of their pictorial palette often used as a mechanism of evocation. Such techniques were poetically used in Joris Ivans' *Regan* (1929), where the use of tonal range and high contrast produced images of Amsterdam throughout a rainstorm that created 'the film maker's poetic diary of a thunderstorm in the city' (Penz and Thomas 1997).

The contemporary work of the Asian directors Wong Kar-Wei and Zhang Yimou brilliantly exploit the power of the implicit and the partially explained, usually portraying these concepts cinematographically rather than through narrative. As in the expressionist films of the 1920s, these also use minimal light focused on a small subject area with large areas of darkness together with the repeated use of reflection and blurred image. These techniques invoke ambiguity and demand a high level of engagement from the audience. In order to dramatise the narrative the editing process often deconstructs figurative understanding and demands that the audience reconstructs the logic by association rather than through explicit storytelling. The flexibility of the filmmaker allows the narrative function not to be depicted in real time. therefore the possibility of reconstruction and interpretation where permutation is infinite is in the control of the director.

Two films in particular stand out in the repertoire, *Chungking Express* (1994) and *In the Mood for Love* (2000), both haunting pieces of cinematography, fashioned largely by the camera style of Christopher Doyle. The foreground themes are of love, loss and time; the background themes are a reflection on the imminent political changes in Hong Kong. Both share a common context, a personal reflection on the city at a meso and micro scale. Compositionally the films have some traces of Italian neo-realism in that scenographically real parts of the city are used – the wall, the doorway, the alley, etc. – together with the use of editorial collage accompanied by heavily influenced musical scores. *Chungking Express* is not only a story of the central characters but also a commentary on urban life. Filmed on location in Chungking Mansions, the building provides corridors of deep shadow, an evocative location for those that drift through the city, and a place that has an aura of sinister squalor. The story is set in both the past and the present, using pictorial reflection, shadow and blurred imagery as a means to convey memory and the passing of time. It is this use of a scenically dark photographic lexicon that visually constructs a story of the city through evocation rather than through spoken narrative or explicit action. The films are shot at length, to facilitate an exhaustive editorial process where the collage of images demonstrates a fascination with urban texture. The way in which the scenes are compiled is undoubtedly stylish; this terminology would normally be considered superficial in a high cultural context, yet it is the most apt description of a fundamental part of the film's delivery: 'Style is substance' and 'surface is depth' (Brunette 2005).

The city in which the story is played out is one of lingering shadows, reflection and half-light. This is not a piece of city described with forensic clarity;

it is a city made of suggested spaces, a place of indistinct memory. The later film, *In the Mood for Love*, replays the same central themes but on this occasion the location is within a building of dark corridors and dimly lit stairwells. Scenographically the images are skilfully patched together, always to create a suggested but never explicit place and shadow is the central component that creates spatial ambiguity. The control over focused light is absolute, leaving the majority of the screen in varying degrees of darkness, where the audience are taxed to construct an understanding from the fragments of a visual jigsaw. Within this film, shadow is nuanced by smoke and rain, where both texture and form combine to create evolving spatial conditions. If one analyses the imagery in both films, shadow is central in creating an aura of emptiness, both spatial and human.

By analysing the use of shadow in this context as both an instrument of enigma and an instrument of territorial demarcation, one could imagine that it could be used within the realms of an architectural vocabulary. If the antithesis of precision (the *sine qua non* of the architectural process) has a sophisticated subtlety, the power of suggestion that exists within film might possibly be used in the production of spatial ideas. At the moment of inception all designers have the opportunity to search for less obvious solutions.

The photographic grammar used by Gary Hill in his seminal installation *Tall Ships*. falls somewhere between film and photography, sharing much compositional language – but its scale and the places of observation create a character in this *oeuvre* that is unique. *Tall Ships* presents a series of interactive sequentially moving images and the crucial relationship this installation has with architecture is that it must use volumetric space to communicate, The installation described as a 'videosphere' is where the individual must experience total immersion. For these images to work they must be presented in total darkness and deep shadow, creating a threshold where visual understanding is challenged. Once the audience enters, a series of movement sensors activate projected images of people seen out of focus at a distance who slowly move into focus and towards the observer. The reviews of this piece focus predominantly on the views of the respondents; this installation provides an extreme experience of space and darkness. To enter the 'event' one must overcome primordial anxiety about the unknown; there is no light and therefore no understanding of the space and no indication of what will happen. Some have refused to enter. A human subliminal understanding is that in order to navigate we must understand the terrain, in order to do this we must see, and in order to see we must have light. Deep darkness, where the eye cannot adjust to levels of miniscule light, leaves the individual vulnerable and with heightened levels of sensitivity (Quasha and Stein, in Mignot and Eleonor 1993).

In contrast the conceptual architectural drawing presents a fixed image that allows some degree of speculation, but however farsighted or impossible the proposal may be, unlike the artist there is an ingrained culture that presentational language should be explicit. The architectural designer is trained to show how things work, and at the end of the architectural process the building has one main purpose: to provide an environmental shelter and these set of un-negotiable imperatives must be met.

However, if these constraints can be abandoned within the world of conceptualisation, there still exists some opportunity to use cross-genres technique where references are both technical, implied and shared. Perhaps the furthest exploration of three-dimensional space that abandons references to classic typologies is the domain of the biomorphic, where synthetic replication or growth of biomimetic skin inhabits a world that has no urban reference. These images of extreme elasticity are a product of the development of powerful and sophisticated digital software which when used in tandem with digitised production techniques produces three-dimensional form. Paradoxically, despite this speculative tool offereing limitless possibilities, it creates a set of permanent boundaries once the processes are complete. The construction of conceptual text shares many of the characteristics of film, in that it can be fictional and therefore not bounded by the realities of time and function. The relationship of territorial description and time can therefore have a highly fluid relationship in text and film, which is a much greater challenge for the architectural speculator.

Painters, whether abstract or figurative, share some of the same constraints, in that the product is captured in one moment in time. The physicality of reading or watching is finite yet the experience of film and text is transient, savoured through the residual trace of memory. The painter and the architect produce a work, conceptual or otherwise, which can be visited once and be revisited. The building, with the exception of a small number of contemporary typologies, is experienced on a daily basis and is understood primarily through the realm of functionality.

The pictorial or contextual description of boundary through light, shadow and line is a challenge within architecture exploration must search for ways in which the unfinished or the enigmatic exist in order to to capture an illusion that suggests rather than describes. With advances in digital forms of representation, the ability to layer and create worlds where there is no defined end suggests an environment – but one that as yet only resides in digital format. Although the realm of computational imagery has become increasingly powerful, it is not appropriate to comment here on the technical virtues of this form of representation; the discussion and exploration concern the realm of physicality and how one might think about a borderless space.

The powerful use of the evocative in text, painting, film and video relies on the audience observing the inexplicit; with varying degrees the narrative can go from a point of conclusion to an extreme territory that is almost void. The middle ground is edited and constructed to give enough clues that the observer can complete 'the picture' with interpretive skills. This mono-directional nature of visual film and painting always allows the observer to be simultaneously aware of the object and the secondary space they occupy, Architectural experience, by contrast, is often one of total immersion, whether architectural space can harness the power of suggestion, unleashing the realm of the imagination, remains to be explored.

The Shadow House, drawn in 1982, simplistically cartoons an idea that lines of demarcation need not be physical and that territorial boundaries are implicitly understood. The implied edge is created by the contrast of light and darkness and the shadows created were to have a dynamic impact according to the time of day, integrated into the composition was the changing relationship between the light source and the solid object. This was an intuitive exercise based on a simple idea and of course had extreme limitations, as the model was never properly tested. However, this was the beginning of a search for a language of suggestion evident in other genres but rarely in an architectural context. The idea of immeasurable boundary – or indeed whether boundary needs definition – was a recurrent theme of conversation both within the logistics of office production and in the less constrained context of the academic studio. There was no clear end to the discussion as one idea segued to the next and the normal construct of logic rarely dominated the conversation. I returned to the drawings 30 years later with only a slightly better understanding of how to direct the exploration. It was important to define the limitations of the narrative and realise that this form of experimentation lacked a clear technical brief. This in many ways was liberating, as the process required the primal, intuitive and reiterative act of small adjustment. The original drawing suggested an enclosure, loosely referred to as a house. This established a hierarchical organisation that had two dominant characteristics, the first was an open series of platforms whose only definition was cast shadow and the second was a sequence of enclosures articulated by bright shafts of light. The model that interpreted these simple principles was constructed in plan with transparent or opalescent plastic and the volumetric enclosure was suggested through wire. The assembly of the model was therefore closer to a constructed drawing than a traditional piece of architecture. At this point the proposal does not attempt to answer the questions functionality but is rather used as a vehicle to test ideas about linearity in space. The model was examined once light and shadow were incorporated and it was used to explore whether a different language of expression could be developed. The exercise produced hundreds of variants where the physical model worked with its cast shadow to create a multiplicity of form, where the solid became indistinguishable from the virtual. In some ways this is little more than theatre, where a set is created for a particular story, but at another level it expanded a language of definition that was neither sought nor tested in the production of a physical building.

As the established Renaissance technique of *sfumato* describes the blending of shadow in painting, the illuminated model displayed a typical range of penumbra, ante-umbra and umbra, giving it a distinct tonal range and depth.

Introducing multiple lighting positions created conditions where reflection, solid material and shadow collided to create labyrinthine complexity together with forms of definition that had multiple levels of distinction. There is now a formal composition that is part physical, part virtual, part reflective, and at its most effective becomes a tool of exploration. By examining both the impied physicality of surface together with the characteristics of illumination, a hybridised model began to emerge. This exercise is in its infancy, and further study might reveal just how much of this built drawing could be usefully inhabited.

Where or what an architectural boundary is is still a source of debate: how much is or can exist intellectually? How or what needs to be depicted physically and where the tangible and the intangible coincide will continue to attract both discussion and experimentation.

THE KANTINE, FRANKFURT

3.1   Detail of façade and roof in open position
3.2   View of roof in open position

WITH PETER COOK

The Städel Academy at Frankfurt is one of the few independent art academies to remain in Germany, where the exploration of film, art and architecture push the boundaries of experimentation. The school was situated in a neo-classical building built in the nineteenth century next to the Städel Museum. Despite its grand demeanour, there were few facilities for the staff and students; the building had been designed for production with no thought to the creative opportunities that arise out of social interaction.

The practice (Cook and Hawley) was approached to design a 'Kantine', a place for eating, drinking and displaying small ad hoc art exhibitions, and this was to be served by a commercial kitchen. There were few spaces within the school where this could be achieved, as the architectural boundaries were inviolate. A small semi-derelict courtyard on the north side of the building, normally littered with the waste material from the sculpture studio, was chosen as the eventual site.

The courtyard was constructed of stone and within it sat six freestanding Doric columns. Whether this had once been a covered space was unexplained, but this curious site already had foundations, a floor and possibly a structure that we could utilise. Deliberation about cost forced the design to keep as much as possible and therefore the challenge was how to build in and around a neo- classical space that had an established and dominant architectural language.

Neo-classicism has a clear protocol where the proportions of the building are defined, the levels clearly stratified and the materials creating a substantial edifice. To adopt the same proportional principles and adhere to the same material language was neither an appropriate expression of the twentieth century nor would it have been seamlessly assimilated; a linguistic copy would have been pastiche. A more interesting proposition was to create a space that could be clear visual counterpoint yet still acknowledged the weight of its architectural surroundings. The concept was to create an architecture that appeared weightless and transparent so that the original boundaries and structure could still be seen. This was to be an enclosure defined by line rather than surface.

concept of lines and transparency began to develop. The decision to use glass for the entire enclosure offered benefits and also serious challenges. The technical issues became an essential part of the design and perhaps came to define the project more than anything else. Environmental issues needed to be addressed: in the summer the heat gain would be substantial and in the winter the heat loss and snow-loading equally dramatic. The possibility of creating effective cross-ventilation was minimal as the space was adjacent to a closed corridor; in discussion with Bollinger we agreed the easiest way to mitigate heat gain was to open the roof, but this was not a suggestion to put vents in the roof but to lift the entire roof off its supporting structure. The engineering problems were particularly complex; these, together with maintaining the concept of minimal line, put pressure on an already limited budget. However the dynamic of the roof structure was inherent to the character of the building.

Steel supports were embedded in the capitals of each of the freestanding columns and these in turn had to be laterally stabilised at high level by tensioned wire. The most critical issue was how to get the roof to lift up and away from the front façade using a system that did not undermine the structural integrity of the glass elevation. The normal construction arrangement of wall and roof is that they are tied together to create structural stability; by removing this it became essential to find alternative ways to stabilise the façade. The roof was lifted by three hydraulic rams fixed into the capitals of the front columns; once fully extended, the entire roof was at 75 degrees to the horizontal and the extended shafts of the rams became part of the linear language.

An interesting symmetry arose in that much of the production of the art school were lines on paper and the building was to resonate the same language, yet it was to be lines in space.

The building needed transparency for the idea to have any visual potentcy, therefore all of the heavy services were confined an adjacent area within the original building, the restaurant and exhibition space were to be located in the old courtyard. In discussion with Klaus Bollinger, our structural engineer, the

3.3 Detail of interior (a, b, c, d)

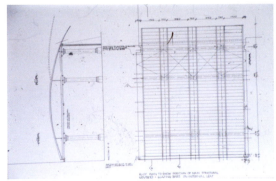

3.4   Detail of façade junction with hydraulic rams

3.5   Roof under construction

3.6   Kantine kitchen

3.7   Roof detail

Tension wires, both internal and external, formed a triangulated structure and supplied the integrity that was needed to stabilise the freestanding façade. All the steel profiles were kept as thin as possible and, together with the tensioned cable system, provided the necessary engineering stability. The building maintained the concept of being little more than a series of lines in space.

The initial drawings were deliberately simple and the only alteration came through minimising the lighting design. Illumination was initially to be provided by as a series of bulbs gripped by attenuated steel rods that would both complement and extend the language of line. These were sacrificed through cost and a much simpler overhead system introduced. The references used throughout the process were rarely architectural; the search was continually for systems that either functionally or opportunistically created spatial impression that contained a minimum of visual surface. These references were more likely to be found in catenary cables on bridge structures, the complex overhead cabling system on railways and in cities such as Tokyo where technical services are exposed overhead. The design process was searching for a system that allowed the building to almost disappear. Perhaps the ultimate goal can be found in film or the description in text where the mind can capture an impression that gradually fades. Architecture is solid and permanent so to chase the idea of ephemera could be futile. However, the difficulty of trying to capture qualities that do not normally exist within solid structures is the most prescient part of the challenge.

3.8   Kantine front elevation with open roof
3.9   Detail of interior structure

BERLIN
SOCIAL HOUSING

WITH PETER COOK

The International Bau Austellung has a historic pedigree that goes back to the beginnings of Modernism and it was perhaps these cyclical exhibitions that pioneered some of the best examples of the modern economic house. The design of social housing, because of its ubiquity, is often ignored and, if the examples of recent history are a reflection of quality, it has all but been relegated. There are of course exceptions but it is an interesting observation that there was still sufficient political idealism and social commitment at the end of the 1980s for Germany and the city of Berlin to host an architectural demonstration project that would be the latest in a long list of publicly funded housing developments that provide templates, to be studied

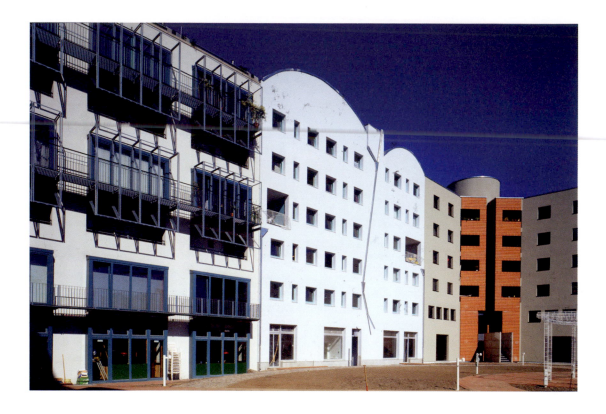

3.16 North elevation

if not copied in years to come. The historic legacy of the IBA across Germany was a roll call of the most influential names associated with the progressive alignment of art and architecture but the housing also provided some of the best paradigms of modern urban living. In 1901 the Mathildenhöhe on the edge of Darmdstadt was a demonstration of the alignment of architectural thinking about domestic living and the input of a vibrant art community.

The subsequent housing was both aesthetic and functional, except that it was built with little concern for the average domestic income; this was an enclave for the financial elite. The indisputable beauty of the Matihldenhöhe left a legacy that needed to be addressed politically and this was to build housing that was efficient, aesthetic and affordable to the vast majority of the working population. The subsequent projects at both Stuttgart and Frankfurt introduced ideas about space planning efficiency, communal engagement and relationship to nature that was both idealistic and also practical. These developments offered new homes for the working population that far exceeded the facilities of their social forebears. The IBA had introduced a model whereby the most interesting and innovative architectural designers were invited to reinterpret modernist housing and address the impact of post-industrialisation with all the effects it had on the lifestyle of the twentieth century.

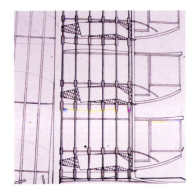

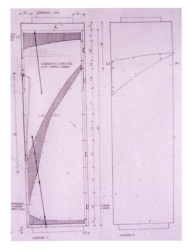

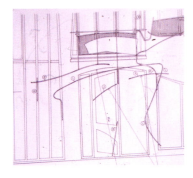

3.17 Early sketch balcony detail

3.18 Early sketch door detail

3.19 Early sketch entrance door and balcony
detail

During the latter half of the twentieth century the dogma of the inter-war years and the tradition of Rationalism had an overbearing influence on architectural philosophy and production in Europe. There can be no doubt that the major influence on the development of Rationalism in Germany could be traced to the neo-classical work of Schinkel and the wider European influence of Gruppo 7, Terragni and the theoretical position of Tafuri. However, it was the work of Oswald Mathias Ungers that had the most powerful contemporary influence in the development of Rationalism in the 1960s and 1970s. The practice of Ungers produced buildings that demonstrated a systematic rigour that was flawless and, as a teacher and theoretician, the ideology extended to younger generations. In this context the developmental language of the IBA bore all the hallmarks of Germany's Rationalist legacy.

Within this context, the comparison of philosophical and aesthetic tradition in the UK was stark. Architectural influences had momentarily swept away the influences of the Brutalists in the 1940s and 1950s a radical, anarchic challenge arose. Many formative thinkers and ultimately practitioners of this era in the UK emanated from the Architectural Association. The architectural practice formed with Peter Cook embodied much of the cultural legacy that emerged from this school and it was with this highly differentiated architectural background that we were approached to contribute to this historic building programme.

The programme of development was entwined with the political machinations that envelop most city councils and the inevitable delays meant that we had more time than usual to both establish an architectural position and to find an executive architect that would work comfortably with our practice. The approach we took offered a clear contrast to the Germanic tradition.

The post-war development of Berlin demonstrated an authoritative systematic rigour that was often mathematically devised and characterised by relentless continuity. The scale of development controlled by the city limited most buildings to be no more than five or six stories; therefore the impression was of low mass and bulk, with horizontal lines of force established by repetitive lines of identical fenestration. There was copious information about the site in Lutzoplatz, where the building was to be constructed; the block was to contain the work from a range of internationally based architects, including Mario Botta, Christian de Portzamparc and more locally Hans Kollhoff and OM Ungers. The attitude we took was to try to create an architectural character that acted as a counterpoint to the general low profile that dominated the IBA developments, particularly in this part of Berlin. The frameworks of references were rooted in a neo-gothic landscape, both architectural and text, existing in both European and English culture. The design was conceived through highly figurative influences, where the formalist approach was intended to deliver a more direct statement, than the cerebrally constructed matrix of Rationalist façades. The most potent image of the recently constructed Berlin housing displayed the dominant language of horizontal repetitive mass. The building in Lutzoplatz however, developed a language that did not abide by stringent rules and showed a form of wilful deviance. One of the most important components of gothic formalism is the use of the vertical line in construction and this became the core language we would use externally. The attenuation of line and the extension or exaggeration of verticality was the necessary counterpoint needed.

The construction of economic housing that has to conform to a matrix of regulatory constraints, performance requirements and severe economic limitations will inevitably undermine a figurative concept that does not rely solely on functionality. Therefore it was fundamental in maintaining the concepts that the spatial requirements enhanced rather than undermined the form. Methodologically there were drawings that were developed as sketches that did little more than acknowledge the boundary and height of the building. In parallel small details were drawn that searched for a language that would exaggerate the idea of the line. These gradually became more organic and there was a suggestion that some of the forms were influenced from a pagan lexicon. This exaggerated linear language was at this stage aspirational rather than realistic: the challenge was how much we could retain. The small details and the larger elevation were constantly being tested, and transforming with each iteration. It was clear that we needed to collaborate with a German architect who were sympathetic to this linguistic typology and not rooted in the contemporary German tradition. Heinrich and Inken Balle had a small practice that produced extraordinary projects influenced by Nervi – their expressionist buildings were startling and unique – and it was with their practice we collaborated on the production of this building. The collaboration became an essential part of the process; as so many architects who build abroad have discovered, initial concepts can be devastated by the un-finessed

hand of the architect with executive control. The Balla office not only provided guidance through the regulatory system but support in interpreting and realising essential parts of the design that did not conform to german standardised models.

The formal motif of the building relied on an emphasis of the vertical line but the gothic exemplars we referred to were very different in scale. It was crucial that the external architectural language was not cosmetic but had a coherent relationship to the spatial organisation of the building. Unlike most social housing that relies on lateral planning, the apartments were designed as duplexes. The apparent perversity had both negative and positive effects. Vertical volume particularly in the living areas could be used expressionistically on the external façade and the increase in internal vertical height was critical in creating an illusion of space. The apartments were subject to all the usual spatial compromises associated with social housing; it was therefore important that the design minimised any sense of restriction. However, the negative aspect was that we had to provide vertical circulation that could otherwise be utilised as functioning floor space. There is a difficult judgement to be made about functionality versus spatial character and this scheme may have sacrificed some functionality but gained a significant increase in light and a greater sense of spatiality. The German byelaws permit that a small percentage of the floor area be used as an unheated winter garden, which gave us the opportunity to utilise this as a double-height space on the façade. Therefore these dominant vertical volumes heavily outlined by lines of steel support became one of the defining aspects of the façade. The unheated double-height glass enclosure

3.20   Façade and interior details (a, b, c, d)

was usually open during the summer and closed during the winter. The space was used by residents for a variety of purposes, but more usually for the growing and protection of plants. The winter garden could be accessed at both the lower and upper levels and had the principal advantage of providing a thermal buffer during the winter months and accelerating air flow to the upper level during the summer. Environmentally an immensely simple construction provided a significant contribution to energy conservation and an elegant glass chamber extended the usable space. While most of the visible aspects of the duplex arrangement were visible from the major façade facing Lutzoplatz, the service components and bedrooms were organised to receive light and ventilation from the rear façade. There was a conscious decision that the dialogue between the front and the back should be contrasting, therefore the back façade became a parody of Teutonic orthodoxy, with a strictly mathematical grid organising the fenestration in contrast to the attenuated and non-orthogonal linear language of the front.

However, there were small elements borrowed from the language of the public façade – a curvilinear balustrade and an angular, diagonal rainwater pipe, a reminder that the aesthetic language, although expressing counterpoint, was thematically united. Once the basic language and the spatial organisation had been established, the form of the roof became an important issue, as the familiar forms of pitches, hips and flat surfaces bore little relationship to the emphatic language of the exterior.

An obvious gambit in the roof space was to continue the principle of providing double-height spaces and the building therefore provided two studio apartments arranged under two arced roofs; the spatial principles were consistent and the linear geometry, both back and front, was comfortably continued. Throughout the process

3.21 Street view

of developing the language of the shell, the internal spatial organisation was the constantly iterated. This process needed to comply with spatial computations that dictated the volumetric ratio of useable to non-useable space and, as these apartments were not a standard lateral arrangement, the computation had to undergo several adaptations. In tandem to establishing the logistical criteria, the impact of local politics and the endless delays quite dramatically affected the budget and inevitable adaptations were made, where the more florid language in the original drawings was compromised. The apartment block was finally completed and contributed an alternative to the controlled language of Lutzoplatz.

It is difficult to chronicle the methodological process of this building, as concepts of gothic pictoriality were compounded with a desire to create an enclosure whose language spoke of lightness and delicacy. The work of Wachsmann was continually referred to, where he both conceptually and structurally was able to make space out of lines. The historic models of the Prater Wheel in Vienna had a majestic presence and seemed to be made of little more than thousands of thin lines. Chedanne's industrial building in the Rue Reamur and the interior of the Gallerie Lafayette were buildings that used the linear language of *art nouveau* to capture an organic vitality that was lost under the edicts of modernism. It would be disingenuous to say that the influences were either philosophically or pragmatically driven; there was an undoubted momentum that came from visual composition and its associations. The relationships between one form to another and how they were woven together defy a linear rationale. There was a desire to break with the traditional procedures and rule systems; the development of ideas was associative and organic.

This process often proceeds silently, with one drawing slowly being adjusted for the next to emerge. The influences are subliminal at the moment of production as the struggle with representational technique takes priority. It is only when there are moments to pause and reflect that both practical and pictorial relationships emerge. To make sense or to describe an order in this process would be to falsely represent what was organic and highly associative. However, at what point does the act of crafting and figurative or functional refinement take place? I believe this happens all the time but usually remains unrecorded.

A building that has no surface reflects the nonsensical idea that buildings can be made of lines in space. However, it is possible to attempt a visual order that suggests the dominance of the line where surface falls into the background and the most powerful force is the line that draws the eye upwards.

OSAKA PAVILION

WITH PETER COOK

The concept of folly within British culture is inextricably linked to landscape and the landscaped garden; there are great historic precedents that link mythology with landscape and monument. Implicit in the word folly is the idea of nonsense, of a structure that has no purpose. The underlying narrative that created the form might be decipherable, but to most it is not. These structures are often belvederes that offer unimpeded views or are used for shelter and perhaps ornamentation. From the eighteenth century emerged many of these indulgent constructions imbued with the quality of delight. It is within this cultural background that the folly at the Osaka Expo was conceived; however, there was a difference in that the pavilions of the eighteenth century were positioned within a context. The orientation, the narrative of the landscape, the horticultural setting and the whims of the patron were all guidelines for an appropriate response. The Osaka Expo had no such references and therefore there had to be an open definition and interpretation of the concept of folly.

The site was the only physical point of reference situated between two water systems. Behind the site to the south was the source of a spring and in front to the north was the lake that it fed; these two physical references were the beginning of a narrative that would shape the ideas that created this folly.

The structure was to physically and metaphorically unite these two water sources –and also allow a certain level of public interaction.

It was important that to acknowledge some aspects of cultural context and the powerful iconography of Kabuki theatre was to become the second significant reference. The use of the mask to disguise and surprise is a potent symbol of enigma and revelation that the design tried to capture. When the public approached the folly they were unaware of its mechanisms; the front of the structure was to be a blank aluminium mask that shielded what was behind. There was one distinctive mark on the aluminium wall and that was one line, a yellow metal wand that for most of the time was motionless. Access to the structure was by steps and, arriving at the top, the visitor had to turn and occupy a small space that disclosed a transparent façade to the rear.

The aluminium mask shielded the view; once inside, the transparent north facing façade revealed the lake, but the vista was only clear occasionally. Within the structure was a water system that was activated every two minutes. The mechanism pumped water through and around the structure to animate certain parts. The initial assault on the senses was the noise of water running over stones beneath the perforated metal entrance bridge. The water was pumped through the structure to a collection of twisted pipes that poured water down the glass façade, periodically distorting the view; the water was then recycled and collected in a small trough concealed below the bridge. When full, the trough would tilt and pour the water out through the aluminium wall into a second trough concealed below the ground level. The sequence was complete once the water

had been tipped into the subterranean trough in which the wand floated and suddenly moved due to the water's turbulence. The folly demonstrated a simple sequence of events using both the visual qualities of water and its inherent capacity to produce energy. The folly was dynamic, surprising and enigmatic, revealing perhaps some of the elusive qualities to be found in the tradition of Kabuki activated by the most evident natural commodity on site, water. The final surprise was the impact at night: as the visitor walked towards the folly the water would activate the wand and the trough of water in which it sat was under-lit so that the moving water would suddenly be reflected onto the aluminium façade, distorting the precision of its surface. The three components that were physically important were the yellow wand that swept across the façade, the bent line of pipes that obscured the gaze and the chaotic lines that flooded the aluminium surface at night.

3.24   Exit stair

3.25   Interior view

3.26   Detail of water pipe

185

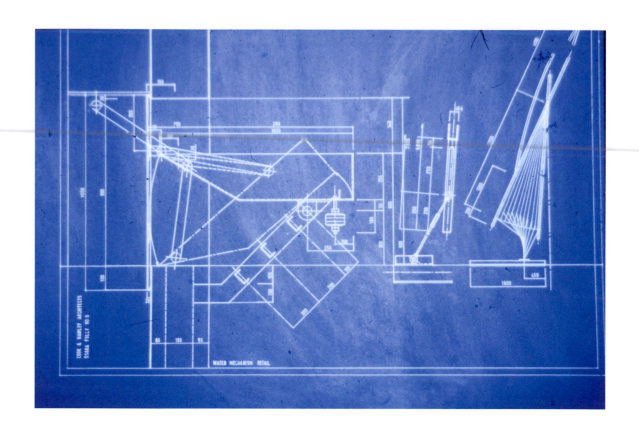

3.27 Drawing of water mechanism

HAMBURG OFFICES

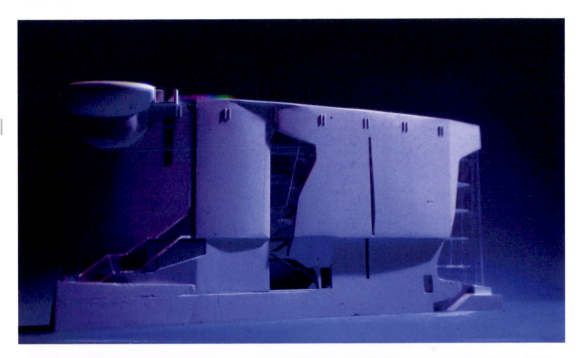

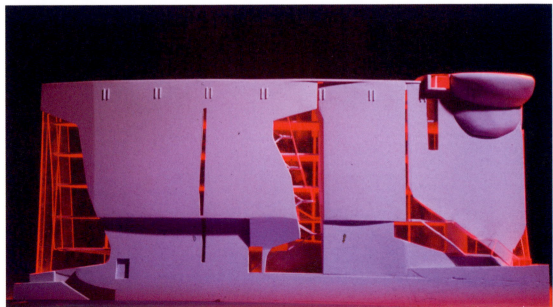

3.28   Exterior view of Hamburg offices day-
and night-time elevations (a, b)

YATAI

3.29 Yatai textile exhibition pavilion,
      constructed frame undressed

THE BLUE HOUSE

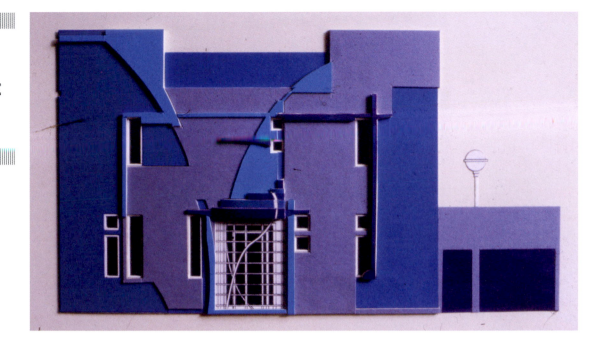

3.30   Blue House north elevation

The Blue House was part of a portfolio of house designs for a development in Landsthul, Germany, where the requirements were to create maximum energy efficiency. Although this is now a standard prerequisite for almost all design, in 1980 there was minimal awareness of how critical this was going to become in the future. The discussions of sustainability remained theoretical and the houses at Landsthul were one of the few pioneering projects of the time. We worked closely with an environmental engineer who established the technical principles the designs had to adhere to. There were five typologies providing accommodation in a number of different spatial configurations. The organisational and positional principles were established to harness as much solar power through passive methods.

The importance of describing the environmental requirements is needed to contextualise the design. The natural energy source came exclusively from sunlight and this became one of the principle influences in the design, both technically and symbolically. The house was situated on the edge of a disused quarry; the building was south-facing and organised around a semi-circular plan to allow the south façade to receive as much light as possible. The principal south-facing space was the living area, which rose through a double-height volume to accommodate a studio gallery. At the rear of this double-height volume was the 'trompe wall', absorbing and subsequently redistributing the heat; the south façade was predominantly constructed of glass to allow maximum light absorption.

However, it was the rear north-facing wall that provided the entrance to the building where the narrative of the house could be expressed. The wall was constructed with 600mm block work and then a render was applied as a surface finish. The fenestration was limited in order to allow as little heat loss as possible. It was through the manipulation of the render that the narrative was told. It was critical that the dynamic of the light was captured; the geographic contours of the location were abstractedly inscribed on the surface, which not only functioned as the entry to the building but also acted as a metaphor for the first chapter of a book where the introduction to the main themes of the story are often told.

The render was applied with different levels of thickness to create surface articulation. The geography of the site could be easily read geometrically and the arc of land on which the house sat was translated into a recognisable form that was profiled on the façade with the application of raised render. There were other contextual features – the presence of water, an escarpment and distant hills – and these were all acknowledged through forms of abstract representation on the façade by manipulating the surface so that the cement finish was differentially articulated. Shadow would be cast by the differentiated surface and as the day passed, so the shadows would lengthen and contract, both metaphorically and physically suggesting that the sun played an integral part in the working of the house.

Fehn memorably talked about the use of light as part of the architectural palette and how the designer needed to respond quite differently according to latitude. Architecture is flat and characterless without the articulation of light, but the Blue House had surfaces that dramatised the use of light and shadow. The nuance described in text is impossible to reproduce with solid surfaces; perhaps the closest reference is the genre of *film noir*, where the self-conscious use of side- and up-lighting not only articulates profiles but also insinuates atmosphere. The front façade of the house obviously does not achieve this level of drama, but it is an inspiring quality to refer to.

MESHED GROUND

Konrad Wachsmann's work was not only definitive for large span engineering in the twentieth century, creating optimal spaces of flexibility, but also for his poetic vision, which appealed to those that imagined his spaces as a never-ending twisting vortex. His observations were about spatial dreams rather than spatial realities and it was these unrealities that persuaded designers to think beyond the boundaries of conventional space. The attraction for me was through one defining comment and that was an observation about the catenary cables of Brooklyn Bridge that were, according to him, the perfect definition of space: they were simply lines, not on paper but in space itself. One imagines that the purity of the object appealed to the tectonic mind but for an architect his description was a mnemonic to be completed in the imagination. Brooklyn Bridge is not enigmatic; it is technically specific but it shares some language with early Piranesi drawings, where the linear construction of the drawing had an evocative quality – both have qualities that attract further thought.

The drawing of *Meshed Ground* was conceived as a frame that had no clear edge or surface, together with the deliberate omission of enclosure, the intention was to create a perspectival space that was constructed only with a lattice-like structure. The system resembles a pergola without the implicit intention to support vegetation. It is absent of function and serves to create a corridor to an undefined point in the distance. The complexity of the frame lacks the functional imperative of the engineering structure, but this independence from structural economy allows the space to develop a more eccentric syntax where unexplained form does not need a technical justification. There was a sub-text to this drawing in that I wanted to see how a form with a strongly structural references could influence a ground scape that then changed morphologically. There was a deliberate syntactical conflict but also a visual interdependence where both aspects of the space were loosely connected. The process of making this drawing was a method of exploration, where the boundaries of formal language are not inhibited by the usual requirements of function or even metaphor. Periodically, these exercises are necessary to test the technical language of transition. Ideas at the outset may be simple, but as the drawing develops the original idea undertakes a transformational change, becoming more complex or perhaps more removed from the original idea. Throughout the process of drawing and painting there will be hundreds of revisions not driven by intellectual directives but by observing the balance of form and making judgements about subsequent adjustments. These abstracted exercises expose one's own ability to translate unformed fluid concepts that drift onto paper and, through the process of drawing capture the layers of mystery that exist in the mind. There is an important element of craft in these exercises; the hand–eye coordination needed for fluent transcription improves only through repetition where the struggle to overcome the gulf between the cerebral and unseen to a legible image that communicates.

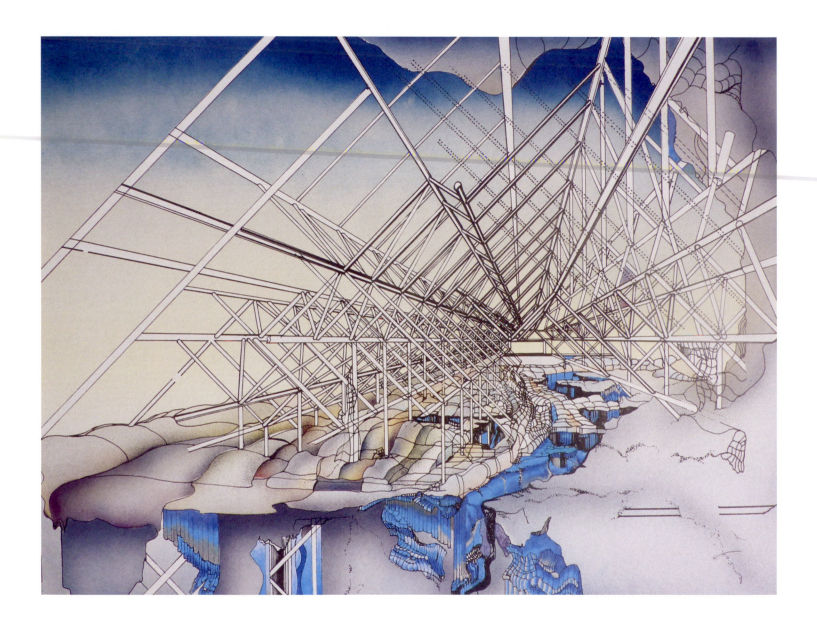

3.31   Meshed ground

WHITEHAVEN

3.32　Duplex apartment view to the sea

3.33 Interior view from within duplex apartment

3.34 Façade at night

3.35   Aerial view of planted roof

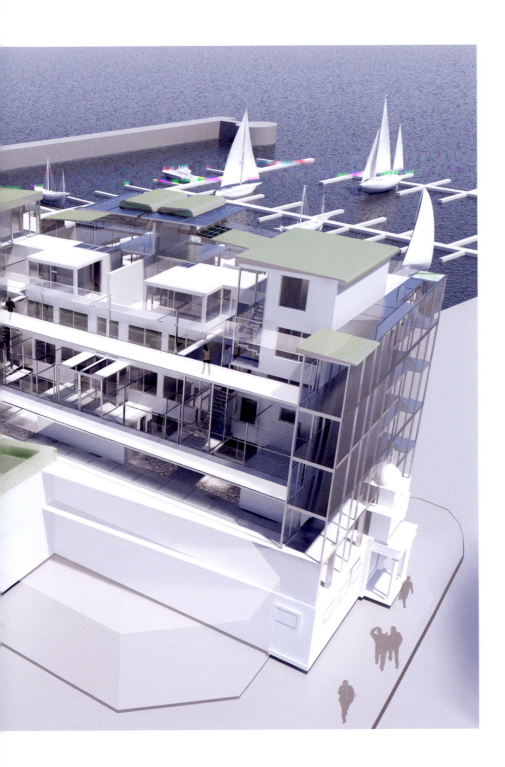

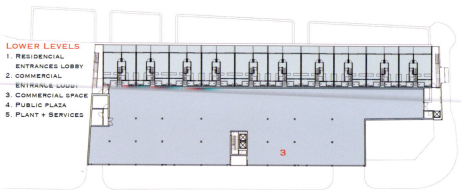

LOWER LEVELS
1. RESIDENCIAL
   ENTRANCES LOBBY
2. COMMERCIAL
   ENTRANCE LOBBY
3. COMMERCIAL SPACE
4. PUBLIC PLAZA
5. PLANT + SERVICES

3

LEVEL 1. OFFICE/ HOUSING

LEVEL 2
UPPER LEVEL
1. ACCESS: LIFTS+STAIRS
2. ROOFTOP GARDEN
3. ENTRANCE
4. BEDROOM 1
5. UTILITY
6. KITCHEN
7. LIVING ROOM
8. BALCONY
9. ACCESS WALKWAY
LOWER LEVEL
10. SHOWER+BATHROOM
11. BEDROOM 2
12. BEDROOM 3

LEVEL 2

3.36   Plan at level 1

3.37   Plan at level 2

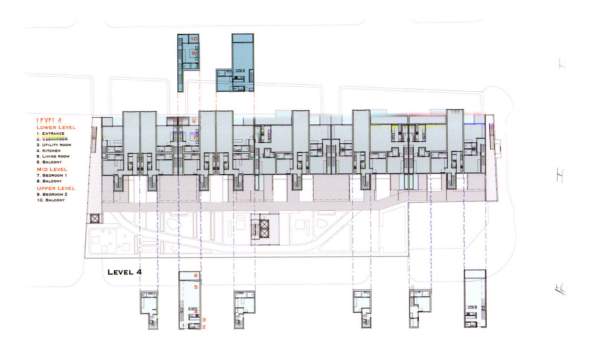

LEVEL 4
LOWER LEVEL
1. ENTRANCE
2. CLOAKROOM
3. UTILITY ROOM
4. KITCHEN
5. LIVING ROOM
6. BALCONY
MID LEVEL
7. BEDROOM 1
8. BALCONY
UPPER LEVEL
9. BEDROOM 2
10. BALCONY

LEVEL 4

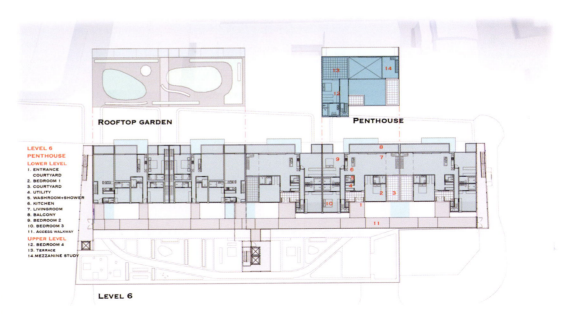

ROOFTOP GARDEN

PENTHOUSE

LEVEL 6
PENTHOUSE
LOWER LEVEL
1. ENTRANCE
   COURTYARD
2. BEDROOM 1
3. COURTYARD
4. UTILITY
5. WASHROOM+SHOWER
6. KITCHEN
7. LIVINGROOM
8. BALCONY
9. BEDROOM 2
10. BEDROOM 3
11. ACCESS WALKWAY
UPPER LEVEL
12. BEDROOM 4
13. TERRACE
14. MEZZANINE STUDY

LEVEL 6

3.38   Plan at level 4

3.39   Plan at level 6

3.40 Rear view to garden

PORCHESTER
BATHS

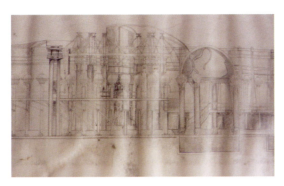 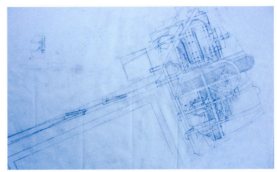

3.41   Pencil detail

3.42   Pencil sketch of plan

3.43   Pencil sketch of Porchester Baths

3.44   Long section through Porchester Baths

THE SHADOW HOUSE

Shadow as a non-substance exists in a variety of tonalities, from the faintest grey halo to deep black that obliterates all in its path. Shadow must have surface in order to be created, as surface will both block the light path and be the plane onto which the shadow is cast. Shadows can be created by a single light source or can be the result of multiple sources to create a range of umbra and penumbra. Dynamic shadow is usually the product of natural light, where the length of the shadow is dependent on the co-tangent of the sun's elevational angle. The natural phenomenon of shadow can be created by mist, cloud and fog, where the nebula drifts to form images that constantly re-form. This non-substance has a character that can have precise definition yet also be so ghost-like as to almost not exist.

Natural shadow is at its most dramatic in northern latitudes where short days and long winter nights create a terrain where every object has an attenuated extension to create a landscape that is criss-crossed with dark lines and blurred boundaries. This is a landscape of luminous drama and quiet subtlety. Peter Høeg describes how shadow becomes the very essence of definition when his detective in *Miss Smilla's Liking for Snow* searches for the footprint that can only be recognised by the faintest line of grey against the whiteness of the snow. Shadow can be read and provides a form of silent narrative. Shadow mythologically has always suggested an ominous presence or, religiously, a halo of shadow was the mark of God. The physicality of shadow is captured in the photographic medium where the action of chemical on paper registers its existence. This does not even need the intervention of complex photographic equipment as the hologram only needs paper with silver nitrate and exposure to the sun. The process of x-ray reveals what cannot be seen by the naked eye through the medium of shadow.

The use of shadow in film has been used not only for visual articulation but also to extend the narrative. Hitchcock was one of the earliest filmmakers to exploit this potential; the iconic scene in *Psycho* has the essence of drama embedded in the use of shadow and its ability to create foreboding. The more articulated use of shadow was developed in *film noir*, where its use in films such as Orson Welles' *Touch of Evil* became an essential ingredient of the atmospheric content. The extension or distortion of shape became a translational tool that was able to convey suggestive narrative in complete silence. Contemporary filmmakers and cinematographers such as Christopher Doyle use dynamic camera technique together with consciously constructed lighting to transform and disguise. The recent portfolio of Hong Kong and Chinese film has demonstrated how the manipulation of shadow can create a complete environment, and it is the fascination of these visual phenomena that prompted the search for an alternative vocabulary that could be used within an architectural palette.

If one imagines that architectural definition can only be achieved by solid construction, the lexicon is unnecessarily limited. The infinite complexity of implicit space, demonstrated in other visual genres, suggests that there might be an opportunity for the principles to be translated It must be emphasised that both before and after, the start of this project, there was never any anticipation that reference to filmic technique and textual description could be harnessed unchanged. The process of observing a technique and its outcome must then be considered through the processes of transformation, where only the simplest of principles are applied. The process of application is an exercise of discovery where an idea is contextually transformed and the consequences are often surprising. In the process of drawing and then constructing the Shadow House, the act of drawing was revelatory and in many instances prompted a completely different course of action that had not been premeditated.

The term 'house' must be understood as both a generic and abstracted term that illustrates an environment that has a relationship to human scale. The project does not have the detail of domestic enclosure, as it only concerns itself with the language of space. At the point of entry a series of stepping stones gradually cohere to form a solid platform. The entrance attempts to challenge the idea of threshold as a definitive line by breaking up a formal platform and allow the transition from public into pseudo-private space to be almost inconsequential. The house is arranged on ascending levels and is divided by a central access ramp that rises to the final platform. The bifurcation of plan clearly delineates the expression of light and shadow into two distinct languages. As the path rises it leads onto three levels, each one higher than the next. Above and external to these spaces is a light source that is obstructed at certain points in order to create definitive lines, made of shadow which provide a demarcation of boundary. The lines imply that not only is one space separate from the other, but also have altered status. There is a notional idea that the daily theatre of activity might be played out on these platforms, whether

3.45   Shadow House plan 2012

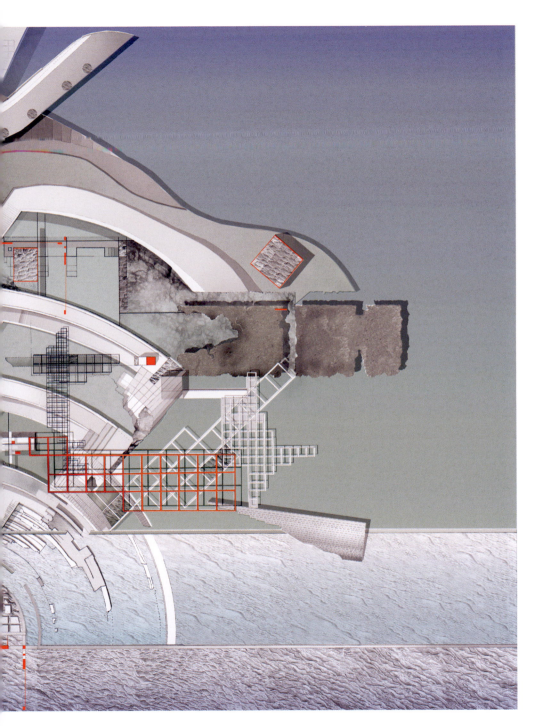

it would be eating, reading, talking; these are areas for more public interaction. The objects both on the platform and the gridded structures above are minimal and only designed to create shadow boundaries The private spaces are to the west of the access ramp. Of course throughout the construction of the model, the physical techniques used were only able to cast shadows that suggested ambivalent rather than specific function. The shadow line that could be seen across each level offered no more restraint than simply an edge. The routes into and out of these spaces were similarly defined. However, the recognition of boundary exists not only within the world of physical reality but also as part of our subconscious, where an understanding of threshold may exist in a number of real and mythical domains. There is usually an understanding that it is safe to walk on surfaces that are visible yet perilous to venture into territory where nothing can be seen; the territorial definition in these spaces is non-existent yet absolutely explicit.

As the route rises, the three intersections lead both to the open semi-public platforms, where most of the definition is described by shadow, and on the other side to three chambers, where the definition is only through light. The contrasting nature of these spaces was quite deliberate as the project needed to explore how both the intercepted and un-intercepted light could be used as a tool to describe space. The three chambers were completely enclosed with the exception of two openings, the first to allow access and an additional aperture to allow a small shaft of light to penetrate and articulate the space.

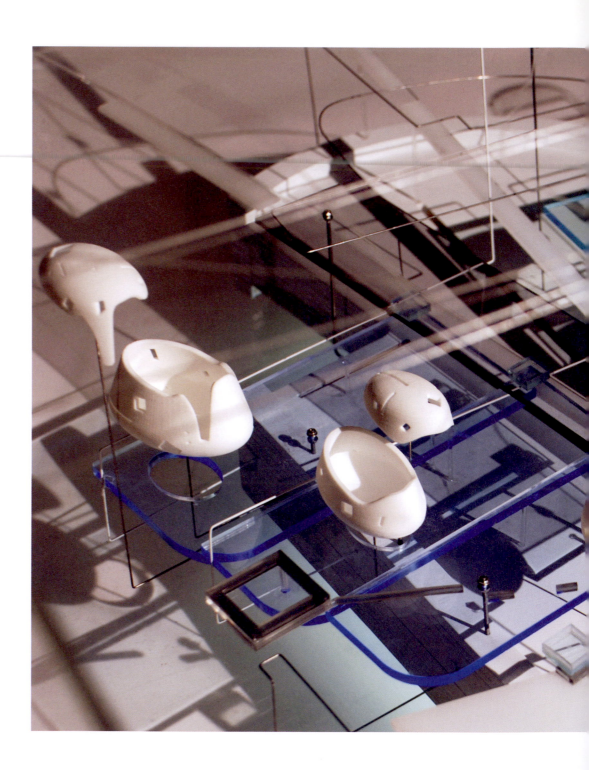

3.46   Detail of Shadow House model 2012

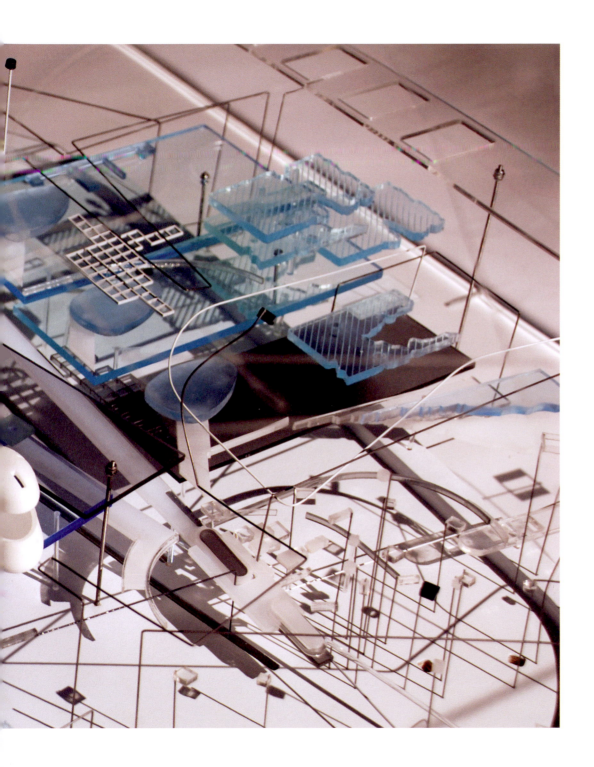

Johannes Schreiter, one of the European pioneers of contemporary stained glass, offered a poetic interpretation of the impact of light as it comes through glass into the dark confines of ecclesiastical space. It was light that brought the space alive with fine shafts that danced and moved, scattering coloured orbs across the floor and into the air. Dark space pierced by light is the only form of definition without which the space is unintelligible. Unlike the flat uniformity of surface illuminated by artificial light, this space was to have the variegated quality of light that fades and of space that fades with it. The idea of boundary and definition are blurred where the dominant space is in darkness. One thinks of certain similarities with cities situated in northern latitudes where the hours of darkness are prolonged during the winter months. Despite artificial light in the centre of the cities, the eye has to search for boundaries, as buildings become only profiles seen against a backdrop that is only slightly lighter.

The drawing evolved into a hybrid that was part architectural and functional and part dream. The overlapping references were from film, text and observation, all of which propelled the ideas forward into an object that unwittingly changed from one idea to multiple ideas, none of which were initially apparent, as in the process of translation they developed new identities.

There is always a struggle to maintain the clarity of concept; the following stage, where a model was constructed, tried to capture the qualities of materiality, this produced another iteration with a modified language. Perspex was chosen as it was visually fragile and was capable of suggesting dissolved boundaries. In retrospect it emerged as an object that only had a distant relationship to the drawing and the original idea. On reflection the concept is still a challenge and still elusive.

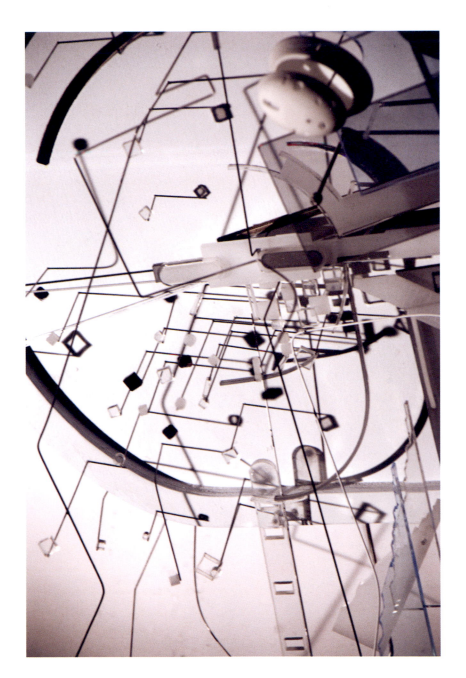

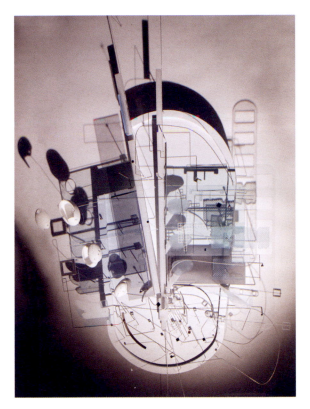

3.47   Shadow House model showing
          entrance detail

3.48   Plan of Shadow House model

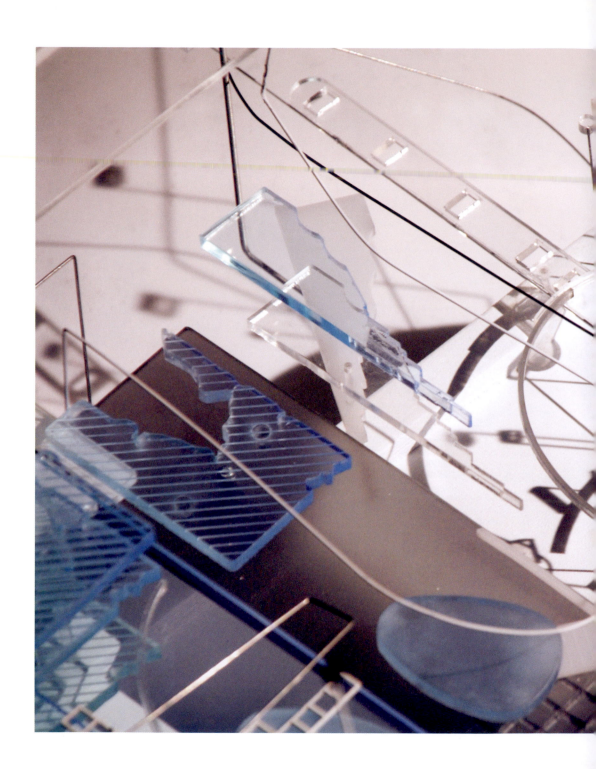

3.49   Entrance defined by shadow detail

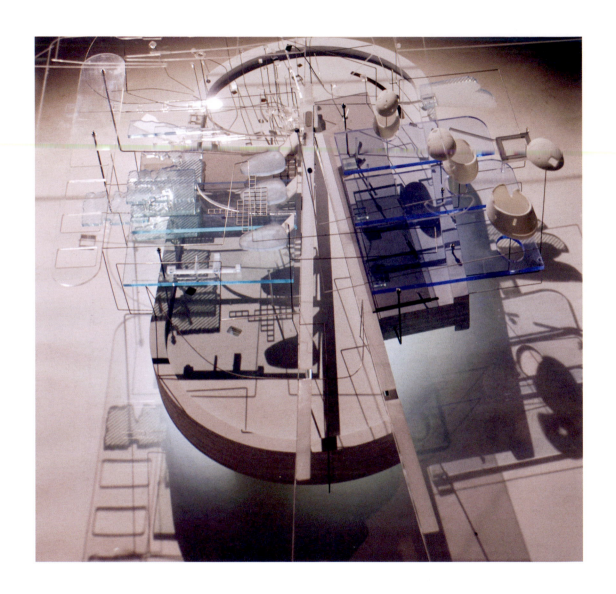

3.50   Shadow studies (a, b, c, d)

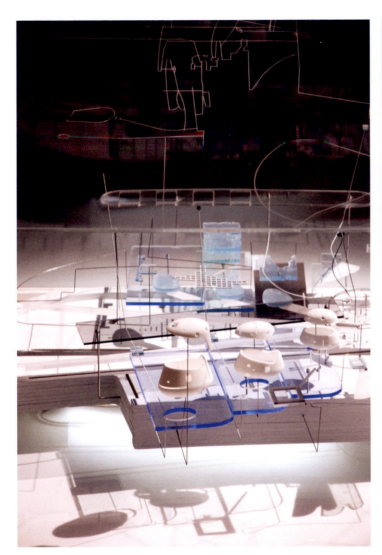
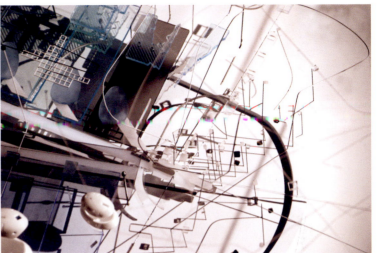

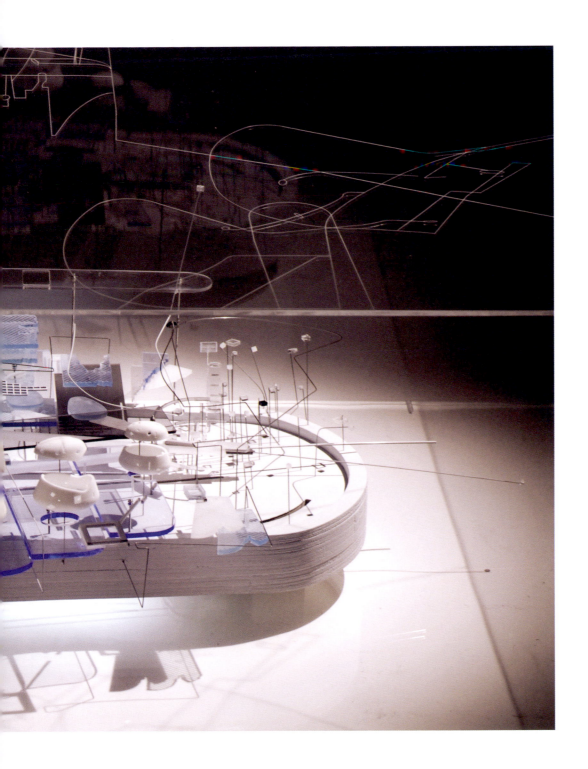

Bibliography

Aellen, Y. and Kienast, E. 2005. *Parkenlagen in Neue Oerlikon*. Zurich: Grun Stadt Zurich.

Amidon, J. 2004. *Moving Horizons: The Landscape Architecture of Kathryn Gustafson and Partners*. Birkhauser Verlag AG.

Ando, T. 2007. *Sunken Courts*. Santa Monica: RAM Publications.

Arata Isozaki Architecture 1960–1990. 1991. New York: Rizzoli International Publications.

Banham, R.B. 1960. *Theory and Design in the First Machine Age*. London: The Architectural Press.

Barthes, R. 1993. *Camera Lucida*. London: Jonathan Cape.

Barthes, R. 2012. *Gary Hill*. Wikipedia list, modified June 2013 [accessed July 2013].

Bawa, D.R. 2002. *Geoffrey Bawa: The Complete Works*. London: Thames and Hudson.

Benitez, C.P. (ed.) 2009. *Contemporary Urban Design*. Aachen: Hentrupp Heyers Fuhrmann Architekten.

Borja-Villel, M.J. 1993. *Tàpies Celebració de la mel*. Exhibition curated by Catalogue by Fundació Antoni Tàpies.

Bragg, M. 1998. *The Seventh Seal*. London: BFI Publishing.

Broome, B. 2012. Knut Hamsen Center Steven Holl Architects. Architectural Record.

Brunette, P. 2005. *Wong Kar-Wai. Contemporary Film Directors*. Urbana, Ill.: University of Illinois Press.

Burckhardt, L. (ed.) 1980. *The Werkbund: Studies in the History and Ideology of the Deutsche Werkbund 1907–1933*. London: Design Council.

Cather, W. 1995. *My Antonia*. New York: Dover Publications Inc.

Collens, G. and Powell, W. (eds) 1999. *Sylvia Crowe*. London: Landscape Design Trust.

Conan, M. (ed.) 2007. *Contemporary Garden Aesthetics, Creations and Interpretations*. Dumbarton Oakes Research Library and Spacemaker Press. Boston: Harvard University Press.

Cooper, D.E. 2006. *A Philosophy of Gardens*. Oxford: Oxford University Press.

Cormier, C. 2010. 'The Blue Stick Garden', in Phaidon (eds) *The Contemporary Garden*. London: Phaidon Press.

Corner, J. (ed.) 1999. *Recovering Landscape*. Princeton: Princeton Architectural Press.

Corner, J. 2006. *Terra Fluxus in Landscape Urbanism: Reader*. Edited by C. Waldheim. Princeton: Princeton Architectural Press.

Corner, J. and Maclean, A. 1996. *Taking Measurements across the American Landscape*. Yale: Yale University Press.

Corris, M. 2010. 'Word and image in art since 1945', in J.D. Hunt, D. Lomas and M. Corris (eds) *Art, Word and Image*. London: Reaktion Books, pp. 253–6.

Cosgrove, D. and Daniels, S. (eds) 1988. *Symbolic Representation of Design and Use of Past Environments*. Cambridge: Cambridge University Press.

Deitch, J. (ed.) 2011. *Art in the Streets*. New York: Rizzoli.

de L'Ecotais, E. and Sayag, A. 1998. *Man Ray: Photography and its Double*. Berkeley: Gingko Press.

Dewy, J. 1929. *Experience Nature and Art in Experience and Nature*. London: Allen and Unwin.

Doyle, C. 2003. *R34G38B25 Images by Christopher Doyle*. London: Systems Design Limited.

Earls, I. 1987. *Renaissance Art: A Topical Dictionary*. New York: Greenwood Press.

Elderfield, J. 1985. *Kurt Schwitters*. London: Thames and Hudson.

Elena, A. 2005. *The Cinema of Abbas Kiarostami*. London: Saqi Books.

Eliel, C.S. et al. 2001. *L'Esprit Nouveau: Purism in Paris*. Los Angeles: Harry N. Abrams.

Evans, R. 1997. *Translations from Drawing to Building*. In AA Documents 2. London: Architectural Association.

Fischer, A. and Loers, V. 1998. *Im Reich der Phantome Fotografie des Unsichtbaren*. Catalogue to accompany the exhibition at Kuntshalle Krems Betriebsges.m.b.H.

Gefeller, A. 2010 'Poles'. Illustrations 19, 37, 38, 07, 44, 45, in C. Lunsford and C. Schaden (eds), *The Japan Series*. Ostfildern: Hatie Cantz Verlag.

Girot, C. 2000. 'Towards a General Theory of Landscape', in *Rehacer paisajes: Architectura del Paisaje en Europa 1994–1999*. Barcelona: Fundacion Caja Arquitectos.

Gombrich, E. 1997. *Shadows: The Depiction of Shadows in Western Art*. New Haven, CT: Yale University Press.

Harrison, C. and Wood, P. 2003. *Art in Theory 1900–2000: An Anthology of Changing Ideas*. London: Blackwell Publishing Ltd.

Harvey, S. and Fieldhouse, K. (eds) 2005. *Notes from the Cultured Landscape*. London: Routledge.

Holl, S. 2007. *Steven Holl: Architecture Spoken*. New York: Rizzoli.

Hunt, D. et al. 2010. *Art, Word and Image*. London: Reaktion Books.

Ichikawa, H. 1986. 'The visible and the invisible', in A. Oshita (ed.) *Utsurohi Sculpture: A Moment of Movement*, Tokyo: Atsushi Oshita, p. 40.

Jardins Imaginaire, Les Habitantes-Paysagistes. 1977. Presse de la Connaissance.

Kaplan, R. and Kaplan, S. 1989. *The Experience of Nature: A Psychological Perspective*. Cambridge: Cambridge University Press.

Lambertini, A. 2007. *Vertical Gardens*. London: Verba Volant.

Leaman, M. 2010. 'Preface', in J.D. Hunt, D. Lomas and M. Corris (eds) *Art, Word and Image*. London: Reaktion Books, pp. 7–13.

Leibowitz, A. 2011. *Pilgrimage*. New York: Jonathan Cape.

Lerup, L. 1989. 'Beyond the Frontier', *Places Print Journal*, Archive Vol. 5, No 3.

Lippard, L. 1966. *Pop Art*. London: Thames and Hudson.

Lomas, D. 2010. '"New in art, they are already soaked in humanity": Word and image 1900–1945', in J.D. Hunt, D. Lomas and M. Corris (eds) *Art, Word and Image*. London: Reaktion Books, pp. 111–115, 121.

Loosma, B. 2000. *Superdutch: New Architecture in the Netherlands*. New York: Princeton Architectural Press.

Lunsford, C. and Schaden, C. 2010. *The Japan Series. Andreas Gefeller*. Ostfildern: Hatje Cantz Verlag.

MacDougall, E.B. 1974. 'The French Formal Garden', in Vol. 3 of *Colloquium on the History of Landscape Architecture*. Boston: Dumbarton Oakes Trustees for Harvard University.

Markus, M. and Remke, A. 2003. *REW. The Individuality and Beauty of the Tag in Writing: Urban Calligraphy and Beyond*. Berlin: Die Gestalten Verlag.

Marx, L. 1964. *The Machine in the Garden: Technology and the Pastoral Ideal in America*. Oxford: Oxford University Press.

Meinig, D. 1979. 'The beholding eye, ten versions of the same scene', in D. Meinig and J. Brinkerhoff (eds) *Interpretations of Ordinary Landscape: Geographical Essays*. Oxford: Oxford University Press, No 34.

Meinig, D. and Brinkerhoff, J. (eds) 1979. *Interpretations of Ordinary Landscape: Geographical Essays*. Oxford: Oxford University Press.

Mignot, D. and Eleonor, L. (eds) 1993. Gary Hill catalogue by Stedelijk Museum, Amsterdam.

Miralles, B. (ed.) 1996. *The Architecture of Enric Miralles: Works and Projects 1975–1995*. New York: The Monacelli Press.

Mojave solar project. Wikipedia (accessed 19 December 2012).

Morley, S. 2003. *Writing on the Wall: Word and Image in Modern Art*. Berkeley: UCLA Press.

Mossop, E. 2006. 'Landscapes of infrastructure', in C. Waldheim (ed.) *The Landscape Urbanism*. New York: Princeton Architectural Press, pp. 164–177.

Mundy, J. (ed.) 2008. *Duchamp, Man Ray, Picabia*. London: Tate Publishing.

Nakaya, F. 1990. *Fog Sculpture*. Fujiko Nakaya, Guggenheim Bilbao. The Collection Online.

Nau, T. 2007. *Evans: Photographer of America*. Basingstoke: Macmillan.

Norberg-Schutz, C. and Postiglione, G. (eds) 1997. *Sverre Fehn: Work, Projects, Writings, 1949–1996*. New York: Monacelli Press.

Novak, B. 1995. *Nature and Culture*. New York: Oxford University Press.

O'Malley, T. and Wolschke-Bulmahn, J. (eds) 1998. *Elysium Britannicum and European Gardening*. Washington: Dumbarton Oakes Research Library and Collection.

Passuth, K. 1985. *Moholy Nagy*. London: Thames and Hudson.

Penz, F. and Thomas, M. (eds) 1997. *The City in Twilight*. London: BFI.

Peter, B. and Wong, K. 2005. *Wong Kar-Wai. Contemporary Film Directors*. Urbana, Ill.: University of Illinois Press.

Phaidon editors. 2010. *The Contemporary Garden*. London: Phaidon.

Richardson, T. (ed.) 2004. *The Vanguard Landscapes and Garden of Martha Schwartz*. London: Thames and Hudson.

Richter, H. 1965. *Dada Art and Anti Art*. London: Thames and Hudson.

Ritchie, D. 1977. *Ozu: Floating Weeds 1959*. Berkeley, CA: University of California Press.

Rivlin, L. 2006. 'Found spaces, freedom of choice in public life', in Q. Stevens and K. Frank (eds) *Loose Space, Possibility and Diversity in Urban Life*. London: Routledge, pp. 38–53.

Ross, D. 1951. *Plato's Theory of Ideas*. Oxford: Oxford University Press.

Schama, S. 1995. *Landscape and Memory*. London: HarperCollins.

Scheou, A. (ed.) 1997. *Itsuko Hasagawa*. Basel: Birkhauser Verlag.

Schwartz, M. and Richardson, T. 2004. *The Vanguard Landscapes and Gardens of Martha Schwartz*. London: Thames and Hudson, pp. 128–35.

Sinnreich, U. (ed.) 2009. *James Turrell: Geometry of Light*. Otsfildern: Hatje Cantz.

Skogskyrkogarden. Wikipedia (accessed 20 December 2012).

Stevens, Q. and Franck, K. (eds) 2006. *Loose Space Possibility and Diversity in Urban Life*. London: Routledge.

Stoichita, V. 1997. *A Short History of the Shadow*. London: Reaktion Books.

Swaffield, S. 2005. *Notes from the Cultured Landscape*. London: Routledge.

Syson, L. with Keith, L. 2011. *Leonardo da Vinci. Painter at the Court of Milan*. London: National Gallery Limited.

Taylor, B.B. 1986. 'The House is a Garden' in *Geoffrey Bawa*. Singapore: Concept Media Pte Ltd.

Treib, M. 2002. 'City Park Rotterdam' in *The Public Garden: The Enclosure and Disclosure of the Public Garden*. Rotterdam: NAI and Architecture International.

Trifonas, P. 2001. *Postmodern Encounters. Barthes and the Empire of Signs*. London: Icon Books.

Vidler, A. 1990. 'The building in pain: The body and architecture in post modern culture', *AA Files*, Spring, pp. 3–10.

Wagstaff, S. (ed.) 2004. *Edward Hopper*. London: Tate Publishing.

Waldheim, C. (ed.) 2006. *Landscape Urbanism Reader*. Princeton: Princeton University Press.

Walker, P. and Simo, M. 1999. *The Legacy of Landscape Architecture: Art or Social Service?* Cambridge: MIT Press.

Williamson, T. 1998. *Polite Landscapes: Gardens and Society in Eighteenth-century England*. Sutton: Sutton Publishing Ltd.

Young, D. and Young, M. 2005. *The Art of the Japanese Garden*. North Clarendon, VT: Tuttle Publishing.

Zajonc, A. 1995. *Catching the Light: The Entwined History of Light and Mind*. Oxford: Oxford University Press.

Index